T0114093

Advance Praise for
Growth into Manhood

"This is a terrific book, loaded with fresh insights and practical encouragement for the man struggling to move into the fullness of his manhood. It goes beyond any other books I've seen for the former homosexual in painting a clear picture of what mature and godly manhood really looks like and how it can be attained. I highly recommend this wonderful resource."

—BOB DAVIES, executive director,
Exodus International—North America

"Alan Medinger is one of the true sages of the Christian ex-gay movement. His life has been blessed by a hard-earned wisdom. In *Growth into Manhood* the reader is given the chance to learn what Alan knows about the qualities of character that define a mature man, about the practical steps a man can take to grow into his fullest potential, and about the paradoxical truth that, in the end, real manhood is 'something we give away.' I highly recommend this inspiring book as a guide for every struggler who, believing that he is really heterosexual, makes the decision to resume the journey into manhood."

—JOSEPH NICOLOSI, PH.D., president, National Association
for Research and Therapy of Homosexuality

"In *Growth into Manhood,* Alan Medinger gives us a practical but never simplistic guide to the journey toward complete manhood. His approach is fatherly—gentle and firm. Its effect on me was to engender greater clarity and courage as I seek to become more manly as a father, husband, and ministry leader. Alan makes a strong case for traditional manhood. He uses his story and decades of ministry to those overcoming homosexuality to substantiate his call. Resolving the same-sex struggle highlights the need for clarity in what real manhood is, how God helps us, and what we must do to grow out of immaturity and into the 'outerdirectedness' that marks whole manhood. He tackles hard issues with sensitivity, forthrightness, and a peaceful authority. I will read *Growth into Manhood* again, intently, for my own becoming and will offer it unreservedly to any man wanting to grow up."

—ANDREW COMISKEY, executive director,
Desert Stream Ministries

resuming the journey

growth into
manhood

alan medinger

WATERBROOK
PRESS

Growth into Manhood
PUBLISHED BY WATERBROOK PRESS
12265 Oracle Boulevard, Suite 200
Colorado Springs, Colorado 80921

ISBN 978-0-87788-306-7

Published in the United States by WaterBrook Multnomah, an imprint of the Crown Publishing Group, a
division of Random House Inc., New York.

WATERBROOK and its deer colophon are registered trademarks of Random House Inc.

Library of Congress Cataloging-in-Publication Data
Medinger, Alan P., 1936-
    Growth into manhood : resuming the journey / Alan P. Medinger.
      p. cm.
    Includes bibliographical references.
    ISBN 978-0-877-88306-7
    1. Homosexuality, Male—Religious aspects—Christianity. 2. Masculinity—
Religious aspects—Christianity. 3. Men (Christian theology). 4. Men—Religious
life. I. Title.

BR115.H6 M43 2000
261.8'357662—dc21

                                                        00-037381

2009

146502721

To the women in my life who have blessed me beyond measure.
To be a son, a husband, and a father to you is purpose
enough for my manhood.

With thanksgiving for all your love and patience:
Enid, my late beloved mother,
Willa, my most precious wife,
and Laura and Beth, my beautiful daughters.

contents

acknowledgments

A man growing into manhood does not do it alone. He needs encouragers, models, and friends. It is the same with the formidable task of writing a book. He needs encouragers, others who have successfully accomplished the task, and friends to support him along the way. I have been blessed with an abundance of each.

I give loving thanks to those people who have shown a special gift as encouragers in my life, in my ministry, and in my writing: Tom Bisset, Frank Watson, Dean Schultz, and Bob Davies, men who have always believed in me and always happened to express their belief just when I most needed to hear it. Thanks also to Joan Guest of Harold Shaw, my champion in getting this book published. And thanks especially to perhaps my greatest encourager, my wife, Willa.

I thank God for the men He has put in my life as role models. In ministry I have been blessed to be able to witness the strong and faithful service of men like Frank Worthen, Ron Scates, Richard Lipka, Phillip Zampino, Rick Wright, and Ed Meeks. On my way to personal growth, God has given me models of Christian manhood in Bob Chase, Bruce McCutcheon, Kevin Mulligan, and David Keating. You will never know how much I learned from you.

No one could grow as a man or in ministry if he did not have the support of loving friends. Again, my cup runneth over. I give special thanks to the staff of Regeneration: Jeff Johnston, Bob Ragan, Lani Bersch, Kris Svensson, Josh Glaser, Laura Suffecool, and Marcie Schuett—my friends as well as my coworkers—who were so patient with me during the long months it took to write this book; to my old college "gang" who have seen all my worst sides and continued to love me; to special friends Jack and Sue O'Neill and Marty and Penny Hylbom.

Finally, I thank all of my fellow laborers in Exodus and related ministries who have inspired me through their teaching and writing and with whom I have shared this wonderful journey of discovering God's plan for setting men and women free from homosexuality: Anita Worthen, Leanne Payne, Andy Comiskey, Joe Nicolosi, and Joe Dallas, and all of the Exodus ministry directors I have colabored with over the past twenty years. It is my prayer that this book will complement and support the mighty work you have done and are doing.

It was a room I had not been in for almost forty years. Back when I was an undergraduate at Johns Hopkins University, it had been the dining hall for the dorms. Now it was a meeting room for student organizations. This Friday evening it was being used by the Hopkins InterVarsity Christian Fellowship group. Two of their leaders had gotten involved in a controversy over homosexuality, and before they engaged in any more dialogue with members of the campus gay community, the Christian students wanted to get themselves better informed about homosexuality. I was a logical speaker. Not only was I an alumnus of the school, but I was the founder and executive director of Regeneration, one of the oldest and largest "ex-gay" ministries in the worldwide Exodus network of ministries for men and women overcoming homosexuality.

Much more than the room had changed over the years. The university had grown tremendously, and the student body was much more diverse. In my day about half of the students were Baltimore boys like me who attended Hopkins, not just because it was a good school, but also because our parents could not afford to send us out of town to college. Now, relatively few of the students were Baltimoreans. When I was at Hopkins, undergraduates were all male and almost all of them white. As I looked at the faces of the hundred-plus students gathered that Friday night, white males were a definite minority. In the 1950s there were no organizations like the InterVarsity group. For most of us, a Christian was a good person—like me—who went to church. That was about all we had in common, so there wasn't much reason to form an organization.

But for me personally the changes in the university, in the room, in the student body were secondary. As I stood there, I thought back to the young man who had been in that room all those years ago; a young man in secret bondage to homosexuality, a "nerdy" type who somehow made it into a fraternity but lived in fear that his brothers would discover his true nature, someone who was already a master of the double life, a man who was religious but did not know the Lord. Now, here I was thirty-nine years later, a Christian, a husband, a father, even a grandfather, a man who was truly comfortable with his manhood, a man who was able to share with joy and confidence what God had done in his life.

As thrilling as it was to experience this extraordinary contrast, my joy and excitement soared even higher when a sudden realization came over me. At the very moment I was standing before the Hopkins InterVarsity group, about forty miles north on Interstate 95, standing in front of another much larger InterVarsity group at the University of Delaware, was Stephen Medinger, my son. Steve, a junior at Delaware, was one of the leaders of the Christian group and co-led its Friday night gatherings. Steve was born eighteen months after I had come out of homosexuality. *Father and son:* never had the phrase had such an impact on me.

Of course I shared with the Hopkins group the story of my seventeen years of active homosexuality, my failed efforts to change by my own strength, and then my dramatic conversion and deliverance from the sexual bondage that had been a part of my homosexuality. There was not time to share with them other profound changes that had occurred in me during the years since my conversion, changes that I could see so clearly that night, changes that had brought me into the fullness of my manhood.

This is not a testimony book (although my full testimony is included as appendix A for those interested), but much of what I have to say is rooted in my experience of growing into manhood, growth that almost stopped when I was a young teenager and didn't resume until after my conversion at age thirty-eight.

We will be looking at how much male homosexuality is, at its core, a matter of undeveloped manhood, and how true healing requires that we grow—even as adults—into our manhood. We will look at how a boy usually grows into manhood, and at what went wrong with us. A central message of this book is that any man can grow into full, comfortable, complete manhood. I will describe how this can happen—even now. Guiding this will be two principles. The first is that every man has to go through certain developmental stages; there is no real shortcut to growth. If we didn't go through these stages as boys, we will have to go through them now. The second principle is that manhood is to a great extent a matter of doing, and we will grow into manhood by doing the things that men do.

On the way, we will examine what a man is, what is the meaning of masculine, and what it is that men do—not just in the cultural sense, but what men do that reflects their universal God-designed manhood. Since we are not looking for simply a generic manhood, we will look at what the special qualities are that God built into men that He wants to see manifested in us. As we look at these, I believe that your desire for your own manhood to develop will start to crowd out any remaining homosexual desire to possess another's manhood.

Because the journey into manhood is anything but easy, we will take a hard, deep look at the obstacles that are encountered on the road to manhood and how they can be overcome. Don't despair before you read this part. As you are thinking of all of the reasons why you skipped out of the growth process as an adolescent, and see that some of the same obstacles to growth are still present today, it might be tempting to throw up your hands and declare that you couldn't make the journey then and you can't now. But you can now; things are different. I hope I can show you how.

I didn't fully understand what God was doing when I resumed my growth into manhood. Many times He provided opportunities for me to grow, and I fought Him all the way. This made my growth process extremely slow. My hope is that this book will provide you with some guidelines that will make your journey go more quickly.

This is not a complete book on overcoming homosexuality. You will need a broader understanding of homosexuality than what is offered here, and most readers will need some healing along the way, healing that comes from prayer and counseling. Others have written well on these subjects, and in appendix C I refer you to their books. This book deals with one aspect of homosexuality, growth, a subject that others have not addressed very completely but one that I am convinced is essential to true healing from homosexuality.

the journey

The road to manhood is a long one. It is a road of learning, trying, failing, trying again, a journey of victories and defeats. Most boys are not even conscious that they are on the road, and few realize when they have reached its primary destination, but the great majority do reach it. For most men it takes from conception to early adulthood to reach that place where, at some deep, inner, unspoken level, they know that they are men. They may not be totally satisfied with the quality of their manhood, but they have no question that they are men, and for better or for worse they will be able to fulfil most of the obligations that are laid on them as men.

Some boys, however, did not reach this destination. At some point the striving became too much, the defeats and failures too painful, so they opted out. They got off the main road, and they took a detour. They arrived at a chronological age that classified them as men, they appeared to have all of the parts that made them men, but deep inside, in place of that nonverbal sense of manhood, there was a void. They did not feel as if they were women—most of them, that is—but somehow, in the world of men, they did not belong.

I was one of those boys. I cannot pinpoint exactly when I took my detour—perhaps somewhere around age eight or ten—but I know when I got back on the main road: I was thirty-eight years old. In the interim, as with so many boys, my detour took me into the world of homosexuality.

As I can see looking back now, I sought in other men the manhood that I desperately wanted but believed could never be mine.

I got back on the road the night in November 1974 when I accepted Christ. This is not a testimony book, but to a significant extent it does draw on my resumed journey, what happened to me after this thirty-eight-year-old "boy" got back on the road. (My full testimony appears in appendix A.) Unlike most adolescents who go through the process of growth into manhood with little conscious awareness of what is going on, I was quite aware. I had the advantage of being able to consciously observe the formation of much of my own manhood. I also had the privilege of watching another man grow up. My son, Stephen, was born eighteen months after my conversion and my coming out of homosexuality. I was able to watch him grow up in the normal way to become a strong, solid Christian man in every respect, a man who would be the joy of any father. Much of what I share in this book is rooted in my experience and a little bit in Steve's.

Although I am not offering my full story here, it is important that I share with you the point at which I came to see that my homosexual problem was largely a problem of undeveloped manhood. My conversion at age thirty-eight was sudden, dramatic—and somewhat unusual. Most people who can identify a specific moment of conversion can point to things about their lives that changed instantly—their own special miracles. For me, two especially dramatic changes happened right away, changes that I have never seen happen in quite the same way to men to whom I have ministered: I fell head over heels in love with my wife and desired her physically, and my sexual attraction to men disappeared. Understandably, I believed that I had been totally delivered from homosexuality, and that's what I started to tell people.

As regards the sexual part of my homosexuality, this was true; twenty-five years have borne this out. But what I did not recognize at the time was that homosexuality is much more than simply the direction of one's sexual attractions. It has two other strong components: emotional neediness and identity. It took much longer to deal with these.

In the first several years after my initial healing, I still had a deep painful longing for some big, strong man to take care of me. It was no longer sexual, but I still longed to be in the presence of a man who would love me, value me, and be my protector. Over about a five-year period God met this need in a wonderful way. In my quiet times I was able to establish such a deep and personal relationship with Jesus that He filled up all of those empty places in me. I came out of that period with what I believe is no more than a normal man's need for male friendship and affirmation. This was my "five-year miracle."

Identity was another matter altogether. This became clear to me quite quickly. In many ways after my conversion I was an eight-year-old boy in a thirty-eight-year-old man's body. As a brand-new Christian I wanted to do everything right, and with God's power available I did not see why I couldn't. But such was not the case, especially as I tried to live out my role as a husband and father. At the time of my conversion I was married and had two daughters, age ten and eleven. I would read a book on what a good Christian husband and father was supposed to do, and it was as if I was being told to run a four-minute mile. I could not do it. I would try to do all of the right things, to initiate, to be assertive, to discipline, to lead my family spiritually. Time and again I would fail.

Outside the home, except in business where I had a clearly defined role, it was the same. Particularly in relationships with other Christian men, I felt totally inadequate. I often felt like a little boy in their presence. Trying to live the role of a Christian man as I was coming to understand it, I felt like some pale, pudgy little guy who gets a tattoo trying to prove that he is a man. I felt ridiculous, like a little boy dressed up in his father's suit. Constantly, I condemned myself for my failures.

These were terribly difficult times, and if I had not had such a profound experience of the reality of the Lord and of His power to change me, I might have given up and simply turned inward in my Christian life. But I had had that profound experience, and so I would just try harder. If I failed in my role of getting enough discipline into my family to have regular devotions, I would just try again. There was no good reason why I couldn't do these things, why I couldn't fulfill my God-given roles.

But there was a reason. I could not do the things that men do, because in many ways I was not a man. I was still a little boy. Physically and intellectually mature, a part of me was stuck in preadolescence. I could not fully and effectively take on my responsibilities as a husband and as a father—as a man—because the qualities needed to play such important and difficult roles had never developed in me.

My first blessed revelation of this fact came to me through Leanne Payne's book *Crisis in Masculinity*.[1] As I read her explanations of what a man is and learned about the true masculine and feminine, I came to realize that I simply had not grown up. I was not freed from my obligation to still fulfill my God-given roles, but I no longer had to condemn myself when I failed. Rather, I had to start growing up. But now, having gained a measure of self-acceptance through Leanne Payne's teaching, I could be patient with myself while I did. What a relief!

So, more than twenty years ago I started down the road of growth into manhood. I want to share this journey with you, to walk with you down this difficult road. If you are anything like the thirty-eight-year-old "boy" that I was, I pray that I can help you walk down a similar road. If you are like that boy, I urge you with all my heart to give it a try. It will be the most difficult trip you have ever taken; at times the pain will be excruciating, but the victories will be joyous beyond measure. And the pain of your failures will only last for a short while; the fruit of your victories will be with you forever.

Why Take Such a Difficult Trip?

Whether you are a homosexual overcomer (a man who is moving from homosexuality to heterosexuality) or a man whose undeveloped manhood led to heterosexual immaturity, this journey is not one you have to take. You can go on the rest of your life at your present level of maturity. Quite likely no disaster will befall you. You will probably still have a job and family and friends. You can still be active in your church and in community life. You might even continue to develop certain specific talents and skills. Life can go on with little change. This happens with countless men who go only so far in the development of their manhood. No one will make you do it, and unless your current behavior is especially risky, continuing as you are will not threaten your survival.

But there are some powerful reasons for taking the trip. The first is that the alternative to growth is not terribly desirable. The alternative to having an identity as a man is to have some other identity. What will it be? Some Christian men deal with homosexuality by seeking to become "nonpracticing homosexuals." This may be an option for some, but many find that so long as they retain a core identity as a homosexual, the nonpracticing part remains extremely difficult, if not impossible, to maintain. Some take hold of and keep the "ex-gay" identity, defining themselves by what they are not, rather than by what they are. Others seek to stay in an "in-between" stage. They remain suspended in a life that God never intended for anyone, a life whose best hope is some sort of asexuality, denying their homosexuality but not yet seeing themselves as heterosexual. Any of these could set a man up for a future of deep regrets as he comes to see how incomplete his life was in some of its most basic elements.

Another reason to take the trip is that the rewards at the end of the road are far, far better than most of us could imagine. As you read on, I hope that I can convince you of this. For me, the rewards of achieving full manhood were worth every bit of the effort and pain; they can be for you also.

A little boy seems to know instinctively that manhood is desirable, something to be grasped. This is why Steve, when he was five or six years old, would bend his elbow, make a muscle, and ask me to feel it. A muscle meant manhood, and he wanted me to affirm his. An adolescent boy sees manhood as a prize to be gained, and the pursuit of manhood is what energizes much of what he does. Manhood is good, very good. To achieve full manhood is to be in a place of confidence and peace. It is to feel adequate—adequate to do all that is reasonably expected of you. To be a man is to be set free from many of the fears that beset you in daily life. It is to be able to take your eyes off of yourself and to be able to look at the world around you as something exciting and challenging and full of potential. This is where the journey can take you, and it is worth everything that it takes to get there.

The third reason to take the trip is the most important of all, because it has to do with God's design and desire for your life. A friend of mine set up an elaborate model-train layout with a rail yard, coal loader, little houses, and stores—the whole works. When the project was first set up, nothing worked right. His locomotive would only run backward, the coal loader scattered coal everywhere but in the coal car, and the streetlights blinked off and on constantly. He had a plan as to how things ought to work, but few of them worked that way, so he found little joy in all his efforts.

We are part of a plan too. If we believe in a creator God, we have to believe that unless He is totally arbitrary and capricious, God has a plan for how we should operate as men—what we should be and how we should live out our manhood. We have to believe that He had a reason for making us different from women and that our growth into maturity has some goals. He has revealed Himself as Father, and we know that every good father desires that his son grow into the fullness of his manhood. Could it be that the perfect Father desires any less for His sons? We may not totally agree on what full and complete manhood is because the models around us for manhood are all flawed, but God has not left us totally ignorant. We can discover much of His plan for us as men. This is one of the purposes of this book.

Even now, you almost certainly have some idea of what God created a man to be and some sense that you are not totally there; maybe not there by a long shot. If it is your desire to be obedient to God and to be a son who brings joy to the Father's heart, then you are called to take the journey. You must be willing to grow into the fullness of manhood. Because He loves you and He wants the best for you, your growth will be a delight to Him.

A ROAD MAP

I want to share with you briefly the main principles that I will use to guide us down this road to manhood. I am convinced that for most men who deal with the problem, homosexuality is at its core an identity problem. Such a man does not feel like a man, at least as he perceives the way other men feel about themselves. Dr. Bill Consiglio referred to this as "gender emptiness."[2] This is a good descriptive term because such a man does feel empty; he is confused and uncertain about his manhood. He doesn't feel like a woman, and he may not yet have taken on a gay or homosexual identity, but he feels empty in some place where he senses he should feel solid. However, his problem is not just that he doesn't feel like a man but, in fact, that he is not a man—in terms of having gone through all of the stages of growth that take most little boys from childhood to full manhood. He had found the process too difficult or too painful, so he took his leave and skipped out of a part of it.

Dr. Joseph Nicolosi, in *Reparative Therapy of Male Homosexuality*, says that these fellows became "kitchen window boys."[3] If you were one of those boys, you withdrew from active involvement in the competitive, rough, physical world of boys, and you became a mere observer of that world, watching from the kitchen window. But it wasn't only the world of playgrounds, ball fields, and tree houses from which you withdrew, you withdrew from the very ground on which your manhood was to be formed. In many respects you put your growth into manhood on hold.

Now, fifteen, twenty, or forty years later, if you want to resume your growth, you will have to venture back out into that world of men and boys. Essentially you are going to have to develop your manhood in the same way that young boys do, through a process of learning, testing, failing, getting back up and testing again, and finally succeeding. *We grow into the fullness of our manhood by doing the things that men do.*

Once you are into this process and have had a few successes—regardless of the failures in between—a reinforcing process will start to set in. As you successfully do the things that men do:

- You will find that you are being affirmed by other men.
- You will start to conform to your own inner sense of what a man is.
- You will start to gain a sense that you are becoming the man God created you to be, and through the Holy Spirit you will know that you are fulfilling His purpose for you as a man.

"Doing the things that men do" may seem terribly superficial—and perhaps, in and of itself, it is—but its consequences are not. As you are affirmed by other men, as you start to conform to your own sense of manhood, and as you find yourself moving in the direction of God's plan for you as a man, profound changes will start to take place in the deepest parts of your being. Your core identity will start to change.

The objective of this book is to help men attain full manhood, so let me explain what I mean by the term. *Full manhood,* or just *manhood,* as used in this book is the state at which:

- We can function comfortably in fulfilling the roles that God has given us as men, and we can take on the responsibilities that others have a right to expect us to fill. As husbands, as fathers, as members of the body of Christ, as citizens, we are expected to fulfill certain roles. In our full manhood, we are able to fulfill these obligations. As we go along, I will tell you more about what these roles and obligations are.

- We will have reached the point at which growing up as men is no longer a major focus of our life. This does not mean that we have become perfect men—there was only one perfect man—but that our growth will start to take place naturally through our normal walk as Christians.

Although this book is written primarily for homosexual overcomers, if other men find some broad truths in it that can help them to develop and accept their own manhood, that would be terrific. In this regard, I want to say to the homosexual struggler that other men *can* get something out of this book because many of the struggles you face are faced by all men; the main difference is that you—and I—went AWOL from the battle for a time.

I am convinced that every man, no matter how late he starts, no matter how gender empty he feels, if he chooses manhood and is willing to accept the opportunities and challenges that God lays before him, can expect in this life to experience full manhood.

growth into manhood:

essential for healing

"I had your phone number in my dresser drawer for three years. I kept putting it off, but I finally had to call you." Statements like this are heard often in the offices of Regeneration. Regeneration is a part of the world-wide Exodus coalition of Christian ministries whose primary focus is to help men and women overcome homosexuality. I sometimes think that if every Christian dealing with homosexuality who has our phone number tucked away in a wallet or dresser drawer were to decide to call us on the same day, the phone lines would overload.

This type of call suggests three things about the caller. First, obviously, he is at some level unhappy with his homosexuality. Second, powerful obstacles—most often ambivalence and fear—have kept him from calling for help. Third, he has finally reached the point at which his homosexuality has given him such distress that he is willing to confront the obstacles; he is willing to address the ambivalence or face the fears.

BARRIERS TO SEEKING HELP

Let's look at these obstacles and the specific areas of distress that the overcomer experiences. The first obstacle has to do with the *nature of addictive-type sins.* Although a man may hate his homosexuality with all of his heart and mind, at the same time there are ways in which he loves it. For many of us, homosexual acting out was for years and years our way of coping with life, a way of escape, of self-comforting, of finding temporary relief from the terrible pain or emptiness we felt inside. We hated it and at the same time we loved it, and in our ambivalence we were paralyzed.

I hated my homosexuality. It led me to do foolish and degrading things. It drove me to take risks that I knew could cost me everything: my wife, my children, my career, even my life. But for ten years in the marriage I clung to it. How could I live without it?

The second great obstacle to seeking help is *fear.* There is the simple fear of the unknown. "If I get involved with this ministry, what will these people get me to do, or what will they do to me? What kind of people are they? Are they some narrow-minded group of fundamentalists, gay bashers in Christian disguise, or at the other extreme, are they peddlers of some kooky new psychological theory?" There is also the fear of revealing oneself, a fear usually rooted in pride or shame. "I have been a Christian for ten years. I should be able to take care of this myself. To admit this problem and to seek help is to admit what a failure I am as a Christian. Perhaps people will even question whether or not I am a Christian." These fears are often most intense in someone who has grown up in a conservative Christian community where the stigma of homosexuality is most severe.

Low self-esteem is very much a part of most male homosexuality. This is one of the principal themes in Dr. William Consiglio's book, *Homosexual No More.* A principal defense against the pain of low self-esteem has been to construct an image—for our own benefit and for others—of a man who is good and righteous and together. So, to stand before another person and say, "I am homosexual," is to tear down the false identity that has offered us the only shred of self-esteem we ever had.

FINALLY, WE'VE HAD ENOUGH—SOURCES OF DISTRESS

Despite these obstacles men do seek help. What is the distress that is so powerful that a man would consider forsaking his addiction and would be willing to walk through such a minefield of fears? If the man is a Christian —and the overwhelming majority of men who come to Exodus ministries have some sort of faith or belief in Christian morality—the distress comes in one or both of two areas.

First and perhaps most obvious it is *distress over his behavior.* He is in terrible conflict over the contradiction between what he believes is good behavior and what he is doing. He may feel like Paul, who wrote in Romans 7 about being driven to do the very things he hates. However, he may feel that Paul's problems must have been minor compared to his. This would be so especially if his behavior goes beyond masturbation and fantasy. (In this book I include fantasy and masturbation as parts of homosexual behavior. Sexual activity with another person will be referred to as *acting out.*) I would estimate that over 90 percent of the men who come to ex-gay ministries come because they sense a great conflict between their behavior and what they believe God wants for them.

The second area of distress has to do with *the direction of his sexual attractions.* He is sexually attracted to men but wants to be attracted to women. With regard to men, the attraction is creating an intense inner longing that he feels will never go away and that he believes, as a Christian, he can never fulfill. The longing may be purely sexual or it may be emotional. Although we tend to think of male homosexuality as focusing on physical attraction and female homosexuality on emotional attraction, in many men there is an almost overwhelming ache to be held by, nurtured by, loved by a man, or by transference, to hold, nurture, and love another man. I have heard men whose degree of sexual promiscuity would be unbelievable by heterosexual standards pour out their pain and cry, "It was not the sex I wanted; it was just someone to love me." I believe them. This unfulfilled longing can be as intense as the purely sexual. Of course, the two cannot be totally separated. Leanne Payne and others have pointed out many times how our sexual desires are often deeper emotional desires that have become eroticized.

The attraction to the same sex is only one side of his distress concerning the nature of his attractions; the other is his lack of attraction to the opposite sex. He feels absolutely no romantic or sexual attractions toward women, but he wants one day to get married and have children. Like other men, he has a sense that much of a man's purpose and fulfillment in life comes through marriage and fatherhood. He wants to feel drawn to a woman, but there is nothing there. The absence of any opposite-sex attraction lies at the root of his sense that he can never lead a normal life, that he is stuck in this place and will never be able to get on with life.

There is a third area of distress that may not come up until the man has started to deal with the first two. This has to do with *his identity as a man.* Because this is not as directly "sexual" as behavior and attractions, he may not at first link it closely with his homosexual condition. Besides, it is so much a part of "who he is" that he may not have even thought that it could be changed. It is not an identity that says simply, "I am gay," but one that goes much deeper. It says, "I am not a man," or at least, "I am not a man like other men." He doesn't measure up. Going back to adolescence, sometimes even earlier, he felt different from other boys, and *different* always translated as "less than" or "inferior to." These feelings continued through the teen years and into adulthood. Even today, in the company of other men, he feels that somehow he is not a part of their world.

Aspects of the Identity Issue

His problems in this regard center in two areas of life. First, he experiences great discomfort or awkwardness in the company of men, particularly groups of men and particularly in unstructured situations. He always feels as though he is outside their world looking in. Often he doesn't share the same interests that other men have, and this sustains his feeling of always standing apart from them.

Second, the identity issue is manifested in his belief—and frequently in his experience—that in many areas he cannot do the things that men do. Not just in the company of other men, but in the family and elsewhere he feels a great inadequacy in exercising the masculine virtues, particularly taking initiative and exercising authority. This may find its expression in his assuming a very passive role in life or, as it does in some men, in his taking on a brittle type of assertiveness that tries to cover up feelings of weakness and insecurity.

Obviously these characteristics can be present in men whose sexual orientation is heterosexual, but there is a fundamental difference in the nature of this shortcoming in the two types of men. In the man with a heterosexual orientation, these insecurities rest on an often subconscious belief: "I am inadequate as a man." In the homosexually oriented man, however, the underlying belief is "I am not a man." Most boys and many men struggle long and hard to prove—largely to themselves—that they are adequate as men. Most of us who grew up homosexually oriented gave up that struggle early on. Believing that we never really could be men, we sought another man's manhood.

Whenever I am asked to describe what happens in the healing of the homosexual man, I address the three areas just described: behavior, attractions, and identity. I explain that the struggler can expect to achieve total or near total victory in the area of behavior, a significant—if not complete —shift in the direction of his sexual attractions, and he can become totally comfortable and at peace with his male identity—his manhood. I am convinced that such change is possible for any man who truly seeks it and who surrenders his life and his sexuality to Jesus.

The Centrality of Identity

Although the healing of the homosexual man is in many ways an indirect process—flowing out of the broader changes in his spiritual life—almost every homosexual overcomer is going to have to confront all three elements of the problem. He will not recover until behavior, attractions, and identity have all been dealt with and to some extent transformed. Although his natural inclination may be to focus on behavior and attractions—because this is where he feels the most distress—I believe that the richest fruit will be borne in his life if he focuses most strongly (and early on) in the area of identity.

This is true for two reasons. *First, identity is more amenable to direct attack than behavior or attractions.* I have yet to meet the man who one day said, "Today I am going to start being attracted to women rather than to men," and, barring the rare bona fide miracle, found that anything really changed. As for behavior, although trying to be obedient will always remain an essential part of the healing process, a change in behavior without a corresponding deep change in identity may be little more than "white knuckle" abstinence. Identity, on the other hand, as I will show, can be changed significantly through a program of conscious choices and specific actions.

The second reason the change process can be furthered so significantly by dealing with the identity issue is because *a man's incomplete male identity is what drives and directs homosexual behavior and attractions.* This broken or incomplete male identity is the steering mechanism that gives direction to our sexual attractions and the engine that powers our sinful behavior. Let's look at this in some detail.

With respect to attractions, the essence of sexual attraction seems to be "differences" or "otherness." Certainly, for the heterosexually oriented man, some sexual attraction may lie in his knowledge that his penis interacting with a woman's vagina can bring extraordinary pleasure. But we all know that there is so much more to sexual attraction than this. What about a woman's breasts? Why are they an object of sexual attraction to a man? These are simply organs that are there to nurse a baby; they have no direct sexual function. What about her hips, the roundness and smoothness of her skin? What about even some things that she does that are intentional, such as letting her hair grow long or wearing lipstick? Why should these things stir up sexual attractions in most men? There may be a number of reasons. A woman's body—her breasts, her roundedness—can stir up a man's desire to be nurtured; her differences may intrigue his appetite for mystery; her vulnerability might trigger his desire for conquest. All of these make sense, but what most draws man to woman sexually is that she is "other." She possesses things that a man does not have in himself.

Those characteristics that a woman has that a man doesn't have, that symbolize woman, draw him to her. They express the feminine and they draw his masculine. The masculine part of a man longs for that other. Looking at it spiritually, the man may be longing for completion, for restoration of that part of him that was removed when woman was created. Or perhaps because male and female together can reflect God more ably than man or woman alone—we were both created in God's image—a man's longing may be for a completion that more fully reflects his Creator.

I am a man, and I look to find my completion in woman. But what if the man does not have the inner sense that he is a man? Will he experience the same attractions to a woman? Will she be his "other"? No, and this is critical. If he feels that he is not complete as a man, his first longing will be not for women but for complete manhood; he will be drawn to the masculine in other males. This will be his "other." This will be his missing rib. This will be his means of attaining completion. It follows, then, that the development of our manhood—finding completion in ourselves—will do great things both to decrease our same-sex attractions and to start drawing us sexually to women.

I said that our incomplete male identity, besides determining the direction of our sexual attractions, is also the engine that drives our homosexual behavior. The enormous power of the homosexual drive is seen in the incredibly foolish, even insane things that many homosexual men will do to make some kind of contact with maleness. What causes an otherwise sensible man to pick up a tough-looking young stranger and take him to his apartment, knowing full well he risks being robbed and beaten or even worse? Why does an intelligent, married business or professional man risk arrest and public humiliation by making sexual contact with another man in a public rest room? Why did I repeatedly go into a gay bar on a main thoroughfare in Baltimore, knowing I could be seen by anyone and have my whole deception uncovered?

We did these things because of the enormity of the craving within us. We were driven to make some kind of contact with anything that represented or symbolized maleness: a hard, tough look, muscles, a man's penis. These were symbols of manhood—the manhood that we did not have—and we were driven, often obsessively, to gaze on them, touch them, smell them, taste them, become one with them in some way. Our incomplete manhood cried out for this, cried out for its missing elements.

Leanne Payne illustrates this craving for manhood with her cannibalism theory. In *The Broken Image* she describes how cannibals eat only the people they admire, believing that by eating them they can acquire some of their traits.[4] This "consuming" drive for manhood in the homosexual male becomes obvious: A man who feels he lacks complete manhood satisfies his need for it through his homosexual behavior, hoping to acquire some of the other man's manhood.

The key point to remember, however, is that the craving for another's manhood is only present in a man who feels he lacks his own manhood. Is that not the case with all covetousness? We crave the things we don't have or believe we don't have. So intense is that craving—so powerful the engine that can drive a man to homosexual behavior—that even when such behavior flies in the face of both his fundamental human desire to protect himself and his most basic religious beliefs, he still cannot stop himself.

The identity issue manifests itself in another way. Many of us see the failure to have been affirmed by men (or conversely the feeling that we were rejected) as a key element in the development of our homosexuality. In this regard, the powerful homosexual drive is a desperate plea from the little boy within: "Won't some man show me that I have some value as a man to a man?" This is not just a craving to ease the pain of low self-esteem. A man may be quite valued by the women in his life, and he may recognize that he has extraordinary gifts in certain areas, but the cry of the little boy is still there. His value must be shown by a man, and the area being valued must express manhood.

As with so many parts of life, especially areas of deeper need, this need can be sexualized. From that point on, a sexual liaison or simply receiving a signal that another man desires him, even if only as a sex object, somehow temporarily satisfies the craving. This accounts for much of what I call "dry cruising" that homosexual men do, going where other men may come on to them, even at a time when sexual contact is not desired. Sometimes, on the way home from work, when I knew I could not explain being more than a half-hour late, I would still stop at a gay bar. I was not looking for a contact but only hoping that some man would show me that he wanted me.

No Shortcut to Growing Up

God could zap any one of us and give us total victory over our sexual sins in an instant. There was such a zapping in my healing in that I was set free from desire for sex with men at the time of my conversion. But because He has a far better plan for us, this is not the way God usually operates. He is not content to see us merely fulfill our desire to stop our sinful behavior, nor is He satisfied to find us merely being turned on to women sexually. He wants us to become the men he created us to be, true men in every respect. He may allow sinful behavior to continue so as to bring us to the point at which we will surrender the powerful stranglehold that has us in bondage. Likewise, He may allow the pain of undeveloped manhood to continue in order to make us finally willing to go through the painful process of growing up into the men He created us to be.

When my children were growing up, I hated to see them get hurt physically. However, I still took the training wheels off their bikes. I would rather see them get a little bloody and bruised than have them never able to ride a bike. I would rather see them try, fall, and try again than see them grow up to be fearful individuals.

If this is your circumstance, does it seem as though God is playing games with you? Is He letting you dangle in the wind in your homosexuality until you finally figure out what you are supposed to do? Certainly not. One of the principal metaphors that God uses to describe the relationship that He wants with us is that of a father and a son. What does any man desire for his son more than that he grow into the fullness of his manhood? If we then, who are sinful, desire this for our sons, how much more must God desire this for us? He who planted in each of us all the attributes of manhood could not want anything less than that these attributes grow and blossom to their fullest. And just as a good father disciplines the son he loves, so will our Father let us suffer in our brokenness until we hear His voice and start to seek the very best that He has for us, our full manhood.

God established the family in which each father would teach his son what it means to be a man. We know that life hasn't always worked out this way. Sin came into the world, and fatherhood, like everything else, became imperfect. However, God's ultimate plan for us has not changed. While His original plan for our lives may have failed through human sin, redemption is ours through Jesus Christ. God will be our Father, and He will walk us through the process that will bring us into our full manhood. All things become new in Jesus Christ.

the way a man develops

We may never see in our lifetimes a decisive resolution to the genes-versus-environment debates that go on with respect to all sorts of human behaviors and conditions. Full understanding eludes us not only because the interactions of genes and environment are so complex but also because with so many types of behavior, various groups have a vested interest in promoting the belief that either one or the other is the determining factor. For example, homosexual activists seem determined to find proof that homosexuality is hard-wired into a child. Their thinking is that if this is believed, then a just society will surely have to recognize homosexuality as an acceptable way of life. On the other hand, those of us who wish to have our change from homosexuality to heterosexuality appear credible are anxious to promote the belief that we were not born that way. On a similar issue, early radical feminists promoted the belief that, except for certain differences related to reproductive roles, men and women are exactly alike, that all of the role and behavior differences we see are the result of environmental influences. Such extreme, politically motivated views receive less acceptance today, and people are coming to believe that environment and heredity together—along with free will, as most Christians can see—play important roles in making us what we are.

How boys become men is a part of this debate, and it is certainly relevant to the theme of this book. Is a little boy born with traits that will almost inevitably lead him to take roles and behave in ways that we see as common to men in our society and other societies? Or does the culture dictate this? From the earliest weeks of their lives, are little boys steered by their parents and the broader community in the direction of assuming the same roles their fathers had? Or is something else, something internal, driving them in this direction?

Certainly I will not resolve this debate here, but I cannot ignore it altogether either. Rather, I will address it by starting with two fairly basic hypotheses, ones that I believe most readers will be able to accept. I will build on them later. In chapter 6, we will deal with many of the inborn markers of a man as we examine the full range of differences between men's and women's bodies. And throughout the book, as we look at how manhood develops, we will be continually addressing environmental factors.

The following two hypotheses are necessary to support the concept of growth into manhood put forth in this book. I hope they will appear acceptable on their face. If not, I urge you to read on anyway and see how they fit into the real world—the almost universal real world—of boys growing into men.

1. Boys have a biological destiny to grow into men: men who are different from women in ways that go well beyond genital design and reproductive functions.

2. Societal structures have always existed to guide the process of growth from boyhood to manhood.

Taken together, these hypotheses do not reflect an extreme viewpoint. I am not claiming that manhood is either all genetic or all learned. If we assume that hypothesis 2 is necessary, not just a fluke that happens to occur in every culture, then we can carry the hypothesis a bit farther and say: Boys are genetically destined to become men, but guidance along the way is necessary or the process may not work out satisfactorily.

FROM BOY TO MAN: WHAT HE BECOMES

From a purely physiological point of view, when a little boy is born, if nothing takes his life prematurely, he will grow up to be a man. Simple, a biological fact. He is born with the raw material to be a man, and the main element needed to facilitate the conversion is time.

Now during a part of this time, someone will have to feed him and protect him from the hostile elements of nature and from any other enemies he might encounter. This being so, we would say that he becomes a man when he can fend for himself in terms of gathering food, providing his own shelter, and otherwise defending himself.

He needs to become a producer or provider, able to procure his basic needs. How old would he be when this occurs? It would depend. If food was plentiful and available for the gathering, and if the elements were not too hostile, early adolescence could quite well mark his full emergence into manhood. However, if nature was not so accommodating and he had to learn how to farm or hunt or fish or go through the supermarket checkout line to survive, manhood would be delayed until he learned these necessary skills.

But that's not quite all. We recognize that man is a member of a species, so he has not reached full manhood until he is sexually mature enough to father his own kind. This takes him at least through puberty.

Following this, if nature is not totally accommodating—and it seldom is—the children that he fathers will likely die and his species with it unless he is willing to take care of the children and mother during the children's earliest years, especially while the children are being nursed. There are creatures—deer, for instance—among whom the father impregnates the mother and has nothing to do with the offspring. But given the long period during which human offspring need care, survival of the race would be doubtful if the man is not ready and willing to assume the role of both husband and father.

But this is merely a biological view of man. Man is more than just an independent biological entity; he is a social creature. If we move from biology to sociology or anthropology, we find that man has never, on a large scale, lived alone or simply within his nuclear family. There has never been a civilization based on hermits or an archipelago of family "islands." Man forms liaisons with other men or other families for the purpose of mutual defense or to organize ways of more efficiently providing for each family's needs. Thus, he is created to function within a larger community or, more likely, within different levels of community. To be a functioning man, he must participate in the life of his immediate community and his larger community or nation, at times being called to defend his community or nation. Today, we say he functions as a citizen.

We still need to go one step further. A man is more than a biological or social creature; he is also a spiritual one. He is not complete until his spiritual self finds expression. He must live out his life in relationship with the God in whose image he was created. First the Jews and then the Christians were taught that this type of relationship was also to take place in community. For Christians, this community is the church. Full manhood requires that a man is able to function as a member of the body of Christ.

So when is full manhood achieved? A boy possesses manhood when he reaches the point at which he is capable of being a provider, a husband, a father, a citizen, and a member of the body of Christ.

But there is still one more dimension to this growth into manhood. Each perspective of manhood has a qualitative side. After God created man, He said that this creation was "very good" (Genesis 1:31). The manhood that every little boy, every adolescent, and every man seeks, that every mother and father desire for their sons, has a qualitative side to it also. The very word *manhood* has a strong qualitative connotation to it. Unless we are speaking in the narrowest of biological terms, when we say that someone is a "real man," we are also expressing our view of the quality of his manhood. Manhood comes not only when we can do what is necessary for us and our human race to survive, but it comes when we do these things well. To achieve manhood is good in and of itself, but some men's manhood is better than others. Certainly, in the context of this book and in line with the aspirations of most readers, complete manhood implies being able to do all of the things that a man does—being a provider, husband, father, citizen, and Christian—and doing them well.

Most of us would agree that we don't expect to do all of this perfectly. There was only one perfect man. And doing "well" is a subjective term. But I believe that we can generally know when to apply it. For example, by the time my son, Stephen, was turning twenty-one, I knew that he was ready to do well as a husband, for he was kind and protective toward his fiancée, and he truly loved her. He also loved children. He has chosen to be a teacher, and children adore him. Also, it was clear that he would have little trouble being firm with children. He was a strong Christian both in terms of being an active witness and in his discipling of others on his college campus. He was firm in his beliefs and loyalties, so he was destined to be a good citizen. On the remaining count he was not there yet. Until he completed his education in another year, he would be hard pressed to be the provider his family would need. Even making allowance for a father's prejudices, I believe that I can identify "well" in Steve. Look around you. Can't you identify it in others, in yourself?

Interestingly, this definition of manhood—being able to be a provider, husband, father, member of the body of Christ, and citizen, and doing all of these things well—is similar to what I wrote several years ago in *Regeneration News* to answer the question "When are you healed from homosexuality?" We are healed when we are ready to do well in assuming all obligations and privileges generally assigned to a man. Central to these is the ability to be an adequate husband and father. Note that I am using the word *ability*. We do not have to actually be living these roles at the present time, and many men will never marry, some because of circumstances and some because of a higher calling to ministry that overrules marriage. Many more will not father children. But it is when we are capable of fulfilling these roles in a satisfactory way that we have reached full manhood and, for many of us, recovery from homosexuality.

It should be clear that *manhood* as used here is not synonymous with "adult male," although *manhood* by definition means "possessing the qualities of an adult male." Adulthood alone does not signify manhood; it is adulthood plus certain qualities different from those possessed by a woman or a child. Furthermore, I am using *manhood* and terms like *full manhood* or *complete manhood* to identify a point in our growth, not its completion. Even after we can do all of these things well, we hope to continue to grow for the rest of our lives in all of our appropriate roles and in all manly virtues.

Many of you reading this who struggle with homosexuality will see that in some areas you have already reached full manhood. The fact that you are serious and sober enough to read a book like this and are willing to consider going down the difficult road suggested here is an indication that much growth into manhood has already taken place. I hope that what has been written in this chapter thus far will affirm you.

For those of you who have not reached the fullness of manhood by all of these criteria, I challenge you to keep moving on. You can make it! You will be able to fulfill all of the purposes that God has for you here on earth—and you will be able to fulfill them well.

How He Gets There

Growth into manhood, going through all of the processes that take us from conception to full maturity, involves an extraordinary number of changes in physiology, intellect and understanding, sexuality, identity, relational skills, and on and on. The individual changes that must take place are probably too many to count. And yet for most boys the process takes place "automatically," that is, with little conscious awareness that the process is taking place. Hence, the vast number of individuals conceived as boys will, if they survive, attain mature manhood. This is not to say perfect manhood, or even a manhood that they are totally content with themselves, but they will become fully functioning men. One major exception to this is the 2 to 5 percent[5] who will grow up unable to fully function as men. These are the ones we identify as homosexual men.

When concerned parents in this gender-confused society ask me what they should do to make sure that their sons grow up with a normal and healthy sexual identity, my first answer is, "Do what's natural and try not to make any mistakes." This sounds glib, but it bears a great deal of truth. The fact that parents in all generations, in all cultures, having all levels of education and skills tend to raise sons—about 97 percent of them—with a clear heterosexual identity indicates that the process is fairly "automatic," to a great extent a matter of doing what comes naturally. Of course parents make mistakes. We will be dealing with some of these—and their corrections—as we proceed on.

The process works most of the time because God created us to be male and female, and because He created the family in which to raise boys and girls into men and women. The process works most of the time in all times and places, among intellectuals and among savages, among Christians and among pagans. Because it flows out of our physical being and out of the family structure, man has historically not needed elaborate theories as to how to raise sons and daughters. However, in today's society, there are a couple of reasons why it can be important to understand the process.

First, we live in a society in which there is no longer a cultural consensus as to what a boy is and what a girl is. Therefore, clarity in this area on our part can help us do a much better job in raising our sons—and in raising ourselves if our manhood still is not fully developed. Both the breakdown of the family and today's absence of strongly held cultural norms makes the raising of sons a much more precarious task.

Second, understanding the process of how manhood develops may enable us to identify what went wrong in some of us, and if there is something we can do to correct what went wrong, this could reap great benefits. This book is based on the belief that we can identify some of those things, and they can now be rectified to a great extent, no matter how many years later.

So let's look at the process whereby manhood is developed. General thinking today is that it follows distinct and identifiable stages. For us to understand what went wrong in our lives, and for the purpose of correcting what went wrong, let us look at these stages. Although there have been many theories put forth with respect to a boy's growth into manhood, most experts today would agree that one way or another, growth encompasses the following steps:

1. Physiological: At the cellular level, in the structure of the body and in the operations of the brain, there is that which is designed male and that which is designed female. Physiological growth starts with conception and continues on at least through puberty.

2. Separating from the mother: This occurs physically in the birth process, supportively in the process of being weaned, and psychologically in the boy's taking on an identity separate from his mother.

3. Identifying with the father or "the man": The boy regards his father and knows that he in some way is like him.

4. Modeling after or imitating the father: The boy wants to be like his father and so watches him and tries to be like him.

5. Testing his manhood: He wants to prove that he is like his father, so he tests himself to be affirmed that he is a man like his father, seeking affirmation first from his father and then from peers.

6. Getting affirmed: He gets feedback from his father or peers that tells him he is indeed a man.

7. Accepting his manhood: Affirmation has been sufficient for him to accept internally that he is a man.

For our discussion, it will be helpful to group these seven steps into three broader phases. The first step of physical formation stands alone as the Physiological phase. The next three steps, separating from the mother, identifying with the father, and modeling himself after the father, constitute a process of taking on an identity as a specific individual and as an individual who is a man. However, as we will see later, this is not a completed process; the identity is provisional at this point. We will call this phase Establishing a Tentative Identity. The last steps, testing manhood, getting it affirmed, and accepting it, represent an ongoing building process that may take place over many years. We will call this phase simply Affirmation.

To summarize, manhood is developed as a boy goes through the three stages, encompassing the seven steps shown in Figure I.

Let's look at each phase.

PHYSIOLOGICAL

The physical formation of a man—that which distinguishes him from a woman—will be discussed in some detail in chapter 6, so I will offer only a few words here. The physical process of the development of a man starts at

FIGURE I. PHASES OF GROWTH INTO MANHOOD

Phases	Steps
I. Physiological	1. Creation and maturity of the male body
II. Establishing a Tentative Identity	2. Separating from the mother
	3. Identifying with the father or "the man"
	4. Modeling
III. Affirmation	5. Testing his manhood
	6. Getting affirmed
	7. Accepting his manhood

conception and goes through puberty and adolescence. These processes differentiate boys from girls not only in their genital and reproductive capacities but in such things as height, musculature, body fat, hemoglobin in the blood, brain formation, and so on. Among men (just as among women) God's love for diversity shows up in the differences between individuals, but there are still common factors that make men men and women women.

Establishing a Tentative Identity

In recent years many books, Christian and secular, have described the process that is seen as forming a male identity. Very briefly, most tend to follow this sort of scenario in the early stages. A little boy, when he comes out of his mother's body, does not even know that he is a distinct entity from his mother. This is understandable; after all he has spent his entire existence to this point encompassed in her body. Nursing and continually being held by her helps keep this perception alive for a while, but then reality sets in. There are times when he is physically separated from her, and there are times when she shows a will separate from his own, so he starts to sense that he is separate. But a separate what?

The theory goes that he looks around to find someone whose existence will reveal to him who he is. He has a need for an identity apart from his mother, and he can't create it out of thin air or theoretical pondering. Aha, he sees Dad or a substitute for Dad. Dad is "other," but somehow, he is like Dad. Dad shows an interest in him, and, needing to have an identity, he connects or identifies with Dad. Then, once the basic need to have an identity apart from the mother is met with the father, and provided he has favorable responses from the father, he decides he wants to be like Dad. He starts imitating the things that Dad does. Dad has become his role model and will be, at least until he encounters other significant boys or men in his life.

This theory of forming a tentative identity seems to make a great deal of sense. It gives us an explanation of how this tiny creature coming out of his mother's body can know in a couple of years that he is a separate person and a male person at that. I saw this in my son, Steve. When he was born, he had a mother and two doting sisters aged twelve and thirteen, almost the equivalent of three mothers. But sometime before he was eighteen months old, he started showing that he knew that he was more like me than like his sisters and mother. That sense never left him. I have to admit that with my background, being only eighteen months out of homosexuality when he was born, I did everything I could to make him clearly aware of his maleness. But Steve's consciousness of gender was not a product of my concerns. A friend's son who just turned two is asking: "Is that a boy?" "Am I a boy?" "Mommy, are you a girl?"

In discussing the process of identifying with the father, I am going to refer to the process of *identification* with the father rather than of the more common *bonding*. I do this because the concept of bonding has certain implications that could present an unnecessary obstacle to a man's delayed growth into manhood.

The image many have of bonding is that it is something that happens suddenly and that it is always with a specific man, usually the little boy's father. Essentially it has been seen as a *sudden connection,* like falling in love. One minute the son and his father (or father substitute) are two separate entities, and the next they are connected. I have known young fathers who would intentionally hold their newborn sons to their bare chests believing that some type of instant bonding would take place. This is a beautiful picture, one that reflects well on the heart of a father who so wants to bless his son, but it presents bonding as an almost mystical event. Bonding in this context is seen as a one-time occurrence, and the implication is that if it doesn't take place very early on, the boy will never develop a healthy, mature manhood. To me the concept of this type of bonding is not acceptable for two reasons.

The first is based on looking at the widespread deterioration of the family in modern society, specifically at the huge number of boys being raised without any adult male in their lives. True, many boys born out of wedlock have the mother's boyfriend or father with whom they can bond, but a great number of boys don't have such father substitutes. They are raised with just mom or in an otherwise all female environment. Despite this fact, I have seen no evidence that indicates we are facing an enormous increase in male homosexuality. Admittedly, it may be too early to identify such a trend, and the restrictions of political correctness might discourage academic institutions from investigating such a phenomenon. But we have seen literally hundreds of studies in the past few years reporting other negative consequences that occur in boys raised without a father. However, no increase in the incidence of homosexuality has shown up.

Identification and modeling, in contrast to bonding, are almost always possible, and they need not take place in the earliest days of a boy's life. If there is no father present, there may be a neighbor or family friend or, unfortunately, the television character or the corner drug pusher. Fatherless boys often seem to identify with the wrong kind of men, but as far as we know, they do take on a male identity in equal proportion to boys with fathers or father figures.

The second reason I question the concept of every little boy's need to bond with a father or father substitute is that if it were an essential part of growing into manhood, then we who never did bond in this way could never grow into the fullness of our manhood in later years. I reject this idea unequivocally. If bonding at an early age was absolutely necessary, then barring an authentic miracle, none of us would be healed. We cannot go back as adults and bond with our fathers or with any man as a baby boy would. We are too different from an infant. Our many experiences, our adult imaginations and analytical abilities, our memories of past experiences, our adult male tendency to sexualize relationships—all of these make us radically different from a child at the point he would have bonded. Our forming a bond with a man today would be nothing like the transaction that takes place between a baby and an adult. And yet many of us do grow into our manhood and do overcome homosexuality.

But something does occur between the time the boy separates from the mother and the time he decides to start acting like his father and other men around him. I call it "identification." The little boy sees that somehow he is different from his mother and his sisters and his grandmother and that he is like those other creatures called men. It may be a slow realization or it may come as a sudden "Aha!" experience, but either way it is key to setting his direction for growth into manhood.

This may seem like splitting hairs. After all, what does it matter whether we call what happens bonding or identification? I believe it does matter. Identification is a far less mysterious thing than bonding, and it is something that could occur at any time, even in adulthood. Hopefully, as you are reading this book, if you have never done so before, you will come to the point at which you will say, "Aha! I am not that different from other men. I am a man, and there is no reason why I can't grow into a full sense of my manhood."

AFFIRMATION

I challenge the central place of bonding in male development for another reason—because we need to shift our focus on the homosexual struggle from establishing a tentative identity to affirmation. Surely some things went wrong in the early years of most of our lives, but most of us did separate from our mothers, and most of us did have some sort of men with whom we could identify. If we did not bond, so be it. In fact, except for the rare transsexual, every one of us came to know at some level that we were male. And even today, an adult man who has been in gender confusion for much of his life can rather easily identify himself intellectually as a man. But what is really needed is affirmation of that identification. This is where our emphasis should lie. This is where the great struggles will occur, for it is through affirmation that our sense of manhood comes to dwell in our deepest parts.

The affirmation process—what happens wherein the boy with a tentative male identity has his manhood affirmed to the extent that at the deepest level he takes on a male identity—is not linear. It does not take place one-two-three and it's done. Rather, it is circular or spiral. The little boy tests, he gets affirmed, he feels a little more of his manhood, and so he tries again in a little more challenging environment. If he takes up weightlifting and gains confidence in his ability to curl forty pounds, he moves up to fifty. Of course sometimes he fails the test. But if the boy has a fairly strong tentative identity and if he lives in a supportive environment, he will keep trying until he makes it.

My son, as a little guy, was not a great athlete. In fact, in both Little League baseball and basketball he seldom got to play. But he loved sports, and he had such a level of confidence in himself that he never quit trying. He never stopped thoroughly enjoying sports. This zeal for sports led him to play varsity football in high school. Today, if other young men are around and he has the time, he will spend hours playing basketball, ice hockey, and tennis. To a limited extent, sports are still a means of testing and getting affirmed in manhood for Steve, but I suspect that at age twenty-three and seemingly quite confident in his manhood, he simply loves sports. Later, we will discuss the tremendous significance sports has for a man in our culture, and we will touch on the way men gravitate toward and take delight in "being physical."

Of course the primary affirmer in the early years usually is Dad. The little boy comes to his dad and makes a muscle, and Dad exclaims, "Awesome!" He wrestles with Dad to try to match his strength. As he approached adolescence, Steve always wanted to arm wrestle with me. He was always testing, always looking for affirmation—eventually always beating me.

But there comes a time when Dad's affirmation isn't enough. Perhaps there is a sense of "He has to approve of me; I'm his kid." Or maybe Dad is the type who doesn't do much affirming. Whatever the reason, in early adolescence the search for affirmation is broadened. It focuses on peers. The testing moves out of the home, typically to the playground. The process is competitive and has the potential to produce some losers and some pain. For this reason many boys will seek an environment where their successes will outnumber their failures. This process almost always takes place in a group environment, and the boy will start fulfilling that strange, almost universal male longing to belong to a group of men. The combination of achieving, being affirmed, and belonging can make this a wonderful experience for a young boy.

I have had several of what I call "golden days" in my life. These are days that stand out as so perfect, so beautiful, that years later I can literally still feel the joy of them. One was the day Stephen graduated from elementary school. It was an absolutely gorgeous June day, and he was ending his time at a wonderful little public school that seemed to belie all of the problems we hear about with public education today. Steve had a pack of friends, some of them going back to nursery school days, whom he was always with. We knew the boys well; they had been to our home many, many times over the years. They all looked handsome, dressed up for the ceremony, and they all behaved in typical boyish fashion. Until they got on the stage for the ceremony, they never stopped moving. Punching each other, chasing one another, the picture they brought to my mind was of a group of puppy dogs playing, all over each other. Steve belonged, and he unconsciously loved being a young boy. Perhaps that day still glows in my memory because I realized that day that Steve was completely on the right track toward manhood.

At some point, and I suspect that it is quite early in adolescence, the testing-and-affirming process appears to plant the final seal of authenticity on a boy's manhood. After this point, rejection by peers or by girls will not take away his deep sense that he is a man. The point at which the testing-and-affirming process leads the boy to a deep, solid sense that he is a man may not be consciously recognized. In fact, by the time he says the proverbial "Today, I am a man," he has probably long since internalized this truth.

The testing-and-affirming process does not end with the establishment of a basic male identity. To a limited extent it goes on with men, sometimes playfully, sometimes neurotically, for much of their lives. In men who feel like men but very inadequate ones, the testing and seeking affirmation can express itself in unhealthy ways: ruthlessness in business, cruelty in relationships, boastfulness, or womanizing. For healthy adult men, however, the testing-and-affirming process is simply an exercise of their God-given desire to prevail.

The testing-and-affirming process is the basis of training for men called to perform in extraordinary ways. Military boot camp is a prime example of this. Men, operating in a group, are put in a position of being tested over and over again—for the most part physically—facing challenges that will be difficult to meet but that the majority will be able to meet. This is the way the marines or the army "makes a man" out of a raw recruit. The testing, and knowing he has met the test, gives the recruit the confidence to be a fighting man when the need arises. I mention this especially to point out that the testing and affirming can take place at any time in a man's life. Just because it was skipped in childhood, don't conclude that it cannot be gone through later.

It is not too late for you.

what went wrong in our lives?

Having addressed the "normal" process that the vast majority of men go through, we saw the steps that bring them to the point at which they have a solid sense of their manhood. Of course, in this sinful and broken world, many may not turn out to be good men, or they themselves may not be very confident of the level or quality of their manhood, but they know without a doubt that they are men and nothing else.

Some of us, however, didn't get that far. For some reason—or reasons—we reached full physical maturity without having a deep inner sense that we were men, or we believed that if we were men, we were profoundly different from other men. Our identity did not rest on a foundation of assumed and almost unconscious manhood. We didn't feel that we were women, but it was as if we were void of any kind of gender identity. We might have identified ourselves as "nonmen," characterized not by what we were, but by what we were not.

Our peers went on and grew according to a common pattern. They had relatively successful relationships with other males, ones that seemed free of the emotional or sexual baggage that so often appeared in our male relationships. They felt entirely different about girls, and most of them were getting married and having children. Life would go on for them in the pattern that had gone on since the beginning of time. For us, it looked as though the cycle had come to a dead end. What happened?

Before we look at what did go wrong in the stages of our development,

I want to pick up on that term *nonmen*. It appears that two distinct things happen on the detour that leads a boy into homosexual adulthood. Unless, at an early age, he is deliberately influenced to do so by another person, he does not simply reach the normal age of acceptance of his manhood and decide, "I am gay." That's the second step. The first step encompasses the period of being a nonman.

He knows that physiologically he is a man, but at the same time he feels that he is different from all the other boys or men around him. His interests, his skills, his relational abilities all seem so different from what other boys have. At some point he notices that his peers are showing sexual attraction to women, while he is attracted to men. He is not in denial about this, but he hasn't put it all together to create an identity for himself out of all these differences. All he knows is that he is different.

TAKING ON THE HOMOSEXUAL IDENTITY

It may be hard for many to believe, but not too many years ago it was not unusual for a man to clearly acknowledge his homosexual longings, to be acting on them, to have no sexual or romantic feelings toward women at all, and still not identify himself as gay or as a homosexual. In fact, at one time, such a man would have been the norm for homosexually oriented men. The whole idea that *homosexual* could describe a *person* rather than just a *behavior* started to evolve only about 150 years ago. Homosexuality as an identity simply did not exist before that.

This lack of recognizing a homosexual identity is not just a historical phenomenon. It is a part of the pattern of individuals moving into homosexuality. As recently as 1971 it was found that the average interval between the time when a person recognized his same-sex attractions and the time when he decided that he was "a homosexual" was about seven years.[6] In my situation, I can remember myself as a thirty-five-year-old man sitting in a gay bar where I had gone to meet someone for sex, feeling sorry "for all those poor gays." This sounds like denial, but I don't believe it was. As I look back on my views at that time, I believe I knew intuitively that these other men had defined themselves in a way that was going to structure and guide their whole lives. I had not. With the strong, gay-affirming messages that come across in the media and with the increase of gay-positive programs in our schools, almost certainly the time between first acknowledging homosexual feelings and taking on a gay identity has shortened.

In growing into manhood, each man is going to have to let go of this false identity, but this is the second step, and we will deal with that later, in chapter 12. Right now, I want to deal with the first step: what went wrong in the earlier developmental stages, those days when the nonman emerged. Somehow we failed to go through all of the stages of developing our manhood. Somewhere we got off track. Either our tentative identity as a man did not take form, or if it did, somewhere along the way it was snuffed out. Something beyond step one in the development of manhood has not happened.

DIFFERENT TYPES OF HOMOSEXUALITY

There has been an evolution in the theories as to what went wrong, that is, what causes homosexuality. As regards male homosexuality, we went from Freud and the dominant-mother theory, to a focus on the deficit in a boy's relationship with his father, to a multicausal model with many lesser theories coming and going.

My interest here is not to go into a great deal of detail on the origins of homosexuality; the reader would be wise to go to the sources that focus primarily on this area. I strongly recommend that you do read Moberly, Satinover, Davies and Rentzel, and Nicolosi (see appendix C). Our objective here is not to offer a broad teaching on the causes of homosexuality, but rather to identify certain specific things that did go wrong so that we can correct, compensate for, undo, or otherwise make them right in ourselves—

even today. To identify the solutions, we must first recognize the problems. As we do this, we will discover that applying the solution is anything but easy. We will see that our past experiences have thrown up some formidable roadblocks on our new path to manhood. But they are not insurmountable, and overcoming these roadblocks will be a major part of the process that will be described in coming chapters.

Before going further, however, we need to spend a little time looking at an important principle: Not all homosexuality is the same. In fact, there appear to be different types or "strains" of male homosexuality that reflect the different drives men are seeking to fulfill homosexually. These different drives come out of different life experiences.

When we think of male homosexuality, we most often picture a man who is driven to seek both sexual and emotional contact with another man. There are physical, romantic, and possibly dependency elements in his homosexuality. In this type of man we almost always find gender-identity deficits or confusion.

Another type is the man who exalts manhood to the extreme. At the same time, he denigrates womanhood, and as an outgrowth of this, he sees a man (usually a younger man or teenage boy) as a more desirable sexual partner. This type of man seldom shows any deficit in manhood. To the contrary, he may be the warrior or super-man type. This phenomenon was seen in the ancient Greeks and Romans and more recently in the Nazis.[7] There may be an element of love for the younger man who is the object of the older man's attractions, but the older man seems driven by male idolatry rather than gender emptiness.

I call a third type of homosexuality, which may not reflect a deep deficit in male identity, "fetish" homosexuality. A man's focus locks on to a certain part of the male body (usually the penis) or a single homosexual act, but he shows little in the way of other homosexual manifestations. There is no emotional longing for a man. His masculine identity is fairly solid, although he may have a fear of women. A variation on this is the man who has some hindrance in his ability to relate to women, so he simply uses homosexual men to gain sexual gratification.

When we see these different forms of homosexual expression, we can be quite sure that we are seeing different patterns of homosexual development. And if the development pattern is different, so are the remedies. The type of homosexual development we are dealing with here, the more common type, seems to be evident in the majority of men who seek help from our ministries. But it is not present in all, and it is important that those who do not fit this pattern identify the real needs and deficits that drive their homosexual desires.

However, most of us did follow a general progression, one in which something was flawed in our relationships with our fathers and in which something major was lacking in our identity as men.

MOBERLY AND "NORMAL" HOMOSEXUALITY

Dr. Elizabeth Moberly in her book *Homosexuality: A New Christian Ethic* described homosexuality as being a reparative drive coming out of a same-sex love deficit.[8] Dr. Moberly's theory received immediate acceptance by most ex-gay ministries because it lined up so well with what we were observing in our clients and with what many of us sensed about our own lives.

She describes how a process starts when a child (we will use boys in our example) experiences a trauma that disrupts his relationship with the same-sex parent (the father). The boy perceives this, whether it is or not, as rejection coming from his father. This is extremely painful for the little boy, and so to keep from feeling further hurt or rejection, he pulls away from his father. Dr. Moberly calls this *defensive detachment*. It is as if the boy is saying to his father, "I am not going to relate to you anymore; then you can't hurt me." By not allowing any kind of strong connection to exist between him and his father, he is far less apt to feel rejection.

Of course, there is then something else that he doesn't receive from his father—his identity as a man. The stage of identification with the father either is aborted or never takes place. He sees Dad as hurtful, and so he does not want to be like him. He fails to model himself after Dad, and in some cases he may react against what he sees his father as being. He is not taking into himself those traits of his father that are characteristically masculine. When he gets into the world of boys, boys who have started to take on some of their fathers' masculine traits—aggressiveness, competitiveness, a focus on the physical world, a desire to expend physical energy—he realizes he is different. In the process, what Dr. Moberly calls *same-sex ambivalence* sets in. He wants what the other boys have, but he resents them. He craves masculinity, but he fears it and gets angry toward those who have it. This same-sex ambivalence continues to mark his relationship with his father and with most other men in his life.

When puberty comes, the boy's natural desire for the masculine, something he now feels he can never possess in himself, turns toward other males. It becomes erotic. He becomes drawn to other men sexually. But, according to Dr. Moberly, the drive is a healthy drive, a reparative drive. The boy actually wants to fulfill basic love, dependency, and identification needs, needs that should have been met by a man. However, a deficit has occurred, and now he is trying to get those needs met in a wrong way, a way that will never achieve its real goal.

Note that Dr. Moberly identified three needs: love, dependency, and identification. Logically, she suggested that these same-sex needs could be met legitimately in nonsexual relationships with same-sex people. When we took hold of her teaching, many in Exodus ministries tended to focus on the unmet need for same-sex love. Perhaps that was to be expected. The hunger that homosexual men feel toward other men certainly feels like a hunger for love. And besides, what better way could there be to overcome homosexuality than by having an unmet love need met by another man? It was suggested by Dr. Moberly and others that the need for same-sex attachment could come from a same-sex therapist or other helper.

THE NEED: SAME-SEX LOVE OR
SAME-SEX AFFIRMATION?

I started to question the thesis of the same-sex love need some years ago after leading a workshop at the Second Congress on the Bible in Washington, D.C. In my talk I placed considerable emphasis on the same-sex love need. Afterward, I was challenged by a member of my class, a Chinese doctor who shared that in the pre-Communist China of his youth, fathers were typically distant authoritative figures. They seldom showed any signs of affection, especially with sons. However, he pointed out, homosexuality was extremely rare in China despite this emotional distance. This rarity of homosexuality in China was also mentioned by psychiatrist author Ruth Tiffany Barnhouse in *Homosexuality: A Symbolic Confusion*.[9]

Remembering this and hearing the histories of many men who came to Regeneration over the years led me to believe that what we were dealing with was not a same-sex love deficit but a deficit in affirmation. The little boy sought affirmation of his manhood by his father and, in his perception at least, never received it. In a highly structured society like pre-Communist China, where male and female roles were rigidly defined and strongly supported by the culture, it was not difficult for a boy to know who he was and who he was destined to be as a man. The father, quite naturally, without having to show any signs of intimacy or affection, could easily affirm the son in his man's role. At the same time, the culture around him would be affirming and esteeming this role.

Another factor leading me to question the central role of the unmet same-sex love need is the observation that in our ministry we meet relatively few men whose fathers were the direct opposite of warm and loving; that is, who were physically brutal. The boy who is physically (not sexually) abused by his father is certainly not getting his same-sex love need met, but in a perverse way the father may be sending a message that he has expectations for the boy that make him worth beating. At least his father notices that he exists. In a warped way the physical nature of the act—man-to-man—could show the boy that he has a manly role. I am not saying that a warm, loving father might not be essential to a boy's healthy development and future emotional well-being, nor that a brutal father won't quite likely leave other emotional and psychological scars. I am suggesting that these elements may not be critical in helping determine the boy's most basic male identity.

The verbally abusive father is another matter altogether, especially if the father's abuse denigrates the son's manhood. Unfavorable comparisons with more manly brothers or showing signs of disappointment in the son's manhood are clearly the antithesis of the affirmation that the boy needs. Yet over and over again men tell us of having grown up with such fathers.

One further observation leads me to question that a same-sex love deficit is central to the development of homosexuality. We do not run into a disproportionate number of homosexual men in our ministries who had no father at all. The total absence of a father does not seem to increase the odds of homosexual development. Joseph Nicolosi writes, "There is clear evidence that boys with absent fathers are capable of heterosexual adjustment if they have not experienced emotional rejection from a significant male figure."[10] Of course, for many boys there was a father substitute, but for many there was not. This latter group certainly did not have their same-sex love needs met, yet we are not seeing that this correlates with homosexuality.

On the other hand, we do see among our clients a disproportionate number of men whose fathers left the family at a critical time in their development, usually through divorce or death. For those who can remember such an event, there is often the recognition that the departure of the father was interpreted by the boy as rejection. The feeling in the heartbroken little boy is *If I had been important to my dad, he would not have left me.* The significant factor here appears to be the boy's sense of rejection by the father, not the absence of the father.

In Dr. Moberly's theory of *defensive detachment*, the word *detachment* has a significance that may have gone unnoticed by many: We can only detach from something to which we were once attached. To detach from his father a boy must have at some point attached to, or identified with, his father. To some degree, flickering though it may have been, he started to establish a tentative male identity (phase two in our development model), but either the identity was barely formed or it was snuffed out. The real or perceived rejection of the son by the father could have done either thing: "Daddy rejected me; I don't want to be like him." His father was not an attractive man after whom he wanted to model himself.

The tentative identity requires affirmation at each level of its formation. Steve came to me and made a muscle, and I told him what a man he was. Steve threw the ball, and I told him what a big boy he was. If consistently I had been too busy to look at his muscle or play ball with him, too tied up with church work or too engrossed in my newspaper, not only would he have missed the affirmation that he needed, but he would have seen my response as rejection—the very opposite of affirmation. My recurring refusal to acknowledge him would have sent a message to him that he was worth less than my paper, less than my job, or less than my church work—worthless. And his worth in his mind equaled his worth as a man. For a man to have rejected him would have been to reject his manhood.

The stereotypical father that many homosexual men would identify as being like their own is the one who is physically present in the family but not engaged with them. In the words of many of our men, "He was there but not there." Many boys, especially those sensitive by nature, will take being ignored as rejection. Little Alex makes a squirrel trap out of a cardboard box, a stick, and a piece of string. Daddy gets home from work a little late and just has time to wash up for dinner. After dinner Alex asks Dad to come outside and see the squirrel trap. Daddy says, "Not now, it's seven o'clock. The news is on." A more aggressive boy would be back at 7:30 telling Dad it's time to go look at the squirrel trap, or in the meantime he would have gone next door and asked his friend's dad to come out and look at it. Not Alex. He is wounded. His father has shown that he is less important than the news. His father has shown that he has no interest in what he does. His father has no interest in him. Intuitively, he may have known that building a squirrel trap was a manly thing to do, but the man has not valued it. The man is not valuing him. Therefore, he has no value as a man.

Where the Process Ran off the Track

Now let's look at how this theory fits with the seven steps of growth into manhood that we described earlier (page 28). This will make quite clear where the problems lie.

It is obvious that almost every one of us completed step one. We do have male bodies, and although some of us in build, muscles, or hairiness may tend to be a bit feminine, our bodies in many ways, even to the genetic coding in each cell, declare that we are men.[11] Even in children born with both sets of genitalia, the chromosomes are clearly male or female.

Regarding step two, although there may still be some unhealthy ties to the mother, in the most essential ways we did separate from her. And even where the mother tie is not adequately broken, often the reason for this is found in the next two steps: identification with the father and modeling. Something negative happened in the relationship with the father that sent the boy back to the mother. Where this is the case, essentially we have not a mother problem but a problem that starts with step three, identification with the father.

This line of thinking is consistent with much that has been written about homosexuality. Psychiatrist Irving Bieber wrote, "We have come to the conclusion that a constructive, supportive, warmly related father *precludes* the possibility of a homosexual son."[12] Clearly implied here is the proposition that a father who is attractive to the son, who encourages the son's identification with him, and who affirms his son's manly qualities during his developing years will overrule even the most clinging mother.

If we have passed the first two steps, we must conclude that the problem lies within the next four steps: identification, modeling, testing, and getting affirmed. Dr. Moberly's defensive detachment offers us a clear picture of what goes wrong in the process.

What happens when a boy detaches from his father at an early age? Regardless of whether the detachment was prompted by actions of the father or came about because of the boy's heightened sensitivities or his wrong interpretations of events, a series of responses is likely:

1. The boy decides that he doesn't want to be like his father. A wall goes up between him and his father. The world of manhood is no longer an attractive one to which he aspires.

2. In fact, he doesn't receive affirmation from the father. Even if the father tries to affirm him at a later stage, his defensive wall may reject the affirmation.

3. He stops identifying with the father, so modeling ceases. He stops taking on his father's manly characteristics. Manly aggression, competitiveness, an enjoyment of physical activities, a desire to prevail don't develop in him.

4. When he gets out into the world of boys who have taken on some of their father's manly qualities, he may be seen as different and fail to achieve their acceptance. Among boys, peer acceptance is expressed not so much by words as by being welcomed into the group. The failure to be accepted becomes a painful form of rejection.

5. His father, who might have affirmed him at an earlier stage but who now sees in his son something unmanly, may be even less apt to affirm and, in fact, may make an issue of his son's sissiness. At its worst, this could be expressed in the father's declaring,

"You'll never be a man." More commonly, this message comes through by way of the father regularly comparing the boy with his more manly brother or by emerging family dynamics in which it is understood that this boy is mother's and another son—or even a daughter—is father's.

6. The world of men becomes an alien and strange place, a world set apart, a place where, if he ventures in, he will only experience humiliation and further rejection.

7. He stops testing.

At this point the process of growth into manhood has for all practical purposes ceased. The boy will not reach the point at which affirmation prompts him to take into himself a solid male identity.

WHAT WENT WRONG: THE LARGER CONTEXT

Earlier, I mentioned the evolution of thinking as regards the causes of male homosexuality—going from the dominant mother theory to the emotionally detached father to a multicausal approach. In the multicausal approach the suggestion is not that Johnny arrived at homosexuality in one way and Billy in another, but that in each individual a number of factors combined to produce a homosexually oriented individual.

Thomas Schmidt in *Straight and Narrow?* makes a strong case for multiple causation. He offers a model for how biology, societal constructionism (society's attitudes and structures), early childhood environment, moral environment, behavioral reinforcement, and individual choice could all contribute to the development of homosexuality in an individual child. He offers the following example to illustrate this. In brackets I have identified the factors as Professor Schmidt has named them:

A boy with a biological disposition to gender non-conforming behavior [biology] is born in a confused culture that associates such behavior with homosexuality [societal constructionism]. The boy has a dysfunctional family in which the mother is overwhelming and the father is ineffectual [early childhood experiences]. The boy grows up with no more moral training than is necessary to keep him out of trouble at home or at school [moral environment]. He experiments with same-sex relations as an adolescent and finds pleasure and companionship [behavioral reinforcement]. As he enters adulthood, he chooses to move to a large city where he can build a life within the homosexual subculture [individual choice].[13]

Obviously, not every element mentioned by Schmidt has to be present, and not every factor is given equal weight. In fact, you can remove almost any element in Schmidt's model, and the remaining components can still foster a homosexual man. Every day we encounter homosexual men whose bodies and brains are clearly masculine in their construction, men who work and play in fields viewed decidedly as masculine, men who grew up in strong Christian homes with clear and reasonable moral standards, men who have chosen to never act out their homosexual feelings, and yet they still have an overriding homosexual problem.

The Moberly model deals primarily with just one of Schmidt's factors—early childhood experience. Yet it is not difficult to see how the others contribute to homosexuality—especially biology. If a boy is born slight of build, poorly coordinated, and without the typical male right-brain visual-spatial specialization (to be explained in chapter 6), then he is apt to do poorly in the activities that prompt affirmation from men and other boys. If he is born with a passive rather than aggressive nature, the first experience of rejection may send him into withdrawal from the world of men rather than lead him to try harder.

But whatever the multiple factors seem to be, one element in the pattern almost always seems to be present: There was an unsatisfactory relationship with the father, and this had critical consequences. Less than one in ten of the men with whom I have worked—those whose homosexuality follows the most common pattern—have said that they had a good, active relationship with their fathers. It does appear that all of the factors described by Schmidt can contribute to the development of homosexuality, but the preeminent circumstance appears to be a lack of identification or involvement with the father, and this at some point aborts the process of modeling, testing, and being affirmed.

is it possible for us now?

Grow up now? Can a thirty-, forty-, fifty-year-old man go back and retrace his steps? Can you go back and live your childhood all over again—doing it "right" this time?

No, you can't. You cannot grow up the way a little boy does. You cannot go out to the ball field with young boys and be one of them—not now. Nor can you relate to adult men as an adolescent boy would. They would never respond to you in the same way as they would to a growing boy. To a great extent manhood is formed and takes shape in relationships with others—primarily men—and you as an adult cannot have the kind of relationships that an eight-, twelve-, or fifteen-year-old boy would have.

We cannot be little boys on the ball field again, but there is one qualifier. I learned how to throw a ball for the first time with Steve. When he was two or three, it was a Whiffle ball thrown from four feet away in the living room. Gradually, we worked up until we both had gloves and were throwing a baseball in the street. I was learning to throw with a young boy. It was far along in the process that Steve found out that I was learning along with him. Frank Worthen shared with me how a number of men in his ministry learned to participate in certain sports by interacting with young relatives or boys in their Sunday school classes. Although this can be a valuable way to learn to do some of the things that men do, and it can benefit us greatly, it is not reliving at a relational level what we missed out on before.

Besides this, for a boy, growth into manhood is usually a natural, unconscious process that flows out of normal physical growth and changing relationships. This happens with little intentional direction or consciousness. The boy has little awareness of the process going on, and this fact itself helps shape the process. But as an adult, you will be aware and this makes the process significantly different. Your growth will be a conscious effort, an undertaking of the mind and the will.

You cannot grow up now the way you would have if things had gone better when you were a boy, but you still have to go through the same processes that any boy goes through. If the steps outlined in chapter 3 are truly necessary for growth into manhood and you skipped some of them or went through them only partially, then at some point you still have to go through them if you are ever to experience full manhood. God heals our physical, emotional, and even our spiritual brokenness, but it is safe to say, God does not heal our immaturity. He wants us to grow out of it.

The process of growth is a part of our humanity. Disease is not a part of God's plan, so God often heals it. Sin is not a part of God's plan, so God provides the means through Jesus Christ to overcome it. Growth *is* a part of God's plan, and God wants every person to experience it. Although the process won't be exactly the same as it would have been had it taken place much earlier, in one way or another, you will have to go through all of the steps that lead to full, mature manhood.

Let's take another look at the steps and see what faces you. What has already been accomplished in your life, and what may yet have to be experienced? In doing this we will be charting out much of what follows in this book. As we discuss these seven steps, personalize them and take an inventory of where you are with respect to each. Here again are the steps, only this time with a column added in which you can describe where you are in the process.

Figure 11. Where I Am Today

Phases	Steps	Where I Am Today
I. Physiological	1. Creation and maturity of the male body	
II. Establishing a Tentative Identity	2. Separating from the mother	
	3. Identifying with the father or "the man"	
	4. Modeling	
III. Affirmation	5. Testing my manhood	
	6. Getting affirmed	
	7. Accepting my manhood	

Physiological

It can be said with little doubt that almost every man reading this book has completed the most important part of this process. Praise God for this. Every cell in your body records your maleness. Although there are wonderful variations in how we are put together, in all of the most important body systems—heart and lungs, genitals, musculature, voice, body hair— you are clearly marked as a man.

However, physiological growth does not stop at birth. Obvious changes continue to take place through adolescence and even beyond. Strength and physical skills may continue to be acquired well into adulthood. It is rare that Major League Baseball names a Most Valuable Player who is only nineteen or twenty years old. Men's bodies were created for doing, and although fundamental changes in your body may not be possible, your growth into manhood—becoming able to do the things that men do—may call for some further development of the raw material that God gave you. In chapter 6 we discuss those things that mark our bodies as male, and in chapter 8, the ways a man lives out his manhood by being "physical."

ESTABLISHING A TENTATIVE IDENTITY

Almost every boy, even those who wound up with the most pervasive homosexual identity, went through this process to some degree. However, for many the process stopped at the most superficial level. The boy knew that he was a male, and he knew that he and Dad had some things in common, but the connection never grew strong enough to empower him to go out into the world of boys to test and prove his manhood.

Separating from the Mother

Quite obviously, in a physical sense, at least a part of this has taken place: You are not living in the womb. You certainly know that you are a separate individual from your mother. But there could remain an excessively strong identification with the mother. The process of shifting primary identification from the mother to the father may not have been completed, most likely because of a nonreceptive father or a nonreleasing mother or some combination of the two.

The majority of the men to whom we minister have satisfactorily made the separation, and this is not an issue for them. It is not too difficult to identify those who haven't. Often they still share a great many of their mother's interests, pastimes, prejudices, aversions, tastes. (We do not include here the mother's Christian faith, morals, and beliefs. God wants a mother to impart those to her sons.)

Prayerfully, ask yourself how much you are like your mother. If many of your models are women (perhaps Judy Garland or Barbra Streisand or Amy Grant or Britney Spears), you may still have too strong an identification with women.

If it didn't happen in early childhood, can the separation from your mother's identity still be completed at this late date? It certainly can. It can come about by an act of your will and by your prayerfully releasing any unhealthy spiritual ties to your mother. We will deal with this specifically in chapter 13.

Identifying with the Father

The fact that a boy would react to real or perceived rejection by his father shows that the boy had made some kind of prior connection with his father. He knew that he and Dad had some things in common. Anatomical and social clues would have shown the boy that he was like Dad. However, some boys didn't carry this very far. They never went from seeing similarities with Dad to believing that they were like Dad and, most significantly, that they wanted to be like Dad. In many such boys their tentative identity as men was dead in the water. If the blockage was due to negative feelings about Dad, something else came about: same-sex ambivalence.

It would be wonderful if you could make the necessary connections with your father even at this late date, but it is unlikely, perhaps impossible. Your father may be deceased, or you may live too far apart. Perhaps his personality has never changed and he is still not free to connect with his son. But there is no reason why your dad has to be one of the men with whom you connect in forming your manhood. Your need is to connect with *men* broadly, and other men are more likely to fill this role.

If you have carried some same-sex ambivalence over from childhood, leaving a part of you still antagonistic toward manhood, this needs to be dealt with. Same-sex ambivalence does not continue into adulthood in every man with a homosexual orientation, but it doesn't have to for the man to retain a homosexual identity; it has already done its damage by aborting the normal growth process in his youth. If you have carried it into adulthood, you will not attain full manhood until the unambiguous declaration is made, "It is good to be a man, and I want to be a man."

This is critical. To go down the difficult path of growth into manhood, you must be able to see that manhood is something you dearly want.

Some who read this book will have passed through same-sex ambivalence and genuinely want to be men, but their view of manhood may be clouded by the veil through which they view their fathers. Healing may be needed here. Others may be in a place where manhood is a mystery. They really don't know what a man is, or their view of manhood is distorted by unattractive stereotypes. One goal of this book is to help such men get a view of manhood that reveals it as something to be desired.

Identification with the man—as a part of establishing a tentative identity—is possible for any of these men, and for most of them, forging such an identification will not be a difficult process. The next several chapters will deal with the theme of understanding manhood and seeing manhood as something that God created as "very good." Where a negative image of his father still controls a man's view of manhood, the answer is usually a spiritual one: forgiveness, repentance, healing. We deal with this in chapter 12.

Modeling

For the little boy, identification with the father and modeling himself after the father are usually inextricably linked. He is like Dad; Dad is good; he will try to be like Dad. The boy does it naively and innocently, and he wants to be like that man in his entirety. I hope you won't go that route today, aiming to be exactly like some role model. Unless the model is Jesus, doing so would risk falling into idolatry. Rather, identify in certain men specific qualities that you desire for yourself, and then try to emulate them. It is common sense to do this, and it is as suitable and as possible for a forty-year-old man to do as it is for a four-year-old boy. After all, imitation is not strange to any of us. There are few adult men who don't do this all their lives, identifying men they admire and trying to develop some of their qualities.

You need to be wary of your specific vulnerabilities, however. Your natural tendency will be to imitate men who personify your own standards of manhood. If your standards still reflect your brokenness, you will choose the wrong models. For example, if your standard is the Greek god Adonis, you will probably not choose your models wisely, and your quest will be fruitless if not downright counterproductive. As you learn to appreciate qualities that represent true, God-designed masculinity, emulation will be your natural response. The upcoming chapters will help with this.

In learning to model yourself appropriately, you will learn to identify the false masculine that is common in the gay community. Also, you will be helped to come to terms with the "symbols" of masculinity, seeing how they can be a help or hindrance in your growth.

Because our thinking, judging, and measuring faculties are much more advanced than they were in childhood—and hopefully our spiritual maturity is also—we will model ourselves in another way. We will look at God's revelation through His creation and His Word, and we will try to discern just who God designed a man to be, and we will model ourselves after him—the man of God's design.

AFFIRMATION

I have implied that the process up to this point is not too difficult. Now we enter the truly tough part: seeking and finding affirmation by testing our manhood. All of the intellectual understanding we gain and all of our spiritual clearing away of sin and false beliefs will not transform our shaky and vulnerable tentative identity into a deep, solid foundation of manhood until the tentative identity has been refined through the mill of testing and of gaining affirmation.

Testing

This is where most of us dropped out before. We were not willing to go through the pain and humiliation that we were certain would be ours in the world of boys and men. The fear of this pain and humiliation is still an overriding issue for many of the men in our ministry. But as they step out into the field of testing, many find that things are different now. This time they know what is at stake.

As boys they didn't know that avoiding difficult and painful experiences would stifle their manhood and steer them toward homosexuality. Most now understand this. As a boy, you were in a process that you didn't understand. You can come to understand it now, and not only that, you can chart your own individual course, testing yourself at your own pace and selecting those challenges that have the potential of reaping the greatest benefit with the least pain. Most important of all, the first time you may not have known the Lord, or if you did, you may not have realized that He would walk with you all through the process. He is with you. He will be your encourager, your coach, your comforter when you fail, and your strength when you try again. You can risk the testing.

Getting Affirmed

Can we today, as adult men, gain the affirmation that eluded us in our childhood, affirmation that will sink so deeply inside us that a solid, unquestioned male identity will start to take shape? This is the core issue. If we can take the tests—and I have already said that we can—will the affirmation we gain be sufficient to plant the seed of confident masculinity in us? I absolutely believe that it will. But again, it won't be the same process that a little boy goes through. There are similarities, however.

First, like a boy, we must be affirmed by men; they are the ones we still see as having the authority to affirm manhood. And like it or not, like a boy, affirmation must come from what we do.

I'd better pause right here. What I have just said will be taken by many, in this day of psychological Christianity, as being a major heresy. What do I mean by affirmed for *what I do?* I should be affirmed for *who I am.* Am I leading you back into the trap of performance orientation? Isn't that the game most homosexual men play much of their lives, doing what will win the approval and acceptance of others, and isn't it ultimately futile and self-defeating? Such objections are valid—ultimately—but not at this point.

Manhood is inseparable from "doing." In a significant way, manhood is like our vocation. To grow in his skills, a young carpenter or artist or accountant needs to be affirmed for the way he builds or paints or keeps a set of books. He won't be encouraged to grow in his trade or profession if he is simply told what a fine fellow he is. Ultimately you will be affirmed for who you are, but in the early stages of growth, you must be affirmed for what you do. Otherwise, all of the affirmation in the world will ring hollow. It will never overcome the lying little voice inside that continues to tell you that you can never be a man.

Being told by a kind soul that you are a "real man," if this opinion is not backed up with real evidence, will not only be meaningless, it could be counterproductive. Hollow compliments, no matter how well intentioned, have the potential of actually affirming the very thing that we least want to believe, that we are little boys being condescended to by the big man. This is why self-esteem programs, unless they are backed up by opportunities for people to actually accomplish something, are doomed to failure.

Manhood is formed in the company of men, and so affirmation must be sought on their terms. This clearly presents a dilemma. You may not like watching football and you may have no ability to fix cars. But a broader understanding of masculinity will expand the areas in which you can recognize and receive affirmation from men. For example, if three men in your church have decided to rebuild the fence around the church playground and they decide to ask you to join them, the very asking will be affirming. Implicit in their asking is the statement that you are one of the men of the church.

Having stressed that the affirmation of men for what we do is essential, let me add that it will not be enough by itself. Affirmation from two more sources will be needed.

Second, you must affirm yourself. Your life will also have to start conforming to your own deepest sense of what a man is, and again this will be based on the evidence—what you do as a man. Every one of us has a deep inner sense of what manhood is. As this sense in you is refined, and as you go through the testing process, you will start to affirm yourself. Your actions and attitudes will start to line up with your deep inner sense of what a man is, and feelings of manhood will sweep over you.

But there is a third source of affirmation that should be obvious to Christians: *the affirmation of the One who above all others has the authority to define us,* the affirmation that comes from the Lord. This is not a pious platitude. I know from experience that affirmation from the Lord—the voice that speaks into our hearts, "Good, my son"—is real and profound in its capacity to encourage us. And this is a confirmation of *who we are.* In fact, Jesus is the only one who knows us totally, so He is the only one who can rightfully affirm us for who we are.

Although this is the bottom line of affirmation, if it is only Christian talk without any experiential content, it will also sour. Early on in my growth into manhood, I heard an ex-gay ministry leader say many times, "You are who God says you are," and "You are a man in Jesus Christ." I agreed with him totally, but then I wondered why I still felt like a ten-year-old boy in the presence of men. There are truths we must grasp and hold on to because they are from God's Word. But until they are made evident in our lives, they may not contribute to growth or healing. Perhaps I was uneasy about this man's teaching because I sensed that there was a disconnection between his words and his real life. This turned out to be true; it was later revealed that he was sexually involved with some of his clients.

We can get all of the affirmation that we need, but getting it may take a while. This is to be expected when something of great value is being formed. We will take a further look at affirmation—in the context of our culture—in chapter 9.

Accepting Manhood

Is it too late to accept your manhood? I know that it isn't. I was thirty-eight years old when I started out on this journey, and today, if I were not called to the ministry of helping people deal with sexual and identity problems, manhood would be almost a nonissue for me. My manhood is just there, and it feels good. I have seen this in many other lives. It can happen in yours. All of this is possible through Him who strengthens us.

"The Program"

I am wary of programs, especially those that tell me that I can achieve my life goals if I will simply follow the recommended seven or ten or thirty steps. I find myself especially resenting the voice that matter-of-factly says, "All you have to do is..." The tone and wording generally reflect the speaker's obvious ignorance of the terrible obstacles that I am up against. Too many men in our ministry heard the voice of a father who neither understood nor sympathized, barking, "Get out there and act like a man!" In this book you may feel at times as though you are hearing these words from me. You may even need to hear these words on occasion, but I hope you will hear them in the context of everything that God is trying to do in your life, and I pray that they come across with the sympathy and under-standing of one who knows how hard a road it is to travel and how high the obstacles are that we encounter on the way to manhood.

Despite my misgivings, a program is offered here. But it is one based on principles, not a following of prescribed steps. The primary principle of the program is also the basis for this book: *We grow into manhood by doing the things that men do.* This sounds quite simple, doesn't it? That this pro-gram is really not so simple is evidenced by the fact that I have written a whole book to convey the message rather than have it carved on one of those nice little plaques they sell in bookstores.

A program is being offered here, but for it to have an effect on your life, it is essential to recognize the context in which the program must be worked out. A computer analogy might be helpful here. On your computer, as important as an individual program is, it is worthless without an operating system, the collection of underlying elements on which the program rests and operates. What is offered here is a program in the same sense, and it, too, will not function without the correct operating system. The operating system in this case consists of the fundamental elements of the Christian life. These include worship and praise, repentance, forgiveness of others, thanksgiving, fellowship with other believers, and above all, a deep personal relationship with Jesus Christ. Ex-gay ministry is really just the application of basic Christian principles to the homosexual condition. The program simply won't work unless these elements of the normal Christian life are present in your day-to-day walk. The same can be said for growth into manhood. Draw on basic Christian principles and be guided by them, and you will meet your goal.

It Is Not Growth Alone

One more essential thing to remember to keep the program in its proper context is that growth is only one of three aspects of overcoming homosexuality. The process of coming out of homosexuality must take place in three arenas: understanding, healing, and growth. These three areas are always involved because God works in all three areas of man: the mind (understanding), the spirit (healing), and the body (growth). Here, *healing* refers to the whole realm where God works supernaturally in us. This would include physical healing, inner healing, deliverance, sudden revelations of truth, strong and immediate convictions of deep sin, and any other way in which a sovereign God chooses to move in power in our lives. *Growth* specifically means gaining the capacity to live our lives in this time and place as the men God created us to be.

Thus far Exodus ministries have focused far more on understanding and healing than on growth. Most of the valuable books that have been available to us until now (see appendix C) have focused on understanding (Moberly, Satinover, and Schmidt) or healing (Payne, Comiskey, and Bergner). Even those that address homosexuality more generally (Worthen, Dallas, Consiglio, and Davies and Rentzel) have not put major emphasis on growth in terms of developing one's true gender identity.

In some ways this is surprising, but in another way it is to be expected. It is surprising because one of the earliest views of male homosexuality was that it represented arrested development: a boy's failure to go fully through all the stages of adolescence. Because of trauma or seriously flawed relationships, he became stuck at a developmental stage far short of full manhood. If a part of him stopped developing, then isn't the obvious solution to help him resume his growth into manhood? It would seem so, but we really haven't seen much therapy or ministry clearly focused on this.

It is also surprising that there has not been more focus on growth since to a large extent homosexuality is seen today as an identity problem. Many people recognize that identity, perhaps especially male identity, is not something that just is but is something that develops. Where a masculine or male identity is not properly developed, isn't the most obvious solution going to be to develop it? This would be growth, but again this has not received much attention in our ministries. Even Leanne Payne's *Crisis in Masculinity*, the book that helped me so much, is much more a vehicle for understanding manhood than it is a handbook for growing into it.

On the other side, the lesser emphasis on growth thus far actually reflects the natural sequence experienced when we first start to come out of homosexuality. We start with an understanding of homosexuality and what went wrong with us. This points us in the direction of the restoration and repairs that need to take place. But when we seek to accomplish the restoration and repairs, we inevitably find that there are things that we simply can't do by ourselves. We need a greater power. That power turns out to be the healing, convicting, revealing, affirming, loving power of Jesus Christ. He helps us do, or stop doing, when our strength isn't up to the task. Through prayer, deliverance, and other ministerings of the Holy Spirit, great obstacles are removed, great walls that held us captive are torn down, and then we start to grow and change.

It is important to point out that this particular sequence (understanding, then healing, then growth) may be applicable only during the early stages of overcoming homosexuality. Later we will continually draw on each area as the need arises, each one complimenting and facilitating the other. Healing through the power of the Holy Spirit may enable us to recognize a whole area of truth, the ignorance of which may have held us in bondage for years. In this situation healing has facilitated understanding. Entering into new stages of growth and moving to new levels of maturity may bring us to a place where we recognize the crippling power that unforgiveness has had over us. Here, growth has led to understanding. As we seek to grow, we may see that we are blocked by pervasive fears and that we don't have the power in ourselves to overcome them. Growth then leads us back to seek healing.

Once they make a real commitment to change, many people make great early progress in overcoming homosexuality through coming to know the truth and through God's healing power. But then comes the time to live out what the understanding has made known and what the healing has made possible. With a course laid out for them and with major obstacles removed, it is time to resume the process of growth that was aborted so many years ago. But some don't take that next step, and if this is the case, all of the understanding in the world and any number of extraordinary healing experiences may be of no avail. Jesus healed the man at the pool at Bethesda, but if the man had not been willing to get up and walk, his encounter with Jesus and the healing he had received would have meant nothing. We must take our understanding and healing out into the real world where God has placed us. This will be in the town and the time in which we live and with the real people whom He has put in our lives. If not, we will be like the man in James 1:23-24 who sees his face in the mirror and then walks away, forgetting what he has just seen. If we never move out of our comfort zones, all the books we read, all the conferences we attend, all the tapes we listen to will have been for naught; we will miss out on so much of life, and we may end up being of little use to God. It is time to start growing into manhood.

Is it possible for you now? It is, but you won't know for sure until you try.

what is a man?

Most little boys grow into manhood without ever giving a conscious thought to the meaning of manhood. In fact, most men would be hard pressed to define manhood.

This came home to me some years ago when I was preparing to teach on manhood and womanhood at an Exodus—North America conference. In preparing for the class, part of my "scientific" research consisted of asking the husbands of my daughter and foster daughter—solid men, both of them—what it meant to be a man. Their responses were identical: a wide-eyed blank stare and "Huh?" I am sure they wondered where I was coming from with such a weird question. They had grown into manhood without ever having felt any need to define or describe what it was they were becoming. The natural course of events, responding to the changes in their bodies and to their changing and expanding environments, had simply carried them along from infancy to adult manhood. No goals were set, no steps were planned, no conscious monitoring of progress took place; they just did what came naturally.

Like it or not, many of us don't have that option. If you are an adult male who has never grown into his full manhood, the route that my sons-in-law took and that the vast majority of men take is not open to you. You cannot just do what comes naturally because it is not "natural" for adult men to go through the stages that a boy goes through. You cannot go through each phase unconsciously because you are already conscious of the process, and this consciousness will have an impact on you every step of the way. You cannot help but monitor your progress. So growth into manhood is a very different thing for an adult man than it is for a boy. On the other hand, the goal is the same, and in many respects you must go through all of the same steps that a boy goes through. However, you will go through them quite differently; you will go through them consciously and deliberately. No other option is open to you. In some ways this makes the process more difficult, in others much easier.

The beginning of this process requires us to understand what manhood is. We have to answer the question that brought the blank stares from my sons-in-law. We seek to define manhood. But when we do, we find out quickly that the simplest definitions of manhood are not very helpful: "Manhood is having the characteristics of an adult male who behaves in a manly way." Well, what is this manly way? "A man is an adult male." This is circular thinking, defining manhood by manhood, and that doesn't work.

We must go much deeper for our definition. Here is how we start: A man is a man both physically and relationally. The *physical* is his adult body, including his brain and all of the functioning systems that enable him to operate. This is what we will examine in the rest of this chapter.

The *relational* has to do with how a man relates to the world around him, including other men, women, nature, and, of course, God. This relational part of him will be governed by what can be called his masculine nature. Therefore, manhood is what characterizes an adult man who has a fully developed masculine nature. We are not defining manhood by manhood, because *masculine* is not the equivalent of maleness or manhood. Understanding this distinction was for me a key in the development of my manhood. This is what we will discuss in the next chapter.

MEN AND WOMEN: THE DIFFERENCE

The title of this chapter is "What Is a Man?" not "What Is Man?" There is a profound difference between these questions. When we define any word or concept, we are describing how this word or concept is distinguished from all other words or concepts. We give it its identity by differentiating it. The question "What is man?" would require that we distinguish man from other creatures in the universe, from animals or birds or even angels. But the question "What is a man?" implicitly calls for us to distinguish a man from other forms of humanity, namely women and children. This is what we will be doing in this chapter, describing how a man is different from women and children—mainly from women, because this is where the most confusion exists and where a true understanding will yield the richest rewards.

Every age and every culture has probably gotten it wrong in some ways regarding the differences between men and women. Historically and in many non-Western cultures today, the differences have been exaggerated. Women have been seen as unfit for certain jobs or roles. Their physical makeup and their reproductive functions have often served to severely limit what was permissible for them to do. When such restrictions started to become firmly established in the culture, legal and religious restrictions were developed to enforce them. The most obvious example of this in modern times would be the restrictions placed on women in strict Muslim countries. Forced to cover almost their entire bodies in public, denied an education, some women are, by our standards, virtual prisoners in their homes.

At the other extreme we have the situation that has arisen in our modern Western culture in which political and social pressure has been exerted to deny that even the most obvious differences exist. Not only have the differences been intentionally denied, but people have actually come to believe that they don't exist. Not too many years ago at a Midwestern university a professor asked his students to get into small groups and decide what the differences were between men and women. Their collective conclusion: Women have the ability to conceive and give birth to children and to nurse them, men don't—period. That's it! At about the same time, when I would discuss differences between men and women in one of our ministry's teaching programs—only physiological differences, mind you —some people would get angry with me for even discussing the subject. These extreme attitudes are fading, but they are still sufficiently present in some settings to preclude rational discussion. In the political realm, the abilities of women to perform in the military in combat is one area where rational discussion is still often not allowed. Even in the church, the topics of women as clergy, deacons, ushers, and teachers of men are hotly, but not necessarily rationally, debated.

In today's Western culture and even in much of the world influenced by it, people's views of manhood and womanhood are unsettled. This has its advantages and its disadvantages. On the negative side, it has damaged family stability as each married couple must work out its own roles because the culture no longer simply assigns them. Many men and women enter marriage with different expectations of the role their spouses will play, and often a struggle for power ensues. Some find their views incompatible, with neither willing to yield to the other, so the marriage breaks up. Others settle into an unhappy truce, letting the conflict go underground. For children, such families provide uncertain role models. Many readers of this book no doubt grew up in homes in which the parents' roles were not clearly defined and in which one or both parents were unhappy with their arrangement or continued to struggle against it.

However, the volatility of our views on men and women has its advantage in that it causes us to step back and look at the fundamentals. We are almost forced to ask, "What is a man? What is man meant for? What is a woman? What is woman meant for?" For the Christian this all translates into the question "How does God want us to live as men and women?"

God has revealed His plans and purposes for us in two ways: through His written Word and through His creation. This is where we need to look for our answers to the question "What is a man?"

BIBLICAL GUIDELINES ON MALE AND FEMALE

This subject has been written about and discussed in the church unceasingly for over fifty years. However, with all of this discussion, we still find that sincere believers arrive at different conclusions. I am not qualified to offer a complete biblical exegesis on male and female roles, nor is it necessary that I do so for the purposes of this book. But the subject is far too relevant to be totally ignored here. As Christians, we cannot chart our growth into manhood without considering what God's Word says about our role as men. Therefore, I offer four broad statements that can be supported by Scripture and that I believe the great majority of Christians can accept:

1. God's plan embraces different roles for men and women.
2. In our collective life together, more often than not God wants men to assume roles of authority.
3. God wants us to maintain outward and visible signs (dress, hair, etc.) as a continuing reminder that He has called men and women to different roles.
4. Men and women are of equal value in the sight of God, and both equally, but differently, reflect His image.

There is nothing radical about these views, and they are consistent with most evangelical and Catholic teaching. (For a brief but helpful study of the subject, offered along the lines of traditional Christian teaching, I recommend *What's the Difference: Manhood and Womanhood Defined According to the Bible* by John Piper.[14])

EVIDENCE FROM CREATION

Most of us believe that God has a purpose for everything He has done, that He is not arbitrary or capricious. It would have to follow that He has a reason for designing men and women differently. As we look at how men's bodies differ from women's and children's, we can start to see the differences that God had in mind for our respective roles and functions. Before we look at specific physical differences, however, it is important to note that in every area of difference that will be discussed, we are talking about averages. In brain structure, in body shape, in lung and heart performance, and in most other areas, there will be overlap. The two generic bell curves shown below illustrate this for one characteristic, although they could stand for any nongenital, nonreproductive characteristic wherein men and women tend to differ.

These curves could stand for height, weight, upper-body strength, body hair, verbal skills—any number of characteristics, some of which we will be discussing. What we see here for height and would see for each characteristic are two phenomena. First, the averages for men and for women are different. Second, there is some overlap; the curves do acknowledge that some women are taller than some men. But the overlap is not what is so significant. What is important is that on average men and women are different. That we as individuals vary in male and female characteristics speaks only

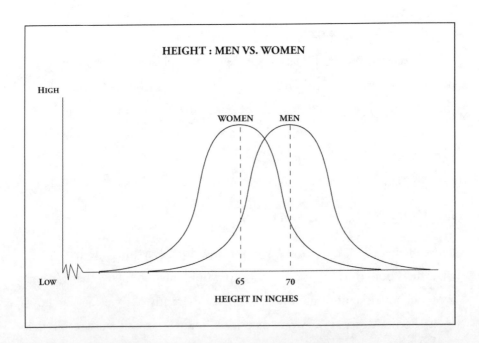

to God's great love for diversity. He wants each of us to be unique, and this is worked out in part by each of us having differing combinations of male and female characteristics. But God does not have a plan for variety without limits. Within this diversity there is order. There is a way that He has created men, and there is a way that He has created women.

Although one doesn't need an advanced degree to know that men's and women's bodies are put together differently—my grandchildren could describe some of the differences fairly well—most people are not aware of how different the average male body is from the average female body. The differences go way beyond those directly associated with reproduction and nursing children. Furthermore, there is a pattern to the differences; they are not just randomly distributed. And as is said quite accurately, form follows function; in looking at male and female bodies, we can see that each was created for somewhat different tasks and roles. There is a specialization built into us to distinguish us as men and women.

EVOLUTION AND CREATION: WHAT WORKS?

Almost every book I used to help me identify male and female physiological differences assumed, as a matter of course, that these differences are the product of evolution. This is not surprising in that to say that we were created would be to commit a heresy of the first order in most secular academic settings.

On the other hand, most Christians believe, using words from the Nicene Creed, in "God the Father almighty, who created heaven and earth." However, many Christians have not thoroughly thought through creation-evolution issues. As a result, the pervasive evolutionary thought in our culture has left many believers with a vague concept that somehow God must have used evolution as a means of creating. For those who think this way, let me share some thoughts.

Author Phillip Johnson writes that the only way a thinking person can fully embrace evolution is if he *first* rejects the idea of intelligent design.[15] There are only two possibilities: either we were designed or we just happened; either some superior intelligence created us or we are the product of a series of cosmic accidents—evolution. A rapidly increasing body of scientific evidence is making it more and more difficult to support *macroevolution,* that is, evolution on the grand scale wherein living beings somehow arose out of inert matter and every species can be traced back to a primeval single-celled creature. The evidence is coming from such diverse fields as microbiology, mathematics, probability analysis, and even the fossil record itself (which shows few, if any, linking species). That the evidence is not causing a wider erosion in belief in macroevolution reveals clearly how many people are determined to deny the existence of a creator. Denying God, or any intelligent design, these people have no choice but to stay with evolution.

But is all evolutionary theory wrong? Can it in any way give us some understanding as to why we are the way we are? Although it is not necessary for understanding why we were made the way we are, *microevolution* fits in with the concept of a creator God. Microevolution teaches that by natural selection certain minor changes occurred over time within a species. For instance, in the animal world, if the best food supplies were to be found high up in trees, those animals with longer necks would thrive. These would have a higher level of survival and, from what we know about genetics, would pass on to their offspring their longer necks. Over time the species could change. Breeders of dogs and horses have known for centuries that by selecting specific animals for breeding, you can increase size, change color, improve speed, or cause changes in any number of characteristics. As a Christian, I have no trouble with this.

Natural selection "creates" what works. Similarly, God, who is rational, creates what works. So whether you believe in God-directed microevolution in bringing about creation and certain small changes or you believe that God in the beginning created us exactly as we are today doesn't really matter for our purpose. In each case, His design reveals His intent for how we should live. Both God and evolution would only create what works. We are the way we are for a purpose.

THE BODY

Let us start by looking at the physiological differences between men and women apart from the brain. We will discuss the brain separately because, although the brain is a part of the body, brain differences between men and women are especially significant and indicative of specific roles for men and women.

A book was recently published with the interesting title *Why Eve Doesn't Have an Adam's Apple.*[16] It is a dictionary of differences between men and women, from "accidents" (men die from accidents at twice the rate of women) to "zinc" (men need 15 mg a day; women 12 mg). For 161 pages the author describes male-female differences, almost all of them physiological differences or things that happen to us because of physiological differences.

From this book and elsewhere, here is a sampling of some of the more significant differences that suggest that men and women are designed for different purposes:

- Height: In the United States, men average five inches—about 7 percent—taller than women.[17]
- Legs: A man's legs are longer in proportion to his trunk than a woman's.[18]
- Muscle-to-fat ratio: At the same weight, a man averages less fat and more muscle than a woman. Men average 15 to 20 percent fat; women 20 to 25 percent. Men have up to 42 percent muscle; women 35 percent.[19]
- Vocal cords: A man's are longer.[20]
- Jawbone: A man's tends to be square; a woman's rounded or pointed.[21]

- Senses: A woman has more acute senses of hearing, smell, and taste.[22]
- Red blood cells: Proportionately a man has more than a woman, enabling him to carry more oxygen to the muscles.[23]
- Bone mass: Women have 30 percent less than men.[24]
- Upper-body strength: A man's is typically two or three times that of a woman.[25]

These differences are not all the product of a man's greater size. Compare a typical man with a typical woman who both happen to be 5'8" tall and weigh 160 pounds, and the man will have longer legs, greater upper-body strength, more bone mass, and less fat than the woman. Some other body differences, such as a woman's wider pelvis, are related to reproduction, but none of the differences mentioned here appears to have a direct relationship to reproduction.

If form follows function, then men more than women are designed for roles involving physical strength. As we will see later, this has far more significance than a man's being able to open a pickle jar or win an arm-wrestling contest.

THE BRAIN

Herein lie the most significant differences between men and women. For the first six or seven weeks of life in the womb, a baby boy and baby girl cannot be distinguished. However, the setup for differences has already taken place. By receiving a Y chromosome from the father rather than an X, a baby becomes destined for manhood. One of the first visible manifestations of this selection occurs in about the seventh week of pregnancy when a flood of testosterone is released on the baby boy. This not only determines that he will have male genitalia and secondary sexual characteristics like the ones just described, but in the words of one author, he gets "brain damaged." A significant number of his brain cells are destroyed. This doesn't happen to little girls, or if it does, it is to a much lesser degree. From that point on, a boy's brain is destined to act differently from a woman's.

The differences in male and female brains have been identified in several ways: through physically examining the brains of deceased persons, through studying how physical damage to brains affects men and women differently, and through electronically measuring where brain activity takes place in response to certain stimuli.

Using general, nonmedical terms, here are some of the known significant differences:

- Men's brains are more specialized than women's. This means that a woman can use an individual part of her brain for several purposes, whereas men tend to use an individual part of the brain for only one purpose.[26]

- Men tend to operate more out of the right side of their brain where visual and spatial abilities reside. Women tend to operate out of both sides of their brains more or less equally.[27]

- Men often have superior hand-eye coordination.[28]

- The areas of a woman's brain devoted to language comprehension and the spoken word are considerably larger than in men, 23.2 percent vs. 12.8 percent respectively, according to one study.[29]

- Women's brains are more integrated than men's. This means a woman can draw quickly on more parts of her brain than a man. The testosterone flood a seven-week-old boy experiences in the womb destroys a part of the corpus callosum, the bundle of nerves that carry information between the two hemispheres of the brain and integrate thinking.[30]

The evidence of these brain differences in men and women abounds in the world around us. Again using averages, consider the following:

- Men excel more often in mathematics and abstract thinking. Until recently there had never been a woman grand master in chess. All major composers of symphonic music have been men.

In an ongoing Johns Hopkins University talent search for youth
with extraordinary mathematical skills, the ratio of boys to girls
at the highest levels of performance was 13 to 1.[31]

- In American universities, over 75 percent of the students planning to major in foreign language are women, while only 14 percent of those planning to major in engineering are women.[32]

- Where men and women suffer similar brain damage from a
stroke or accident, women generally recover more quickly and
more completely. They have a superior ability to use other parts
of their brains to substitute for the damaged areas.[33]

- Reading and speech disorders are far more common among boys
than girls. A boy's greater brain specialization handicaps him in
being able to use alternative parts of his brain when one part
doesn't function well.[34]

Many male-female differences we either accept without thinking or
look on as amusing stereotypes. Most often, however, they reflect the brain
differences being discussed here. A man is watching television and talking
to his wife at the same time. She is upset because she doesn't believe that he
can do both at the same time. He can; the compartmentalization of his
thinking process enables him to do so. We joke of women's intuition, but
almost certainly it reflects the greater integration of a woman's brain; she
can pull together thoughts, feelings, images, memories from different parts
of the brain and integrate them almost instantly to arrive at an understanding. When my wife and I are presented with a problem involving
human relationships, she will arrive at the solution almost immediately,
while I can take hours, even days, to arrive at the same conclusion. But she
doesn't know how she arrived at the conclusion, and I do because I had to
work it out consciously, step-by-step.

Then there is the matter of giving directions. One time I called a woman
who I knew was a strong feminist to ask her to give me directions on how
to get somewhere. Her response? "Let me put my husband on the line."

Women have greater difficulty thinking abstractly of north or south, left or right. A woman's directions will abound with landmarks but be skimpy on distances and compass points.

There is one other area of brain-caused differences that merits specific attention. It is the area of greater male aggression and domination. Where this reflects pathological behavior, such as men's far greater propensity toward criminal and violent behavior, much is being studied and written. However, where it might reflect prevailing inborn differences between men and women that lead to patriarchy or male domination, few writers are brave enough to address the subject. An exception is sociologist Steven Goldberg, who in *Why Men Rule: A Theory of Male Dominance* and other books has been willing to weather a firestorm of feminist flak and examine the subject in a scholarly way.

Dr. Goldberg writes that *every* society ever known has been patriarchal and that men dominate in three areas: (1) they occupy the upper hierarchical positions; (2) they are dominant in whatever roles the society recognizes as high status; and (3) in male-female interactions, the man always plays the dominant role.[35] Although countless individual men and women don't fit these patterns, in cultures at large, in every place and every age, such male dominance has been present.

Because the phenomenon is so universal—scholars have written about thousands of cultures and tribes—Goldberg believes that it must have a physiological cause. He identifies this cause as the masculinization of the brain that takes place in boys in the womb when hormonal action causes the structures of the central nervous system that promote dominance behavior to develop earlier and more extensively. Then during and after puberty males have a greater sensitivity to the hormone testosterone, causing them to react much more readily to certain stimuli with dominant behavior.[36]

The opposition to Goldberg's theory, and indeed the opposition to any suggestion of innate male-female differences, comes largely from those who believe that we are blank slates at birth, that all pervasive male-female differences are taught, the product of socialization by the culture in which a child grows up. There is not time to debate that issue here, but let me simply say that with so many of these differences being universal, with specific brain-structure differences having been identified, and with Scripture supporting, not just describing, differences in male and female roles, I have to believe that our Creator designed us to function differently.

Why is it necessary for a man seeking to grow out of homosexuality and into manhood to consider all of this? It is important for several reasons:

1. Many people are convinced that what men and what women do is totally dictated by the society in which they find themselves, and this puts us on the defensive. If the behaviors discussed in this book are all merely reflections of custom or societal prejudices, then we are totally free to accept or reject them. However, if the differences are built into us, such rejection will hinder the growth process being offered here.

2. In rejecting the world of men, a world in which they are uncomfortable, some homosexual overcomers are in effect declaring that "it shouldn't be that way." Naively (or arrogantly) they want men to live on their terms, and if the way a man lives is totally arbitrary, it is more reasonable for them to call for the world to change rather than for them to change.

3. Seeing the way men are made can point out areas to the overcomer in which he has never fully developed along normal male patterns. This will show him areas where he needs to grow and areas in which, if he doesn't measure up to the male norm, he will have to compensate if he is going to grow into manhood.

4. Understanding what men are leads us to see what men do, the next step in our journey that we will examine after looking into one other important way in which men and women differ.

understanding the masculine

I said earlier that a man is a man both physically and relationally. We have just looked at what distinguishes a man physically; now we will look at what distinguishes him relationally. This requires that we examine the fascinating subject of the masculine and the feminine.

Can you define the word *masculine?* I would expect that almost every reader of this book has a strong *sense* of what masculine is, and if you are a homosexual overcomer, I suspect that you have a heightened sensitivity to the masculine. At the same time, unless you have read some books on the subject or have thought about it deeply, I doubt that you can *define* it. Certainly, you might be able to describe some attributes that are masculine— strength, muscles, a deep voice, an authoritative manner, toughness, manly self-confidence—but can you define it? Where does it come from? Is there some common trait, is there some sort of fountainhead of masculinity out of which the masculine attributes flow, a source that some men have more access to than others, that maybe you wish you had more access to?

Almost without exception, men with a homosexual orientation do have a heightened sense of the masculine. It may be a love-hate attitude. It is easy to picture the effete gay man who ridicules the big, dumb jock but at the same time would almost sell his soul to rest his head on that man's chest and have that man's big, strong arms wrapped around him. In the gay community the craving for the masculine often gets expressed in exaggerated ways: tight jeans, T-shirts that reveal bulging muscles, cruelty, and domination. In fact, the whole leather scene is a parody of that which is truly masculine, and although the majority of homosexual men may not be drawn to leather and sadomasochism, this part of gay culture is highly visible because it offers the symbols of hard, strong, raw masculinity to which so many homosexual men are drawn. For many men, craving for the masculine is the central driving force in their homosexuality, as it once was for me.

To deal with this drive for the masculine, we need to understand what it is that we are really driven to, not in its sexualized and symbolic manifestations, but in terms of the true masculine, the masculine that God wants every man to possess. When we find it and we discover that it can be ours, we will have found a key that opens the door to our growth into manhood and out of homosexuality.

As we discuss this concept of the masculine, I will be drawing greatly on the teaching of Leanne Payne, especially as offered in her book *Crisis in Masculinity*. For my own development as a man, Leanne Payne gave me a theory that I was able to turn into life experiences. I share those experiences here in an effort to help you achieve the fullness of manhood. During your journey, you would be wise to read *Crisis in Masculinity* and get the full depth of her teaching.

The masculine is difficult to define because it is not a tangible thing, like a man or a muscle. It is not a force like energy or torque that can be described in quantitative terms. In the strictest sense I am not sure it is even something that we can describe in spiritual terms. Trying to define it can quickly lead us into circular thinking. "Masculine means having the qualities found especially in men. Men are those creatures who have masculine qualities." However, we can get by this difficulty. Let's start by looking at three parameters, three statements, that I believe most people can readily accept. These will give us a foundation on which to build an understanding of the masculine.

The masculine can only be understood in relation to the feminine. In a way this is similar to our only being able to understand darkness in relationship to light, or cold to hot. They are at the same time both contrasting and complementary. They are opposite ends of a continuum. One gives meaning to the other. Later on, however, we will see that these analogies are not perfect, in that where you have more light you have less darkness and where you have more heat you have less cold, but where you have more masculinity, you do not necessarily have less femininity.

Masculine and feminine are far broader concepts than male and female. Although some dictionaries may use *gender* and *sex* as synonyms, to truly understand what it means to be a man you have to distinguish between the two. In C. S. Lewis's *Perelandra*, the protagonist, Ransom, declares:

> Gender is a reality and a more fundamental reality than sex. Sex is, in fact, merely the adaptation to organic life of a fundamental polarity which divides all created beings. Female sex is simply one of the things which has feminine gender; there are many others and Masculine and Feminine meet us on planes of reality where male and female would be simply meaningless…. The male and female of organic creatures are rather faint and blurred reflections of masculine and feminine…. Their reproductive functions, their differences in shape and size partly exhibit, partly also confuse and misrepresent, the real polarity.[37]

Lewis is saying that gender is a far broader concept than sex. The universality of gender, its transcendence, shows up in our tendency to assign gender to nonhuman objects. Though English is one of the few Western languages that does not assign gender to its nouns, a ship is usually "she" as is a cat of undetermined sex, while a dog whose sex is not known automatically becomes "he." Although their definition is difficult, the masculine and the feminine seem to be all about us, leading us to intuitively recognize them. As we proceed and start to define them, you will see how your intuitive understanding makes great sense.

God embodies both the masculine and the feminine, and He is the source of both. I gained this understanding from the writings of Earle Fox, especially his *Biblical Sexuality and the Battle for Science.*[38] It is because God embodies both the masculine and feminine that they are so universal. All of creation in some way reflects its Creator, therefore its masculine and feminine qualities must come from our Creator. Scripture is clear that God is not a man; therefore God cannot be male or female. But He does embody those qualities that we—male and female, created in His image—reflect. Those qualities include the masculine and the feminine. As we proceed further and describe the masculine and the feminine, we will see why God revealed Himself primarily in masculine terms.

Now, let's describe the masculine and the feminine by contrasting one to the other and then go on to tell how an understanding of these two qualities can be a key that opens the door into manhood.

The Masculine Is That Which Is Outer Directed; The Feminine Is That Which Is Inner Directed

The masculine faces the world: It is oriented to things; it explores; it climbs. Its energy is directed toward the physical: measuring, moving, building, conquering. The feminine looks inward toward feeling, sensing, knowing in the deepest sense. Its energy is directed toward relationships, coming together, nurturing, helping. Rather than moving out into the world, it draws the world around it into itself. Both the masculine and the feminine are relational, but the masculine relational drive is toward the physical, toward working and playing together; the feminine drive is toward being together. In fact, another way to describe this same contrast is masculine *doing* and feminine *being*.

The male body is designed for the masculine in the sense that a man's larger frame, his greater physical strength, his analytical and compartmentalized brain all make him more outer directed and object oriented. The woman on the other hand, in her capacity as a life bearer and nurturer and in her greater capacity for intuitive understanding and for communication, is especially equipped for the feminine. Even in our sexual parts, the male is outer directed, the woman inner. He moves out into the woman. She receives him.

The Essence of Masculinity Is Initiation;
The Essence of Femininity Is Response

A second way of understanding the masculine and feminine is also found in C. S. Lewis, that the masculine is initiation and the feminine response. It is the masculine part of us that decides to start a new project, move to a new country, initiate marriage. The feminine will be the helper, the encourager, the supporter of another's plan or dream. The masculine loves to try new things; the feminine takes joy in helping and serving. The masculine proposes; the feminine accepts.

Herein we can see why God the Father has revealed Himself first of all in masculine terms. He is the ultimate initiator. All things come from Him. He is the Alpha. In our relationship with the Son, Jesus must always be the bridegroom and we must be the bride; it can never be the other way around. We can only respond to Jesus; we cannot be the initiator to Him. Jesus, on the other hand, embodies the feminine in response to the Father. He is totally obedient and responsive to Him. Again quoting C. S. Lewis, God "is so masculine that we are all feminine in relation to him."[39]

Masculine Authority; Feminine Power

A third contrast that can help us understand the mystery of the masculine and the feminine, although it is a little more difficult to grasp, comes from Earle Fox. It is the idea that the masculine wields authority while the feminine wields power. Yet doesn't this contradict the physical realm in which the male has far greater strength? It does only if we equate power with physical strength. But we see more than one type of power around us. There is the power that is physical strength that can lift two hundred pounds or open the pickle jar, but there is also a power that endures, that does not vacillate, that is like glue or solder and holds things together. This is the power of the feminine. In the family, the woman, the one primarily embodying the feminine, is the one in almost all cultures who holds the family together. She makes the home and does the most to establish relationships among husband, wife, and children. This takes a special kind of power that is less often present in the man.

To understand authority and the masculine, we again look to God. God is the ultimate authority (masculine). It is He who determines how we should live our lives. However, He is also the source and sustainer of life (feminine). He holds us in His hand and He sustains our lives day by day. Fox points out a meaningful connection between God's revelation of Himself as Father and His authority.

> The Hebrew word for "father" is AB, as in Abraham, "father of many" or abba, "daddy." The root meaning of AB in Hebrew is "he who decides." God, of course, is the ultimate Decider, and in that sense the ultimate Father. [40]

As we look at God's most basic structure whereby we live in relationships—the family—we see that the man (the husband and the father) has been given the role of AB, the decider. To go along with this authority, God has given the man greater physical strength and special decision-making abilities that will enable him to protect the family from hostile forces and to provide for its well-being.

Masculine Truth; Feminine Mercy

There is a fourth way in which we can contrast the masculine and the feminine: The masculine seeks truth; the feminine, mercy. Let me explain this by way of illustration. My wife, Willa, and I were driving with some guests, a younger couple and their daughter, to a little state aquarium near Fort Fisher, North Carolina. Willa asked me matter-of-factly, "Can we say that Sarah is our granddaughter?" Her motivation was to relieve the younger couple of having to pay the admission price for their daughter. Willa and I are members of the Baltimore Zoo, and this gives us—and our grandchildren —free admission to zoos and aquariums all over the country. "No!" I responded with mock outrage. "I'm not going to lie and risk my soul for the sake of a two-dollar ticket." I was needling Willa, but my response reflected both the strong beliefs that I hold and my tendency to act on principle. Willa's suggestion reflected her wanting to be kind and helpful to the couple (although I later thought that, knowing what my response would be, she just might have been rattling my cage a little).

Willa and I were expressing our respective masculine and feminine roles: mine toward truth or principle, hers toward love or mercy. This contrast between the masculine and the feminine is the stuff around which dramas are written. The father discovers that his beloved son has committed a terrible crime and forces him to turn himself in to the authorities. The mother pleads with him not to. The masculine operates on principle; the feminine is moved by compassion. The masculine looks to the long-term good; the feminine looks at the immediate human need. The masculine has a passion for truth, the feminine for love.

A severe imbalance between the two in one individual can spell disaster, providing either a brutal legalist or a moral relativist. Writing for *Christianity Today*, author Frederica Mathewes-Green declares, "A classic image is that male justice is too harsh, too prone to blind legalism. Women are thought to temper this with compassion, by considering human variables and calling for mercy." She points out the potential for harm from either side: "Where cold legalism binds men, women slip into the quicksand of rationalization."[41] I see no other area where the complementarity of the masculine and feminine is more necessary, or the balance more difficult to attain. The person heavily slanted toward principle thinks that others are weak. The person inclined toward mercy sees the opposite as heartless. The two are perfectly reconciled in God and in no one else. In Psalm 85:10, we are told that in God "righteousness and peace will kiss each other."

What I have described is a cluster of attributes that we have defined as masculine: the capacity to initiate, an outer directedness, the ability to exercise authority or make decisions, and a passion for truth—all related to one another with the common thread of masculine *doing*. And we also have a cluster of attributes that we have defined as feminine: the capacity to respond, an inner directedness, the power that gives and sustains life, and a strong predilection toward love or mercy—all tied together with the common thread of feminine *being*. Although a precise definition may be elusive, I have no doubt that most of us can recognize the masculine and the feminine when we encounter them, and when we do, we know intuitively that they are good. The masculine and feminine are of God, and therefore both are very good.

RELATING TO MAN AND WOMAN

Now let us relate the masculine and the feminine to man and woman, and to the particular problems that many of us have encountered. What was God's intent when He created mankind in the form of male and female? What happened to cause some of us to wander away from God's plan in our development? Three rather simple principles can lead us into truth in this area:

- Every person, male and female, embodies the masculine and the feminine.
- By God's design the masculine should be predominant in the man, and the feminine in the woman.
- Homosexuality in the male reflects a man's failure to develop his masculine qualities.

All Masculine and Feminine

We have already alluded to the first principle, how we all embody both the masculine and the feminine. First, because we are made in the image of God and God encompasses both the masculine and the feminine, we, too, reflect both. Second, God gave us the picture of a one-flesh union when a man and woman unite in marriage, not a picture of two halves coming together. Before I was married, I was not half a person. The same is true for my wife. Our coming together created something mysteriously wonderful, something that did not exist before. Together we reflect God more fully than either of us could individually, and yet the image of God was present in each of us individually from our very conception.

As a practical matter, every one of us is called upon and is able to exercise both masculine and feminine gifts at different times. There are times—as with my children or grandchildren—when I must be able to be a nurturer, times when under the authority of others, I must be able to respond.

Try to think of what a woman would be like who had none of the masculine in her: totally inner directed, totally responsive, morally vacuous. She could not cope either as a single person or as a wife and mother, but perhaps only as a woman dependent on her husband. Think of the man who has no feminine qualities in him: no ability to respond to others, no capacity to feel or understand the deeper things of life. He would most likely wind up being a brute who could only hurt those around him.

The Masculine Predominates in Men; the Feminine in Women

Regarding the second principle, our bodies offer convincing evidence. Man's greater physical strength makes him better able to cope with a hostile world, whether he encounters it as a field to be plowed, a tiger to be slain, or a human enemy to be kept from ravaging his home. Generally, his brain is better able to design the bridge or the house, to plot the strategies that are needed to accomplish a goal. His capacity to compartmentalize his thinking, to separate analytical thought from feelings, enables him to become more focused on objective truth. Even his greater size supports him in his calling to initiate and take command.

The woman, on the other hand, with her softer body, is the natural nurturer. Her need to be present to nurse her younger children makes her the sustainer and constant presence and strength in the home. Her integrated, intuitive brain gives her a superior ability to respond to human needs and problems.

In chapter 6, I offered four broad principles that can be derived from Scripture regarding men and women (page 71). A brief look at the roles that God assigned to men and women in Scripture further supports the preeminence of the masculine in men and the feminine in women. Mary is assigned the role of being the life bearer for the Son of God. The roles of priest and king, roles of authority, were always given to men. Prophets and judges, on the other hand, could be men or women, as they manifested both masculine truth and feminine understanding. The apostles sent out to bring the gospel to the world were men, but much of the strength of the early church came from the women who supported them and in whose houses the early fellowships gathered.

Homosexuality Reflects a Failure to Develop Masculinity

Concerning the third principle, the problem in the homosexual man is not that he has too much of the feminine but too little of the masculine. Can there also be too much of the feminine? Could we have too great a capacity to nurture, to communicate, to understand, too great an ability to respond and help? No, any man who has a surplus of these things is blessed and is likely to be a blessing to others. Maybe in your homosexual struggles you have thought that you are too sensitive, too verbal, too intuitive. I don't think you can be. Look at yourself again. Do these qualities make your life difficult? Are they what hold you back from getting on with your life? I doubt it. Isn't it your inability to initiate, to exercise authority, to function as you are expected to do in the physical world of men that gives you such distress?

The problem with male homosexuality is not an excess of the feminine but a deficit in the masculine. We never adequately developed the masculine side of our being. This is not the only problem at the root of male homosexuality, and I am not saying that it is present in every struggler, but it has been in most of the men whom I have encountered in this ministry over the last twenty years.

The good news—the really great news—is that it is not too late to develop the masculine part of you. The true masculine is not in the size of your muscles, the depth of your voice or the hair on your body, but is in something that God has already planted in you, that you can develop even today if you are willing to resume the growth process. You can pick up where you left off years ago, and in the process you will become free to be the man you were created to be. Your body, your abilities to function as a man in every aspect of life, your core identity will all come together, and you will have grown into manhood.

what men do

Now we are going to look at four "things that men do." They are active: being physical, desiring to prevail, leading, and relating to other men. This is the part of the book that I fear could come across sounding like the words that I resented so much: "All you have to do is…" "A man is a leader, so get out there and lead…"

This *is* the "All you have to do…" portion, but I promise not to leave you there. After suggesting how the overcomer can actually do these things in chapter 9, then refining what men do qualitatively in chapter 10, I will address in chapters 11 and 12 the obstacles that will be encountered. You may find that that is the key part of the process, conquering those internal barriers—most of them emotional—that block growth.

In dealing with the things men do, I am addressing a broad spectrum of traits. Some readers may already be comfortable and adept at one or even all of these traits. If so, read this chapter just the same. Earlier I addressed the fact that there are men who are well-developed in every aspect of their manhood but still lack a deep inner sense that they are men. If you are one of these men, my prayer is that this chapter may affirm you and help in healing your distorted image of yourself. You may gain a greater appreciation for what you can do and who you already are.

All four of the things that men do that I will be discussing in this chapter—being physical, desiring to prevail, leading, and relating to other men—were horrendous challenges in my life. But it was facing these challenges and coming through them until they were no longer great challenges that marked my growth into manhood.

Let's take a look at these fundamentals of manhood.

MEN ARE PHYSICAL

By this I mean that they have a drive to utilize their strength, to expend energy, and to build things, and they find that this being physical brings them great satisfaction. There is a vital relationship between manhood and being physical, and coming to understand this is going to be critical in any man's growth into manhood.

Earlier I described how I observed that my son, Steve, and his elementary school buddies always seemed to have a boundless supply of energy just waiting to be released. However, it isn't only ten-year-olds who manifest this. When my wife's large family gathers for an outing, if there is a pool table, a Ping-Pong table, a horseshoe pit, or a place to shoot clay pigeons, the men quickly forsake standing around chatting, and they are off to the physical activity. Whenever men and women gather and they are free to do what they prefer, you are likely to see the men drawn toward action, toward doing physical things.

But this idea of men being physical stirs up all sorts of objections. Before we look at how being physical is expressed in a man's life, let's address some of these objections. First of all, isn't it terribly simplistic to say that muscles and physical actions are the measure of a man's worth? This is not what I am saying. I am not addressing worth, but rather something more akin to gifts. The gift of strength might be compared to the gift of good musical pitch. It would be good if I could sing on key, but the fact that I can't does not give me less worth. It does, however, restrict my participation in the world of my wife's musical friends. Similarly, a lack of manly strength and other traits can restrict my participation in the world of men.

Then there is the fact that most people, if they were to assign a hierarchy to gifts or attributes would rank the physical at the bottom, well below spiritual, intellectual, social, and artistic skills and attributes. Modern culture reveals a strange ambivalence here, however. We esteem the college professor far more than the ditchdigger because the former works with his mind and the latter with his back. Yet at the same time, physical appearance is of ultimate importance, and the greatest rewards in terms of adulation and income are awarded to the athlete.

Many of us are going to resist linking manhood with being physical because it was our failure to measure up in the physical world of men and boys that brought us so much pain in the first place. In recalling my teen years, nothing stands out as more painful than my consistently miserable performance in gym class. Nothing drove home to me more relentlessly that I was different from—and therefore inferior to—other boys. Although intellectually I belittled sports and "dumb jocks," there is little I would not have given to be instantly transformed into a superb athlete, no longer having to experience so much humiliation.

Some will resist linking manhood with the physical because they know what a "gay" thing this is. For many, perhaps most, homosexual men the male physique is the ultimate expression of manhood. Although many of us knew, even when we were in the homosexual life, that this is ridiculous, this knowledge did not keep us from an essentially idolatrous focus on the male body. This is demonstrated everywhere in gay culture today as a quick review of almost any gay magazine or paper will show.

Finally, for many Christians, especially those of us who have struggled with pervasive sexual sin, the body has been a great hindrance to our leading a righteous life. It is the body that is the home of those infernal appetites that would dominate us and draw us away from the Lord. I remember the friend who led me to the Lord saying, when we were both brand-new Christians, "Wouldn't it be wonderful if we didn't have these bodies?" This concept has frequently crept into the church. As Christians we commonly refer to our battle against "the flesh," falsely equating the flesh with just the physical body.

So we have all of this: the philosophical belief that the body is always of lesser importance, our own painful experiences of our bodies failing to perform up to the standards of other men, our propensity to idolize the male body, and the Christian tendency to see the body (the flesh) as always opposed to the spirit and therefore negative. And now we want to regard the body as something good? Yes, absolutely.

God sees the body as good. He gave us our male bodies with their special abilities as a gift. God made our bodies and declared them "very good" (Genesis 1:31). The body is the temple of the Holy Spirit (1 Corinthians 6:19). We are called to present our bodies "as a living sacrifice, holy and acceptable to God" (Romans 12:1). Our bodies are members of Christ (1 Corinthians 6:15).

Our bodies, at least in this life, are inseparable from who we are. It is only while we are in our bodies that we can fulfill all that God calls us to be and to do here on earth. True, our spirits and our flesh are in a battle, but remember, *the flesh* encompasses more than just our physical body; it also encompasses our mind, our emotions, and our will. We do not reject our minds, emotions, or wills because they are subject to sin. Instead, we seek to sanctify them, to make them fit for use by the Lord.

In looking at our sanctified bodies, then, let's start by looking at what God did with us as men. God did not give us just any bodies; He gave us the bodies of men. This means that, contrasted with women, He gave us an extra measure of strength in terms of muscle size, and He gave us the heart and lung capacity to support those muscles. He gave man a brain that would tend to focus on the physical world. God does nothing arbitrarily, so we have to assume that He intended for men to use their extra strength in certain ways.

To Adam was given the primary responsibility to "subdue" the earth and to "have dominion" over all of God's creation, responsibilities that would take physical strength and energy. When God created the family, the roles of protector and primary provider fell to the physically stronger man. Our bodies give us an idea of God's purpose for us as men. It is reasonable, then, that we usually find in a healthy man a person who not only accepts his responsibility to use his strengths for God's purposes but who also gains a sense of fulfillment both from using these strengths and from knowing that he has a reservoir of them to call on whenever it is required.

If it is the nature of man to be physical, then being physical will bring out man's true nature. If it is his nature to be physical, a man will discover that being physical will nourish, energize, and fulfill him.

"Fish gotta swim; birds gotta fly" is how an old song expressed every creature's need to fulfill its purpose. We once had a black Labrador retriever, a dog that had been bred to retrieve, especially around water. Fetching objects was her gift. Even more than that, it was her purpose and passion. In the car, whenever we drove by a lake or river, she would get extremely agitated and start to whimper. When we let her out, she would quickly find a stick, drop it at our feet, and wait. Whether we threw it into the water or on the land, she would fetch it and fetch it and fetch it, almost to the point of exhaustion. She was exercising her purpose in life, and she loved it.

Similarly, I have heard people with musical gifts say how frustrated they are when they don't have an outlet in which to express their gift: a pianist who has no piano available, or a singer who has no choir or chorus to join. Their gifts long for expression. There is a parallel here with a man's being physical. Strength, energy, building—these components of being physical—are like gifts, and they cry out for expression in men. The distribution of these gifts varies greatly from man to man, but all men have something "physical" in them longing to be released.

For a number of years our ministry has had softball games as a kind of therapy for our men. After the games we have seen how even the men who were most coerced into playing left the ball field with a surprising sense of fulfillment and satisfaction.

To know how we should use our bodies as men, we need to look at the attributes that were especially built into men. I see three—strength, energy, and a propensity to design and build—that have a special male character and that, if developed, exercised, and used for good, will not only please the Lord, but will help bring us fulfillment in our manhood. Let's look at each individually.

Strength

I want to address specifically the muscular strength of men. Men have other strengths, such as self-discipline, and as we saw before, there is the strength in women that brings forth life, the strength that holds things together. But here I want to focus on physical strength, the use of the added musculature and the supporting organs that God has given us as men. It will be impossible to understand manhood and how we can grow into it without addressing this subject.

First, we need to make an important distinction, particularly for those of us with a homosexual background. Physical strength and the "beautiful" male body are two very, very different things. The man with the perfectly formed "pecs and lats," the man with the tiny waist and the sculptured biceps, is very much a creation of modern male narcissism. I am not saying he did not exist before—Greek and Renaissance statues show that he did—but over most of history the "beautiful" male body has not been synonymous with physical strength.

Take a look at the physically strong men in our culture prior to the last fifty or sixty years. Photographs taken in the early twentieth century will show you two types of strong men: the lean wiry man, perhaps the farmer or the coal miner, and the big barrel-chested man, the man who drove the delivery wagon or served as the bouncer in the local saloon. The first had arms that were thin and sinewy, and the latter had a huge trunk shaped like the barrels that some of them lifted.

Look at the movies of the 1930s and the strong men who inhabited them: John Wayne, Clark Gable, Victor McLaughlin. These were men with broad shoulders and bulk, but if they ever took their shirts off—and they seldom did—we didn't see the carefully sculptured bodies we see today. Even Charles Atlas, "The World's Most Perfectly Developed Man," whose ads spoke to young boys from the backs of comic books for a couple of generations selling his "dynamic tension" program (so that we "ninety-eight-pound weaklings" would no longer get sand kicked in our faces), did not have the muscular definition of the modern weightlifting American.

Today's excessive focus on the perfectly muscled body, by both homosexual and heterosexual men, comes from our increased craving to comply with the fashions of the age and from the male insecurity that is so pronounced in this age of gender confusion. In the popular view today, muscles define manhood more than strength does, and in fact muscles often count for more than character, kindness, or decency. This is different than seeing our physical strength as one of the legitimate attributes of our manhood.

Our sense of strength is not borne out in the mirror or by having others admire our physiques, but rather by our starting to feel good about our bodies and having the knowledge that our bodies can do most of the things they are reasonably called on to do.

You cannot totally separate the concepts of man and strength. *Strong man* and the positive connotations of that phrase are so etched into our psyche that to have any real sense of one's own manhood, one is going to have to feel strong. Remember, a key element in growing into manhood is the development of an inner sense or perception of ourselves as whole men. Self-perception is vital here. For men overcoming homosexuality, or for that matter, any men insecure in their manhood, developing physical strength will have a powerful and positive effect on self-identity, giving shape to the new solid core out of which we encounter the world. It will be a key element in forming our self-confidence, a factor in giving us a manly calmness, an antidote to fear and self-consciousness.

Healthy men enjoy using their strength. In some ways this is tied in with our masculine desire to prevail, but it is not always prevailing in the competitive sense. In many situations it is merely a challenge to oneself, wherein the accomplishment of a physical feat gives a man a feeling of strength and fulfillment as a man. This was God's plan for us.

Energy

Comparative studies of boys and girls in unstructured situations typically reveal that girls group together and talk while boys engage in constant physical activity. I observed this energy in Steve all through his growing years. I remember one particular summer day when he and his buddies spent eight hours, almost continuously, going from tennis to basketball to baseball. Parents are prone to say about their sons, "Where does all of the energy come from?" Somehow it comes from their being boys.

A man's energy is a reflection of the masculine in him. A man with energy initiates; he takes on new things. A man with energy is outer directed, ready and willing to interact with the world around him. A man with energy will exercise authority because he knows he has the resources at his command to back up what he says.

The stereotypical nonenergetic man in our culture today is the couch potato. After dinner he flops in front of the television and then for the evening exerts no more energy than is necessary to operate the remote control and to make an occasional excursion into the kitchen for another beer and some pretzels. The couch potato initiates nothing: He does not move outward into the world but merely soaks up what he sees on the tube. He builds nothing. He probably complains a lot about the world and about politics, but he does nothing to improve either. He is all talk.

Although this caricature may seem humorous, the reality of this type of man is sad. Almost certainly he is failing to fulfill his obligations as a husband, as a father, as a Christian (if he is one), and as a citizen or member of the community. Some of us had fathers like this, although the vehicle by which he retreated into himself may have been different. In the book *Broken Dreams,* a young man describes his growth into homosexuality. As he describes various significant events or crises in his family's life, inevitably his father was "reading the paper."[42]

Inactivity, of course, breeds inactivity. The less we do, the more our bodies resist any kind of exertion. Inactivity dissipates energy.

Energetic men, on the other hand, are charismatic men. They exude life; they spread enthusiasm. Most psychologically and spiritually healthy men have a propensity toward physical action. The word *vigor*, describing a high level of energy, has only positive connotations. A look at Christian men who have accomplished outstanding things for the Lord in recent years—Billy Graham, Pope John Paul II, Josh McDowell, or Bill Hybels—will reveal men with high levels of energy. They used this energy creatively.

Designing and Building

There are two types of creativity, that which interprets and that which constructs. Interpretative creativity is feminine. The poet, the songwriter, the dancer, and the painter delve into the deeper meaning of things and express them in new ways. The inventor, the scientist, and the cabinetmaker are creative in the sense of making something new and lasting, something solid and tangible. This is constructive creativity and it is masculine. It flows out of the masculine outer directedness, the masculine focus on things, on its desire to prevail and endure.

Men tend to want to design and build. They tinker and analyze in order to understand the physical world around them, and behind the tinkering often lies the belief "I can make something better of this." Men seem to find great joy in this. Man's bent toward designing, building, and tinkering was wonderfully satirized in the personality of Tim "the Tool Man" Taylor on the sitcom *Home Improvement.* Trying to mechanize his wife's shoe rack, installing a superpowerful motor in the dishwasher, year after year tinkering with the car in his garage, Taylor personified the masculine drive to make things work better. Although the outcome of his efforts was usually disastrous, so intense was his desire to redesign and build that he never stopped coming up with new projects.

Most often it is men who are drawn to vocations that are mechanical or analytical or involve construction. Even at a time when women have gained entry into many occupations formerly closed off to them, certain fields (auto mechanics, for example) remain overwhelmingly male.

More so than with strength and energy, a man's ability to design and build in the physical or structural sense is limited by the equipment he was born with. His brain structure will determine visual-spatial abilities, and these in turn give him the mathematical and mechanical abilities that are at the heart of designing and building. However, there are areas of "construction" that do not require strong natural visual-spatial or mechanical gifts. I rank fairly low on the visual-spatial scale, and yet I have found wonderfully fulfilling outlets for my desire to create and build: building a ministry, for example.

In every area in which we are given the ability to create, there lurks the potential for pride. "Look at this mousetrap I designed. Only a true genius could create such a marvel." There is a real danger here, but I find that an excessive fear of pride causes many Christian men to miss out on the joy of creating. We do need to be wary of the pride that declares, "What a wonderful fellow I am." But we often use the word *pride* with a different meaning, one that is not wrong. With respect to specific accomplishments, when we say *pride,* quite likely we really mean "satisfaction."

God shared with mankind the role of being a creator—in the children we bring forth, in our custodianship of His earth, and in the building of the kingdom. When the first great act of creation was completed and God looked at it and said that it was very good, surely He must have felt satisfaction and joy at the work of His hands. I believe He would have us do the same. Some years ago, I built a large wooden storage shed behind my house. No one has ever come up to me and spontaneously declared, "My, what a wonderful storage shed," and I know that many men would have done a better job. Nevertheless, over the years every time I have used the shed, I have felt a glow of satisfaction at the work of my hands. In this little way, I fulfilled one of my purposes as a man.

MEN DESIRE TO PREVAIL

How many girls do you know who spend untold hours in front of a computer screen playing video games, those packaged programs in which the hero is constantly being bopped on the head, falling into a pit, or having to face an endless stream of ferocious enemies? Chances are, not many. How about boys? This is a boy sort of thing. Some may suspect that the attraction is in the violence found in many of these games. I don't think so. Many boys are equally drawn to video sports games that contain little or no violence. I think what we see in these boys is a man's natural desire to prevail.

This desire shows up in little boys from the time they are first able to wrestle with their dads or with other boys. In the little boy and in the grown man, it is always the same thing: the desire to overcome certain obstacles in order to achieve a specific goal. The two elements—obstacles and a goal—are always present.

The desire to prevail is essential in a man if he is to fulfill his duties and obligations as a man. Fortunately, the exercise of this desire (practicing it, so to speak) tends to be tremendously fulfilling to a man. It energizes him. It lifts his spirits. Often it is downright fun.

Like strength, the desire to prevail is developed with exercise. The raw material is in all men, but without exercise it will grow puny and leave us without the capacity to do the things that men do. In less affluent societies, the struggle for survival can provide all the challenges needed to develop this quality. In our culture the most obvious vehicle undertaken for its development is sports. Sports exemplify overcoming obstacles (the other player or team) to achieve a goal (winning). The statement attributed to the duke of Wellington, "The battle of Waterloo was won on the playing fields of Eton," reflected the English view that sports develop in men the qualities needed to prevail.

We immediately link the desire to prevail with sports because sports involve two other manly traits: strength and the desire to expend energy. But the desire to prevail can be fulfilled in many other ways. The boy who achieves the rank of eagle scout, the young man who wins a chess championship, the teenage boy who wins the debating tournament, all have overcome obstacles to attain a goal.

The obstacles to be overcome can take countless forms. They can come in the form of other people, conditions of nature, past personal limitations, even something like one's propensity to engage in lust. The only requirement is that the obstacles be formidable. Otherwise the prevailing becomes less significant and less satisfying.

To prevail, a man operates out of his masculine side and goes on the offensive. The opposite is to operate out of his feminine side and go on the defensive.

The desire to prevail is one of the things that makes men "ends oriented." This is needed in an increasingly feminized culture that has devalued ends in favor of means. I remember being taught in my liberal church in the 1960s that when a group of people were working together on a project, achieving the goal was secondary to how the people working on the project interacted with one another. The feminine relating was more highly valued than the masculine doing. This emphasis is reflected in our political life today, wherein a leader's accomplishments are considered less important than the compassion he shows. In short, who the man is becomes more important than what he has done. Some public-education curriculum emphasizes self-acceptance more than achieving good grades.

Obviously men (or anyone else) can be too driven to achieve ends or goals. The ruthless businessman who doesn't care whom he hurts on his way to the top exemplifies the masculine focus on ends taken too far. As with truth and compassion, this is an area where a lack of balance can spell disaster. And, as with truth and compassion, balance is not easy to achieve. Within each of us there needs to be a degree of balance between ends and means, but in community, most often the responsibility for staying focused on ends will fall to men, and women will be focused on means.

In discussing how a boy grows into a man in chapter 3, a part of the process described was testing. A boy tests his tentative manhood to gain affirmation. A man's desire to prevail is both the culmination of that process and its continuation. A developed man believes that he *can* prevail. The healthy man enjoys continuing to test. Perhaps his continuing to exercise his desire to prevail is similar to a man's continuing to exercise physically. If he stops, he will soon lose strength or his capacity to prevail.

The desire to prevail gives expression to the masculine outer directedness and to the masculine emphasis on truth. Exercising the desire to prevail produces endurance. It enhances a man's capacity to sacrifice himself for another person or for a cause. It sustains him in his role as protector of his family and his community.

The desire to prevail can be directed toward evil ends, toward dominating, controlling, or suppressing other people. This does not make the quality evil; it is simply the misuse of a gift. Fundamentally, the desire to prevail is a gift, and it is therefore good. We see this when we consider its opposite: the willingness to give up. In this light we can see that the desire to prevail is a part of one of man's noblest attributes, courage.

As much as any man in history, the apostle Paul manifested the desire to prevail. At first it was misdirected in his relentless persecution of the church. But after his conversion he completely redirected it, and he endured afflictions, hardships, calamities, beatings, imprisonments, and so on (2 Corinthians 6:4-5) for the single-minded purpose of spreading the gospel. At the same time, he never used any means that would bring discredit to his Lord and to His cause.

Men Lead

If, when I was twenty-one years old, someone had come to me and said, "A man leads," I would have replied, "Yeah, sure, some men do, and so do some women." If he had responded with, "No, that's not what I mean. A man is obligated to lead," I would have rejected his statement out of hand. What he said would have had no relevance to my life. I had not experienced it in my home, and I was certain that I was meant to be a follower. Besides, nothing frightened me more than the thought of leadership. When my turn came, I chose to fulfill my military obligation as an enlisted man in the reserves rather than train to be an officer in college ROTC. In college I studied for a career in accounting because I thought that keeping the books would keep me safe from having to play any kind of leadership role.

After my conversion, the Holy Spirit gradually revealed to me that, being a man, I was required to lead. It was not an option; it was an obligation. First, in my family, then in my job and my church, and ultimately in my ministry I was called to lead. I came to see that this was not just my situation, not just that my circumstances had put me in a place where I had to lead. But leading was one of the things that men did. It was one of the obligations laid on all of us as men.

History certainly shows that men lead. Rulers and national leaders have been overwhelmingly male, and this cuts across all cultures. Once you get beyond Queen Elizabeth I, Catherine the Great, and Joan of Arc, you are hard pressed to find women whose leadership matched that of the hundreds of male leaders their countries have seen. In the military and in the corporate world today, top leadership is overwhelmingly male. History affirms that some women can be great leaders, but by and large, leadership falls to men.

Jesus chose only male leaders. Although women played a critical role in His ministry and in the establishment of the church, He chose only men to be His apostles. It is not reasonable to assume that He did this simply to go along with the culture. Over and over again He showed that He was willing to violate the customs of the religious establishment of His time.

Men lead because leadership is an expression of the masculine: The leader initiates, he exercises authority, his passion for the truth is reflected in his faithfulness to a vision, and he is outward directed, called to have an impact on the world. To men, the primary bearers of the masculine, these gifts were predominantly given. We are all called to utilize the gifts that we are given, for the benefit of others and for the glory of God. Therefore, men are called to be leaders in the family, in the church, and in the community.

I cannot emphasize too much that leadership is an obligation, not a privilege. Jesus gave us the example of the servant leader. "He who is greatest among you shall be your servant" (Matthew 23:11). The world is crying out for men who will be leaders. The need for true leaders is indeed great in the home, where so many men have abdicated their God-given role of leadership; in the church, which can so readily become feminized; and in political and economic life, where what passes for leadership is many times only self-promotion.

You may be agreeing in principle that, yes, men usually make the best leaders and, yes, men are called to fill leadership roles, but you are simply not able. You are certain that you don't have what it takes. It may well be true that you are not ready to take on a major leadership role—even headship in a family—but if you look at what is required of a leader, you will be able to see that the potential is in you. Here is what a leader does:

1. *He has the vision for what needs to be accomplished.* He is the custodian of this vision or goal for the organization, and he regularly communicates it to others. The goal or vision may be his own, it may be from God, or if he has come on board an existing venture, the vision or goal may have been assigned to him. If it is an assigned goal, from an organization or from God, he must make it his own, he must believe in it.

2. *He will translate this vision into action.* He does this by planning and by assigning tasks to others.

3. *He is willing to make personal sacrifices.* The leader cannot call others to do more than he is willing to do himself. His sacrifice may be more than time or money. He is willing to forsake the approval of others when getting the task accomplished requires it.

4. *He loves the people under his authority.* This love will serve as counterbalance to his intense focus on the goal of the group or organization. This love will empower him to do what is good for his people, not just what pleases them. This love will open his eyes to the gifts that other people have, and in turn this will lead him to respect and trust them. He will be motivated to achieving the goal of the project more out of his desire to see others blessed than to aggrandize himself.

5. *He bears responsibility.* In the event of problems or failure, he forsakes justifying himself or making excuses. The buck stops with him. But in a way it doesn't; he can take his problems and failures one more step up the hierarchical ladder. The Lord will always help him bear his burdens.

Describing these duties as I have, we see the masculine qualities in all of this—initiating, sacrificing, forsaking others' approval—and this may at first make leadership look even more formidable than it did before. But look again at these duties; there is nothing that most men can't develop. Nothing was said about a leader having to be six foot six, deep and commanding in voice, tremendously articulate, or extremely extroverted. If this is what it took to be a leader, then many of today's leaders could never lead.

What is required of a leader is that he exercise the masculine virtues of initiating, exercising authority, and standing on principle. You may feel that this is exactly what you lack, but the good news is that you are not required to scale the face of the mountain; you can take the trail that circles upward around it. Each small venture that you make into leadership will strengthen the masculine in you, and this will equip you to take the next step and so on until you are able to lead with a degree of comfort and confidence.

But leadership is not easy. The greatest obstacles to leadership among homosexual overcomers lie in their low self-esteem and their fear of rejection, which will be addressed in chapter 11. Leadership is still not terribly easy for me. I am still too much of a people pleaser, but I marvel at what God has done and is continuing to do. And even in the midst of some struggles, I take comfort and affirmation in knowing that when I lead, I am fulfilling one of my central duties as a man.

MEN RELATE TO OTHER MEN

There is little doubt that the phenomenal success of various men's movements, including Promise Keepers, in past years has reflected a spiritual hunger in men that is not being met elsewhere in today's world. However, these movements have also flourished because they have provided a means of meeting another great need in today's men: the need to connect in relationships with other men. I am not sure that Promise Keepers or anyone else fully understands the nature of this need. I say this because I keep seeing this need for association with other men being interpreted as and turned into a related but quite different need: the need for intimacy. Although men, like all people, have a need for intimacy, by and large, this is a secondary need in men, and I suspect that intimacy is not what the men's movement has been so effective in meeting. Let me explain this by illustration.

I was a member of a Promise Keepers group at my previous church. Every Monday morning four to seven of us would meet for breakfast at a local restaurant. We sat around a large table in the public part of the restaurant, and after opening with a brief prayer, we engaged in some small talk while we ate. Then we had a Bible study, did some sharing, and at the end said a few prayers. Some men had to leave promptly for work so we did this all in exactly one hour. Although we all were part of a charismatic church where people were supposed to "let it all hang out," we never seemed to get into any really deep sharing. No one shared their pain or fears; no one expressed their loneliness or feelings of inadequacy. I tried to get us to share a little deeper, but no one picked up on it. It just wasn't in the culture of this group.

And yet the group seemed to meet the profound needs of its members. This was most evident in the situation of one man whose wife died of cancer after being gravely ill for a long while. All through her illness, this man attended the meetings as often as he could, and he was overheard telling someone that it was from his Promise Keepers group that he received the most help. How? I really couldn't see it at the time. We deeply loved this man and his wife, but no one ever expressed this verbally. He never wept in our midst, and we never consoled him. We prayed for him, his wife, and their children every week, and our prayers were sincere, but they were not profound or lengthy. And yet this is where he felt comforted and strengthened.

A tremendous amount of what goes on between men—the really important stuff—is not verbal. But in today's feminized culture we don't recognize this; we see the goal of our meaningful relationships as being a deep intimacy that must be expressed in a verbal and emotional openness to one another. But men and women are so different in how we relate to one another: Women are almost always verbal, men far less so.

If we are to understand what it means to be a man, let's put aside for the moment the concept of intimacy and look at what I will call connecting relationships. Outside of marriage, I am convinced that a man has a greater need for rather simple connecting relationships than he does for intimacy. I base this on my observations over the years, primarily of single men. I have found few men who function well without connecting relationships, while many with such relationships do fairly well even though they don't have anyone with whom they are truly intimate.

Let me define my terms here. I am using *connecting relationship* to describe the condition that exists between two people, or among a group of people, who connect at some important level. In this sense I think the connection is somewhat stronger than friendship, which may involve simply an enjoyment of one another, but it does not go as far as true intimacy where people are as honest with one another as they can be and are willing to be extremely vulnerable. In a connecting relationship, emotions may not be as visible as in an intimate relationship, but important emotional needs can be met nevertheless.

Our little Promise Keepers group was not intimate, but what we had was more than friendship. There are four basic characteristics of this type of relationship, which men are drawn to and in which they seem to thrive.

First, our group was voluntary. We can work in the midst of a busy office or live in the midst of a sizable family and yet feel terribly isolated. Being put together physically with other people doesn't do it. We have to choose to be with those people, and they with us. The fact that the other men *want* to be with me may be a key factor in making these relationships so fulfilling. They are inherently affirming.

Second, we had shared interests, goals, values, and beliefs—not mutual needs. We were all Christians earnestly wanting to live out our Christianity in our homes, our workplaces, and the community, all of us finding this difficult at times. Our relationships, being based on these common interests, goals, and beliefs, focused outward. Because we shared a common belief that our best guidance for how we should live is found in God's Word, we were sharing an adventure of discovery together. We were finding what for us were new principles. Outer directed, making new discoveries, uncovering new principles, all these things fed our masculine natures. Relationships like this are life-giving for men. Although needs are always important, to let them be the focus of our common life together can be life draining for men. Besides, somehow we seemed to be meeting needs without focusing on them.

Having shared common experiences may substitute for common beliefs. For years my wife and I were part of a small home group where, even being in our fifties, we were the youngsters. All three of the other men in the group had seen combat in World War II. They had been in different theaters of operations, even in different branches of the armed forces, but the common experiences of having left their homes in Baltimore while still in their teens and having been thrust into a world where violence and death were all around them gave them a sense that each knew something of the others that most people cannot know.

If you have been involved with an ex-gay group, you may have sensed the often unspoken feeling that your fellow overcomers are men and women who truly understand you. This makes a connection. However, sharing common experiences, as good as that might be, focuses on the past; shared beliefs and values are more dynamic. They will carry us through the future in all sorts of experiences and therefore better cement our connecting relationships.

A third characteristic of our relationship was that we liked each other. We enjoyed being together. This made possible a great freedom in the way we interacted, in our challenges, in our sparring, in our giving and receiving admonitions. Because we liked each other, we were free to be ourselves and speak the truth to one another.

Finally, we were all men. We loved our wives and our children and loved being with them. We loved things we did together as couples, but it is truly different being with a group that is exclusively male. Perhaps in the company of other men, we know intuitively that we are understood, and therefore a lot of the intimate verbal exchange—an area in which many men don't do well—is simply not necessary. A mutual understanding rooted in our common manhood may let us skip over all that verbal stuff and get right to the issues.

What I have said here is quite simple: Men thrive on relationships that are all male and are voluntary, where the men share beliefs and values, and where they like each other. There is in all men a desire to be better men, and men know instinctively that this kind of relationship provides a great environment for growth as men. Iron does sharpen iron, and healthy, growing men do challenge each other to be better men.

So here we have what men do: They are physical, they have a desire to prevail, they lead, and they relate to other men. Now, how do we get from here to there? How do we do these fundamental things that mark men as men and start to apply them in ways that will increase our own inner sense manhood? How do we do the things that men do?

doing the things that men do

We will grow into manhood by doing the things that men do. Every time I write this I can see the red flags go up. The first red flag is the one that says, "Blind, dumb conformity. Real men fix cars, watch *Monday Night Football,* drink beer, belch a lot, and tell dirty jokes, right? These are things that men do. Conformity to some cultural stereotypes is going to make me a man? What if I don't want to fix a car, I don't like football, I think beer tastes terrible, my digestive system is fine without belching, thank you, and dirty jokes are stupid? So I can't be a real man, right?"

The second red flag asks accusingly, "By whose standards do we decide what men do? Twenty-first-century American, ancient Hebrew, modern Eskimo, seventeenth-century Japanese? Whose culture are we going to use, or can I just pick one—or must I live according to the spirit of this age?"

A third red flag may be the thought that this doesn't make any sense at all. "I couldn't do the things that boys do, so I was rejected by my father and my peers, and this led me to be homosexual. Because I am homosexual, I can't do the things that men do. If I could, I would, and I wouldn't be homosexual." I hope I can lead you to lower your red flags.

COMING TO TERMS WITH THE CULTURE

As we discussed in chapter 6, God created man with certain physical attributes that were distinctive to man and different from woman. On average, men could do some things better than women, and women some things better than men. This created a complementarity. No doubt this worked out to be more functional than putting all of the attributes in every human being.

Besides, God wanted us to be relational creatures, so He gave us different gifts—different from individual to individual, and different between men and women—so that we would work together. With respect to men and women, these different gifts created the complementarity that would serve as the basis for His primary building block for the human community, the family.

Every culture has drawn on these peculiar male and female attributes in ways that would best serve all of the community, the tribe, or the nation. Every culture in recorded history has defined roles for men and women and marked those roles by certain practices, symbols, and customs.

It is interesting to talk to parents who have tried to resist traditional male and female roles and to impose a more androgynous ideology on their children. We had a friend who tried with all her might to keep her boy from male cultural stereotypes. But to no avail. He would not play with his dolls, and absent a toy gun, a simple stick would suffice for shooting bad guys. We hear stories like this over and over. This reflects both the prevailing power of cultural influences and the fact that most gender roles reflect physical, and thus innate, differences between men and women.

Not only have all cultures established differing norms and roles for men and women, but from culture to culture and age to age, from the most primitive to the most modern, there have been strong similarities in the specific roles that were established. Men's roles have primarily focused on the physical, such as hunting, fishing, and fighting, and on the interaction with the larger community, such as war, law, and governing. Women's roles have mostly revolved around the home: raising children, cooking, teaching, relationships with neighbors. Where a family's livelihood was earned in or near the home, as with tending crops or livestock, or in a trade conducted out of the home, the culture might assign the duty to either the man or the woman or to both.

An objection might be raised that roles are similar from culture to culture because men imposed them and took the best for themselves. But then, in some cultures, why didn't women impose the roles according to what suited them best? Even the assigning of roles is a role—one that is peculiar to men. But isn't this because men are physically stronger and can impose their ideas of roles? No doubt, there is some truth in this, but it just bears out a primary point that I am trying to make: Roles, at least in part, reflect our physical differences.

One additional factor helps to determine, and especially to maintain, defined male and female roles in almost any community: religion. Because different roles and norms for men and women were seen as good and beneficial, they have always been incorporated into religious beliefs and practices. Sometimes this was done by men, but within the Judeo-Christian traditions, believers would hold that this was done by God's working through His people. It is meaningful that among the cultures about which most of us have some knowledge, Judeo-Christian culture has been the most protective of women and children. Our history in this regard has been far from perfect, but one is hard pressed to find a culture that has developed a more satisfactory system than that which is a part of our Judeo-Christian heritage. I believe that this is God guiding His people.

Scripture supports the idea that God wants men and women to maintain both symbolic and role differences. Regardless of how you interpret what the Bible says about women's ordination or leadership, we cannot ignore the fact that Scripture speaks to differing roles in teaching and in functioning in roles of authority (1 Timothy 2:12). Furthermore, we are shown that different roles were evident among the men and women who walked with Jesus and among the men and women who comprised the early church. Paul's direction as to whose head should not be covered and whose should (1 Corinthians 11:4-15) is a clear indication of our Lord's intent that we maintain visible symbols that would remind us of male and female differences.

In no culture are gender roles ideal, but that is not the point here. The point is that every culture has its norms for men and women. Furthermore, if you don't want to be a hermit, you must live in a culture. And assuming you do not aspire to be a hermit, you not only must live in a culture, you must live in the culture in which you have been placed. You could choose to move to another culture, but if you did, you would not escape gender roles but would simply confront different ones. Not only must you live in the culture in which you are placed—or have placed yourself—but you must live as a man in that culture. And as a man in a culture, you have two choices: You can choose to live generally according to the standards of the culture, or you can choose to be a nonconformist, to defy the norms of the culture.

For those who wish to grow into manhood, I believe that I can make a strong case that living according to the standards of the culture is the better way to go. There must be one caveat in this, of course. As Christians, especially as Christians living in an increasingly non-Christian culture, our view of how to live as a man in our society must be submitted to God's clear biblical plan for His people. Where the culture contradicts what we know as Christians to be godly behavior, we must not conform. If the culture has come to show the successful or real man as being hard drinking, womanizing, abusive, and narcissistic, there may be much that we have to reject. Otherwise, coming to terms with the culture in a way that accepts it rather than fights it will have three decided advantages for us. Let me explain.

First, your life will start to align with your own deep sense of manhood. Deep inside each of us is a sense of what a man should be. Even in the most gay of men, there is a recognition of that which is truly manly. Even if he rejects and scorns it, he knows what it is. Some of it may be born in us, some of it is surely picked up in our earliest relationships, and certainly to a significant degree it has been formed by our culture, but its source really doesn't matter. What matters is that it is there, it is real, it is deeply embedded in us, and it has a major impact on our lives. This sense is in every little boy and in every adolescent.

We can cry out that no behavioral expression really determines manhood—and this is mostly true—but still there rests in the heart of every man an ability to recognize true manhood, and this recognition is illuminated by certain manly attitudes and behaviors. When we act like men, when we do the things that men do, we bring ourselves into conformity with our own deepest sense of what manhood is. We feel like men when we do the things that men do, and feeling like men, perhaps more than anything else, forms the male identity. Our every act that conforms to our inner sense of manhood is like pouring a little more concrete into the mold that will eventually be filled and form a complete, strong, and healthy man.

As mentioned before, Regeneration hosts summer softball games for the men in the ministry. They are played in a protective environment. The first games were played on a field between a horse farm, the woods, and a church. The games are mostly limited to men from a homosexual background. (My son, Steve, was the first "straight" allowed to play, although now a few others for whom this is a ministry join us regularly.) These games have been among the most therapeutic things our ministry has ever done. In this low-risk situation, most of our men found that there really was nothing wrong with their hand-eye coordination. Almost to a man, they were better at the game than they thought they would be. After these games one could actually see the identity changes in some of these men. Doing what men do in our culture—playing softball—makes a connection with that deep unconscious sense of manhood that we all carry within us. Experiences like this transform us bit by bit as we find ourselves able to function in ways that match our deepest sense of manhood.

Second, other men will affirm you. When you were a little boy, most likely Mom loved and accepted you totally, but that didn't do much for your manhood, did it? Even today, you probably have lady friends who think you are just great. Perhaps certain children in your life think you are terrific. These things are wonderful, and they are not to be belittled. But do they do anything for your feeling of manhood? A little maybe, but probably not much.

But what happens when the men at work ask you to go to a ball game with them or when the men at church ask you to help them repair some storm damage at a widow's house? Isn't this what gives you a real shot of affirmation? Don't these things start to form in you the idea that you really are like other men?

Our most powerful affirmations as men will always come from other men. Unconsciously, we know that men are experts in manhood. They are the ones qualified to affirm manhood. Their affirmation comes in two ways: by their words and by your acceptance into their world. In both situations cultural considerations are paramount.

For the words of men to have a significant impact in affirming you, they must affirm you for the things that men do. "You are such a fine person" or "My, that's a beautiful flower arrangement" do not affirm your manhood. It is nice to receive compliments, but not all compliments affirm manhood. "You did a terrific job leading that group" or "That picnic table you built is great"—these words coming from a man affirm manhood. I know some of this sounds shallow, even juvenile, but it is reality. We need the words of affirmation that we did not receive as little boys. We need them to come from men, and we need them to be offered in the context of what men do because doing is a trait of manhood.

The other way that men affirm us is by accepting us into their world. There is a world of men; it is where men gather to work, to play, to debate. Most men are not aware of it, but it's like a club, and there is only one requirement for admission: You have to be a man to get in. Every time you are invited into that world, they are acknowledging that you are a man. They are affirming your manhood. But you have to be willing to join in. You have to be willing to go to the ball game or to build the fence on the church property. You have to be willing to do what men do in the culture of these men. Their simply asking you to join them has some affirming value, but being with them, joining with them in the context of what men do, will offer far greater affirmation.

Third, the Holy Spirit will affirm you. Later we will talk about the qualities and the purposes of manhood. For now, let's just say that God has purposes for your manhood, purposes to be lived out in the family, in the church, and in the world. When you do the things that men do, often you are fulfilling those purposes, and the Holy Spirit will affirm you. You will be doing the things that the Father wants His son to do, and you will sense His approval.

You do have a choice. You can go your own way and see what happens, or you can enter the world of men and see what blessings and growth you might find there. Making this choice is coming to terms with the culture.

For those of you still struggling with the conformity issue, you may get some relief when we discuss the God-given uniqueness of every man in chapter 13. For those of you clinging to your individualism (the type that is the spirit of this age), I will have some words for you later also. But for now, let's move on with doing the things that men do.

Make It Real

Jake wanted badly to be a "real man." He felt weak and squishy, as though he were some sort of alien creature around other men. So he undertook his manhood project. He started lifting weights until he had gained some respectable biceps and pecs. He got himself a tattoo. He bought a pickup truck with a gun rack on it and got a big dog to ride in the front seat with him. And he got a whole new wardrobe of rugged, manly clothes from L. L. Bean. He even developed a sort of swagger so that no one could possibly consider him a pansy anymore.

And now Jake ventured out into the world as a new man. Guess what happened? Right, almost nothing. Except for some guys at the gay bar, no one seemed to notice the difference. Worst of all, he didn't feel any different. This is understandable when you realize that Jake was only *posing* as a man. He was simply wearing symbols of manhood. He was still the same squishy little guy, and deep inside he knew it. The guys in the gay bar appreciated the new Jake because they had focused for so long on a false type of manhood that they had lost their ability to distinguish the bogus from the genuine article.

Jake could not find his manhood at L. L. Bean, the truck dealership, or the tattoo parlor. He would have to grow into it the way every boy does. He had to go back to the steps of manhood and pick up where he had left off. He had to go back to step seven, testing. He had to do the things that men do and seek the affirmation that is a necessary part of growth. It wouldn't do any good to just look like a man; he had to act like one in ways that affirmed his manhood.

TESTING

Suppose your goal, rather than attaining manhood, is to get admitted into a certain college, and you need to earn certain scores on the Scholastic Aptitude Test (SAT) in order to gain admittance. It is pretty clear what you would do. You would

1. sign up for the test,
2. prepare yourself through your high school studies and possibly by taking an SAT-preparation course,
3. go to where the tests are given,
4. take the test,
5. try again if you didn't do well the first time.

Growth into manhood requires that you take tests also, tests in doing the things that men do. In going about this you follow the exact same steps just listed for taking the SAT. Consider them as they apply to your growth into manhood:

1. Sign Up for the Test

This means making the decision that you want manhood and that you are willing to pay the price for achieving it. You know that it will be difficult, that there will be times of failure and humiliation, and that you will be moving into places you have been afraid to enter before. Pondering these difficulties and recognizing the pain you may experience, you are counting the cost. Recognizing that manhood is a prize worth sacrificing for, you count the cost and make the decision to take the tests. You commit to yourself and to God to do what is necessary to go down the road and take the tests.

2. Prepare for the Test

You may find that much preparation has already taken place, but it may not be complete, or you may see that the isolated experiences of preparation have not come together to affirm you in your manhood. This is what happened to me. In retrospect, I see my twenty-six years in the business world—much of it in roles that I would never have chosen for myself—as God's providing tests for me. Forced into roles of leadership, associating daily with manly men, meeting challenges in the competitive world of real-estate development, many of the parts of my manhood were being formed, although it would be years before the pieces would come together to form a man. Examine your life—take an inventory—and I am sure you will find that you have already gone through many experiences that can be building blocks for your manhood. Think about them, grasp them, and consciously make them a part of your growth.

But there are things that you must do deliberately now to prepare yourself for the tests:

- You need to be dealing with your homosexuality at every level. Early in the book I mentioned that growth into manhood is but one part of overcoming homosexuality, and it is usually one of the later stages in the process. To whatever extent possible, you need to be involved in an ex-gay ministry, going to conferences, reading books, going through a Living Waters or New Directions program. Whatever resources are available, take advantage of them. Along with growth, you need understanding and probably some healing. These resources will provide them.

- You need to find another man to help you. You need someone who will encourage you and hold you accountable, one who will listen to you share your struggles. He could be an accountability partner, a spiritual director, or a knowledgeable counselor. If you are in a support group, he might be your group leader or the leader of your ministry. It is better that the person be a man because your relationship with him will be part of the healing process.

- Most importantly, you need to repent of any sins that have heretofore blocked your journey into manhood. Most of the big steps in my life have started with a spiritual transaction, and usually it's the same transaction—repentance. Repentance is easy. The difficult part is becoming aware of and owning up to the sin that is hindering my walk as a Christian. But once I have discovered a serious sin in my life, after the initial burning sting of conviction has worn off, I am excited because I know that with sin, unlike some emotional or psychological problems, we have a ready remedy: repentance, confession, and the cleansing blood of Jesus Christ.

As you prayerfully examine your life, the Holy Spirit may show you certain sins that, if still carried with you, will be like mighty weights around your shoulders, making every growth step much more difficult.

Here are some of the deeper sins that are common among men coming out of homosexuality, sins relevant to our topic here. They are sins that can undermine your willingness to grow up in the world of men. I have had to deal with each of them in my own growth into manhood.

Allowing Fear to Control You

Fear is a legitimate emotion in the face of imminent danger. But ongoing fears, that in the long run hinder us from doing what God would have us do, are expressions of our lack of trust in God and are therefore sinful. The fear that caused you to bail out of the aggressive physical world of boys many years ago may still be a paralyzing factor in your life. The recognition that your life has been controlled by your fears rather than by God's promises could be an enormous step. After you repent of this and choose to live life differently, you will still face fears, but you will have a far greater power to overcome and not be controlled by them. As with most lifestyle sins, your fears may get hold of you again from time to time and you may have to repent many times. Repeating Paul's words "I can do all things in him who strengthens me" (Philippians 4:13) can be a powerful force in not letting fear gain control of you.

Extreme Self-Protection

This is another response that God builds into us for a purpose—to protect life and limb. But if it assumes a paramount place in our lives and reflects a determination to avoid all pain in life, it has turned sinful. It is often enmeshed with other "self" sins: self-centeredness, self-pity, selfishness, even narcissism (self-glorification).

Sloth

What a great old word! Sloth is one of the seven deadly sins that the church enumerated early in its history. The word itself has the power to convict because it paints such a clear picture of a blob of a creature lying around doing little but meeting its own most basic needs. In some homosexual men, their refusal to be physical, their resistance to engaging in the world of men may have bred in them habits of sloth and inaction. As a result, their bodies may have failed to develop the strength and energy that would make it easy for them to be physical and active in the world. Whether sloth comes from an attitude of idleness or from not caring for our bodies, it keeps us from readily doing the things that men do, and it is a sin that needs repentance.

Being Excessively Effete

We don't find the word *effete* in either the Ten Commandments or the seven deadly sins, but it is a wonderfully expressive word. The dictionary describes being effete as lacking vigor, force of character, or moral stamina, being decadent, soft, or overrefined. The Greek word *malakoi* used in 1 Corinthians 6:9 is sometimes translated "effeminate" and sometimes as "homosexual offenders." It may have a meaning close to *effete.* For our purposes, *effete* means "having an extreme focus on personal comfort." The story my wife connects with such a person is "The Princess and the Pea," the story of a princess whose sleep was disturbed by one tiny pea placed under a tall stack of mattresses, thereby proving she was a princess. Such self-focus can easily restrict what a man does with his body. He will never want to get sweaty or grubby or do anything that is apt to cause physical discomfort. He has created artificial barriers that limit how he will function as a man and will keep him out of the world of men.

Pride

Most homosexual men have extremely low self-esteem, so pride is often not easily discerned. The homosexual man may give himself worth through his possessions, his appearance, his popularity, or even through his sensitivity, and this worth needs to be bolstered by an external layer of pride. For many men this pride is quite brittle and easily shattered, but some are quite adept at maintaining and protecting it. However, it must die if the true man is to emerge. The frightened little boy buried beneath this false persona must come out and take his first scary steps into the world of manhood. The false man must die so that the true man can start to grow. Recognition and repentance are essential for this to occur.

A deep conviction of sin is a rare and precious thing. This book will not convict you of any sin; the Holy Spirit does that. But file these thoughts away in your heart, and perhaps one day the Spirit will use them to bring you to that conviction that is so painful for the moment but so liberating in the long run.

3. Go to Where the Tests Are Given

Like the student taking the SAT, you must find where the test is given if you are to take it. The tests of manhood are given primarily in the world of men. You have to move into their arena of action; don't expect them to move into yours. The primary key to entry into a place of testing is your willingness to say yes: yes to men's invitation to join them, yes to someone who asks you to take a leadership role, yes to God's voice when He tells you to stop contemplating and start acting. Many tests will be presented to you. You only need to accept them. For example, opportunities to practice leadership are especially abundant. The church, your employer, the world, all cry out for men who will take leadership roles.

The world of men willing to do things with other men is not that crowded. There are many lonely men out there, looking for a friend to do something with. Be flexible and willing to go with what another man wants to do. Although the activity might not be to your choosing, the companionship will bring its own rewards. And you will be doing the things that men do.

In some circumstances you may need to seek out your own tests. This is how our Regeneration softball games came about. We knew that our terrible feelings of inadequacy in sports were a major factor in our lack of a sense of manhood, so we chose to venture onto the ball field.

The decisions are yours as to where you will do your testing. Wisdom would dictate that you choose your places carefully. Here are some suggestions to guide you:

- Choose a test you are likely to pass. We can learn from failures, but most often we are built up by a series of successes, each of which encourages us to move on to a slightly more challenging level of testing. The possibility of failure must be present or the test is meaningless, but it is in passing the tests that confidence is built.

- Take the tests among sympathetic men. Initially, at least, it is wise to take the tests among men who are not likely to ridicule you or be angry at your failure. Hopefully, the men of your church would constitute such a group. Even if they don't know your motivation for participating in an activity with them, if they are mature Christians, they may sense your struggles and assume the role of good fathers or brothers.

- To the extent possible, take the tests among strong men. Healthy men are made stronger in the presence of strong men. If you are starting to grow as a man, being in the presence of strong men will help lift you up to their level of strength. Be willing to fight through a period of feeling intimidated before you start to feel comfortable in their presence. The rewards will make the struggle worthwhile.

- Take the test where the consequences of failure will not be too great. If it is a leadership role and you don't do the best job in the world, will others suffer significantly? If it is a sports event, are you playing where the whole world will see you if you fumble?

- Try to keep a sense of humor. What a blessing it is to be able not to take ourselves so seriously. In our first Regeneration softball game, there was a lot of humor and harmless self-mockery. One man deliberately asked if we were going to rehearse before we played an actual game. Another, on reaching first base, declared, "It took me twenty years to get here." One of our members, a schoolteacher, offered to bring baseball gloves for us. We all had a laugh when we tried them on. He was an elementary school teacher! Try to step back and look at what you are doing as if it were a game, maybe a secret game of your own. Remember, if you fail, by tomorrow probably no one but you will remember your failure.

4. Take the Test

Going back to our SAT analogy, preparation—or reading this book—will be of no avail if you do not take the test.

5. Try Again If You Don't Do Well the First Time

Unless a student aces the SAT the first time, the school counselor will always recommend retaking the test. Growth into manhood involves many, many tests, and every man fails some of the time. Expect that, and be determined to try again.

But I'm Different

Remember the bell curves and how on the male curve some of us would fall way to the left, perhaps even overlapping the female curve? Craig comes up to me and says, "Okay, I'm short, small-boned, and smooth-skinned. I have poor hand-eye coordination. I am a wonderful communicator, and I flunked math and physics. It's these things that pushed me out of the world of boys growing up. How am I going to do the things that men do? How is it going to be any different now?" A lot of readers may be thinking just such thoughts right now.

I discussed earlier how we now believe that many factors may have contributed to our homosexuality, and certainly being innately less "male" as regards secondary sexual characteristics could be one of them. Being by nature different in these ways may be what led to our being rejected by our fathers or peers. Being less aggressive by nature may have contributed to our decision to retreat from the world of men rather than stay and fight for our position in it. Studies have shown that early childhood feminine behavior is one of the strongest predictors of adult homosexuality.[43] What I am recognizing is that many homosexually oriented men are at a real disadvantage in doing the things that men do. Where does that take us?

I'd like to be able to tell the Craigs out there that they should grow five inches taller, thicken up their bones, grow some hair on their chests, and improve their visual-spatial aptitudes, but I don't think that would help much. What we have to say is, yes, it will be harder for you than for some men. I have already suggested some ways to make the task easier, but strategies and techniques are not enough. Courage and determination to overcome obstacles come from a man's heart and from his spirit. This may be where the rubber meets the road for you. Ultimately, there is no easy way to go down what, for you, might be an especially difficult road. But let me offer a few points that might help you along the way:

1. Be a man of prayer. Bring Jesus into every challenge. Many times I wrestled with Jesus before I took a step that I was fearful of taking or when I had to try again after a series of failures. I found that He was always there, encouraging me to try, consoling me when I failed, and affirming me when I succeeded.

2. Keep reminding yourself that every man has to overcome special obstacles in some area of his life. The man with an IQ of 105 is going to have a much tougher time getting through college than the man whose IQ is 135, but many make it. The sports world is full of athletes who had to overcome physical handicaps. Don't allow self-pity to get a foothold.

3. Realize that the very act of trying to be a man is a manly thing. We have here the opposite of a Catch-22 situation. In a way you can't lose, because every time you put forth an effort at achieving manhood, regardless of your failure or success in achieving the immediate goal, you have increased your manhood. Simply trying to be a man is one of the things that men do.

Gradually, your tests will move out of the world of safe environments, and the bar will be raised higher and higher, but that's always the way growth takes place.

the qualities of a man

For most people, the concept of manhood brings with it very positive qualities, and these qualities are what make manhood desirable. "He is a real man" is always said as a compliment. Implied in "real man" are all sorts of good qualities. No one, not even a little boy, wants to be *just* a man. No parents dream that their sons simply attain a generic sort of manhood. The little boy may want to be a *big* man or a *strong* man. The father may want his son to be *brave* or *wise*. A mother may want her son to be a *loving* or *gentle* man. The concept of manhood evokes positive feelings in most of us because of the qualities we associate with manhood.

These qualities are different from the attributes described in chapter 7 (men are physical and desire to prevail, lead, and relate to other men). Those attributes are neutral; they can even be manifested in evil ways. Attila the Hun had these attributes in abundance, but his manhood is not the type to which we as Christians should aspire. The qualities we are talking about here are all positive, and they are a part of what makes manhood desirable and useful for God's purposes.

No doubt the man you aspire to be has certain positive qualities, whether you have consciously contemplated them or not. So let's look at some of the qualities that make manhood appealing and desirable. Picturing yourself as a man with these qualities will help motivate you for the journey ahead and may give you some direction as you chart your particular course for growth into manhood.

First, however, we will look at how we come to know these qualities through role models.

ROLE MODELS

The perfect model for every man is Jesus. Scripture says that day by day we are to grow into the likeness of Him. He lives in us, and we in Him, so our identities should start to merge into His. Each of us is a part of His body, so even if we don't reflect the fullness of His glory, some of it can shine through us.

But Jesus is perfect, and you and I are far from perfect. It is clear to me from the way I lived yesterday, and the day before, and the day before that, that He remains a distant model for me. Only as the Holy Spirit works change in me can I hope to be more like Him. This is happening, but, oh, what a slow process. If you are honest, I suspect you feel the same way.

Meanwhile you and I can use some interim models, men a little more like us, men who are flawed like us but at the same time have qualities that we can emulate. There are such men. To encounter them is one reason why God placed us in a body, why we need to be living out our lives with other believers. Godly men can model for us godly qualities that we seek to acquire. On a broader basis the church has put forth the saints and heroes of history as men after whom we can model ourselves.

As mentioned in chapter 3, a baby boy is apt to pick one man as a model, usually his father, and that man represents all of manhood. A little later a small boy might pick a man who has some particular characteristic that he wants, such as strength or courage, and that man, not just his strength and courage, becomes the model. In both the baby and the little boy, there is not yet an ability to discriminate between the good and bad in an individual, so the model becomes wholly the man he wants to be.

You and I need role models, but our models should be men who embody certain characteristics that we desire; they should not be men whom we try to imitate in every respect. As mentioned earlier, this can become idolatry. It can become not only a sin but also a sign that we lack realism in the way we look at other men. In looking at other men, we should consciously identify both their qualities that are worth emulating and their flaws. The flaws make the other characteristics of these men seem attainable.

Men from a homosexual background have a tendency to gravitate to extremes, either to canonize or demonize other men, sometimes the same man at different points in the relationship. Some of you can recall how obvious this was when the new lover came along. For a period of time he was perfection; he was everything. This relationship surely was meant to be forever, and you had finally met the one who embodied everything you had ever looked for in a man. Six months later, what a change. What a selfish person he was, how he had deceived you, how he had taken advantage of you.

You had assigned to him all of the qualities you wanted in a man. He wore them for a while, enjoying the adulation, but eventually neither you nor he could carry on the charade any longer. His real character started to show. You couldn't deny it any longer and so you felt betrayed. All along the man had been a creation of your needs.

I see a variation of this in men coming out of homosexuality who still have strong unmet needs for male affirmation. Mike, in our ministry, was such a person. If any man showed an interest in him or in any way affirmed him, Mike was sure that he had found his best friend for life. This was especially so if the man was not from a homosexual background. Mike assigned almost godlike qualities to him.

Eventually, of course, the new friend's feet of clay would be exposed. One or two times he would let Mike down, and Mike, true to his own lack of maturity, would do a 180-degree turn. This man was no longer a friend. Either he had changed, or Mike had been wrong about him all along. In reality, Mike's view of this man had been formed not on a careful and mature evaluation of his qualities, but rather on the extent to which he fulfilled Mike's needs. For Mike, any man who affirmed him embraced great qualities; any man who did not was readily dismissed.

In selecting role models we have to be careful to look for specific qualities and not to assign qualities to men we like. There are some men with whom I don't particularly desire a close friendship but who represent qualities that I believe the Lord would have me develop.

As we start to look at the qualities of manhood, we should think of men we know who possess them. This will remove the qualities from the abstract and put flesh on them. Seen in other men, you will be able to see these qualities in a realistic way. In your church, at work, in your family, what are the traits that make certain men especially appealing as men? There are many positive qualities that can be associated with manhood, but here we are going to look at six: decisiveness, humility, courage, joy, discipline, and loving Jesus.

One man might embody one or any number of them. That doesn't matter. What is important is to see how they are lived out. How does the quality that you desire manifest itself in this man? Where does it seem to be coming from (from his prayer life, from his habits of charity, from his zeal for holiness)? By and large these characteristics are not inborn but are developed, and they can become a part of you.

One more thought on modeling. With the perfection of Jesus as a background, with a grasp of what we were created to be as men, with an understanding of the masculine, and with living examples of manhood in the saints around us, we may develop in ourselves an image of a composite role model, one who embodies all that we believe we can realistically aspire to, one who is the man we want to be. Formed in prayer and illumined by the Holy Spirit, we may see in this image the man we are to become.

A MAN EXHIBITS DECISIVENESS

Men are decisive. Perhaps I should say that men *should* be decisive, because it appears to me that in these days most men are not decisive, and their families and communities suffer for it. This is one of those areas in which the flaws that are common to men are found in exaggerated form among many homosexually oriented men. Here's an example.

A woman in our ministry told of an experience that she had with five ex-gay men at an Exodus conference. It was their night off, and she and the five men were going out to dinner, a welcome break in an arduous week. They left the campus and headed downtown, and there they stood on a street corner for almost half an hour unable to decide where to go. None of the men would express a firm opinion out of fear that he would offend or that the place he suggested would not work out well and he would be blamed. After hearing a seemingly endless repetition of "I don't care" and "What do you want to do?" the woman finally said in exasperation, "Well I'm going to so-and-so's," and the men followed her.

Characteristics of the Indecisive Male

I can identify five elements that are common in the personalities of many men to whom we minister that make them indecisive. I have battled with several of them myself for much of my life.

1. Being a People Pleaser

If I were to single out what is to me the most unattractive personality characteristic that seems to go with male homosexuality, it would be people pleasing. One time I commented to a large group of male overcomers, speaking of our childhood, "We were good little boys, weren't we?" Every head nodded in agreement. And then when I said, "We were as phony as we could be, weren't we?" the heads all nodded again. Perhaps because we felt rejection by our peers, we craved approval by others, especially those in authority: Mom, the teacher, the pastor. In people pleasing we tried to be what we thought other people wanted us to be, all the while knowing that this was not really who we were. This was our initiation into leading double lives. It was cunning, it was deceitful, and often it was cowardly.

Many parents, when they come to Regeneration after just finding out about their son's homosexuality, will say, "He was the best of our children, the one who gave us the least trouble." Often they tell us how good he was in school and that he was always at the church. Although they haven't yet put it into words, what frequently is most painful to these parents is the realization that after twenty-plus years, they didn't really know their son, and he had never trusted their love enough to be honest with them. This is typical of the anguish that people pleasers cause other people. "I can't make a decision because it might displease you and then you won't like me anymore." This isn't kindness; it's manipulation.

2. Having an Inordinate Fear of Rejection

This is similar to people pleasing but goes a little deeper. "I can't make a decision because if it's the wrong one or you don't like it, you might reject me." This ties in with male homosexuality because, for so many, a real or perceived rejection by the father, and subsequently by peers, lies at the root of their homosexuality. The pain of that rejection is still buried deep within us after we have grown up. An inner voice seems to be ever present, saying, "I can't stand it if he rejects me." Of course, this is not true, but it is a thought based on feeling, not on rational thinking. This root of rejection can be a spiritual stranglehold and often requires serious inner healing through prayer.

3. Fearing Being Wrong

This element has a strong connection with the first. "If I make a wrong decision, I will look like a fool. I will be humiliated." This attitude grows out of a fundamental insecurity, and for many of us it is related to our insecurities as men. It goes back, of course, to the low self-esteem that lies at the root of homosexuality. A man who is sure of himself is not inordinately afraid of being wrong.

4. Wanting to Keep All Our Options Open

When we decide, we are deciding *for* one thing and *against* all of the other options open to us. When you decide to join First Baptist, you are deciding against joining Grace Apostolic. When you decide to attend the University of Maryland, you are deciding against Georgetown. When you are accepting a job with AT&T, you are deciding not to work for Microsoft or to go to the foreign mission field. With every decision you make, you are denying yourself all of the other options that have been open to you, and men from a homosexual background often don't do well with self-denial. For years I wanted to have a wife and children and respectability, and at the same time I wanted to have sex with other men. So for years I straddled the fence, living with a foot in both worlds, never able to make the terrible decision to deny myself one or the other.

5. Not Having Firmly Formulated Beliefs

Another factor that contributes to men's indecisiveness is that many men have no fundamental beliefs on which decisions can be grounded. They have no clear values that immediately click in and make decisions clear. If, when Willa was pregnant with Stephen, tests had shown that he would have Down syndrome, we would not have had to struggle with whether to have an abortion. Based on our beliefs, that would have been taking an innocent human life and was therefore out of the question. At a more mundane level, when I do my income tax, I don't struggle with what to put down because I won't lie on such matters.

Most of the men in our ministry, and hopefully most of you reading this book, have clearly formulated beliefs, giving a firm basis for decision making. The majority of people who come to Exodus ministries come because their strong Christian beliefs tell them that homosexual behavior is wrong, and they cannot reconcile a homosexual lifestyle with what they know the Lord wants for them. This is a great advantage that many of you have in making decisions: You have strong Christian beliefs.

To be indecisive sabotages a man in a number of the roles that he is called to play as a man: his roles of leader, protector, and doer. There may be no greater hindrance to effective leadership than indecisiveness. The basic role of any leader is to make decisions. People will not follow a leader for long if he is unable to make decisions. My weak leadership in the early years of Regeneration was largely due to my inability to make decisions. My vacillations and procrastination regularly caused people to question what I was doing. Because I always wanted the approval of the people in the group and was afraid to risk offending them, I was a terrible leader. If we hadn't been the only game in town, or more accurately the only such ministry on the East Coast, the ministry might not have survived my early weak leadership.

A man is a doer; he functions actively in the world. Indecisiveness hinders action. I have discovered that most of the time when I have failed to do something that was expected of me, it has not been that I had too much to do but that I had been putting off deciding what to do. When we say that a man is decisive—and this is always a compliment—we mean that he quickly decides what to do and then gets it done.

An indecisive man puts those who look to him for security in a place where they feel at risk and exposed. One time I heard Willa tell a friend what a great surge of love she felt for me right after I had told her a firm no on some matter. When Stephen was a young boy, I could see his security and his appreciation for me rise after I laid down some firm limits for him.

Deciding Against Indecisiveness

For a man to be effective as a leader, as a doer, and as a protector, he must be able to make decisions. In situations that come up in which his decision is required, he must not only direct and cause action, but he must also often have to say no. This is where decisiveness meets its hardest test. "If I say no to what they want to do, they won't like me. They will criticize me. They will reject me." A man is a person who can say no without a lot of apologies and endless justifications for his position.

A special problem may be faced by those men who are by nature passive. This is not a passivity that is rooted in fear, but rather one that appears to be inborn. It seems that such men came into the world with an exceptional willingness to accept what is. Their attitude is "It's no big deal. It will work out." Such a man is blessed in that he is unlikely to hold a grudge, and he may never develop an ulcer. However, being decisive will be especially difficult for him, and even if his laissez-faire attitude means that he doesn't pay a price for being this way, others around him may. But this man, as well as those whose passivity is rooted in fear, can do things that will help him grow in this basic characteristic of manhood. Here are some suggestions.

1. Be Willing to Be Wrong

Make the decision that you are willing to be wrong, to be disliked, to be rejected for your decisions. You will be some of the time. There is no way around this. Rightly or wrongly, there are times when your decisions will meet with strong disapproval from those affected by them, and there will be times when, in retrospect, you will know that you were wrong. Will this be painful? Yes, it will. Will it kill you? No, it won't. Is it worth it? Only you can decide. The only other option you have is to wait until you are absolutely certain that your decision is right and that no one will attack you for having made it. Of course, this means that you will never make any decisions. When faced with a decision, count the cost, imagine what the worst-case consequences could be if it's wrong, and then determine if you are willing to take the risk. Believe me, the consequences are seldom as bad as we fear, and they are almost always quickly forgotten by those you've upset and by you.

2. Define Your Beliefs and Commit to Them Fully

Our son, Stephen, was such a passive child that it worried us. In nursery school other children would take his toys away from him, but he would do nothing. Largely at the insistence of his sisters, we taught him to be more aggressive and to start establishing some boundaries. He did grow up to be easygoing, and he would today, as a young adult, be quite passive except for two things: One, he developed clear, strong Christian beliefs; and two, he truly cares for other people. He has developed a passion for the Lord and for other people that has made him quite decisive in matters of right and wrong and regarding the spiritual, physical, and emotional well-being of the people in his life.

If you are weak in your beliefs, start trying to articulate them. Write them down. Then prayerfully try to expand them into a full set of beliefs that you want to have as guides for your life. Ask God to start giving you a passion for these things. Also ask Him to increase your love for the people who need you in the role of leader and protector. This can be a slow process, and I am not sure it can be contrived on our own, but with the Lord it is possible.

3. Start Being Decisive with the Little Things

One of the first things that efficiency experts tell busy people is to develop the habit of handling each piece of paper only one time. If a letter, invitation, bill, or order comes to you, decide right away what you are going to do with it. Maybe it can go right to a file, maybe into the trash, maybe it requires a quick phone call, maybe it goes in the unpaid-bills folder, maybe you can do something with it and immediately forward it to the next person. Whatever you do, don't put it down on the pile with all of the other papers that are piled up on your desk, almost assuring that you will be picking it up over and over again in the coming weeks. When a wedding invitation comes, most of the time, I go right to the calendar to see if we are available, immediately fill in the return card, and put it in the mail.

This is a small exercise, but it can start to develop a pattern of decision making in you.

I think that one reason our Lord chose Peter to lead the apostles was that he was so decisive. True, he often did the wrong things, often made a spectacle of himself, but he was a man of action and a man of passionate beliefs. God could use this kind of man to do incredible things. God wants you to be a man He can work with. He can work with your errors; He cannot work with your inaction.

A MAN SHOWS COURAGE

Often you will hear someone refer to a man as a "rock." It refers to a solid, strong, dependable man. If we embrace the picture of a man as a rock, each of us will find ourselves looking at different facets of this rock. One will see his physical or moral strength, another his desire to prevail, another his decisiveness, some his courage. As with viewing the different facets of a diamond, each person is seeing the same man but from slightly different angles. In fact, all of these qualities—strength, prevailing, decisiveness, and courage—blend into one another. Each embodies a part of the other, but at the same time each conveys a different quality. Certainly courage has its own character, and because it so dramatically embodies what we hope to see in a man, I think it is worthy of serious consideration.

Courage is simply the willingness to do something despite the possibility of being hurt. The potential hurt may be the ultimate one, death, as in the case of a soldier going into combat or of a fireman or policeman in his daily work. It might be physical pain or injury or, as is often the case, suffering a blow to one's self-esteem.

For many of us who have dealt with homosexuality from early childhood to the present, the risk that most threatened us was humiliation or damage to our self-esteem. This may still be so for you today. Every new task, everything that looks difficult, everything that you think you can't do has the potential of bringing humiliation and damaging your already fragile self-esteem. These are hurts that you may fear much more than physical pain. This is psychological pain, and your memories of it may be powerful.

If a present challenge links you to feelings of shame, humiliation, or rejection that come out of situations in your past, you face a formidable obstacle. Although the link with past hurts may not be conscious, at a deeper level you may face a powerful inhibitor that keeps you from doing what a part of you wants to do. If other boys humiliated you on the ball field, to participate in competitive team sports today can be like venturing into the jungle of your greatest fears. You might remember how weak or foolish or incompetent you must have seemed to others. Self-protection manifests itself as a lack of courage.

Our need to examine courage becomes apparent when we look at some of the worst attributes that we see among homosexual men. We have already mentioned how being a people pleaser reflects a lack of courage. The people pleaser, or the man who seeks to be all things to all people, reveals a powerful fear of rejection. Chameleon-like, he will become whatever will bring him approval. We worked with one man who was a much-loved brother in Christ, but in our counseling sessions with him he could only say what he thought we wanted to hear. If he thought we wanted him to be remorseful, he showed remorse. If he thought that victory in his personal life would please us, he was victorious. He could never be honest about his failings, because either he feared our disapproval or he felt obligated to be a "success" after all our efforts to help him. Needless to say, we never were able to help him very much.

Men whom our ministries encounter are often extraordinarily non-confrontational. One man who sincerely wanted help in his homosexual struggles contacted Regeneration sporadically for ten years, always by phone. He supported us financially and always had encouraging words for us. But he would never come to meetings. His reason: His mother didn't know about his struggle, and he wouldn't be able to tell her where he was going one night a week. He feared her disapproval too much.

The precise opposite of courage is cowardice. We have courageous men and we have cowardly men. We have courageous acts and we have cowardly acts. Cowardice is the unwillingness to do the right thing because of the risk or consequence it entails. Despite the fact that we live in a culture that doesn't highly value manly virtues, the word *coward* still carries with it contempt. To call someone a coward may be the ultimate assault on his manhood. Even the Bible says that cowards are fit for the lake of fire (Revelation 21:8).

From personal experience, I know that a single cowardly act can leave painful memories for years. It is not unlike those feelings that come from acknowledging that we failed to say a loving word to a close relative when we could have, and now it is too late because he or she is no longer with us. Early in our marriage my wife and I and two other couples were at Baltimore's Memorial Stadium watching an Orioles game. Five or six rough-looking men sitting directly in front of us were feeling their beers, and one of them made some insulting remarks to my wife. Given their number, their size, and their condition, I said nothing. She has forgiven me, and I know the Lord has forgiven me, and my silence was certainly expedient, but if today I could exchange a slightly crooked nose and a few stitches in my chin to be free of that memory, I would consider it a good trade. To paraphrase Shakespeare, "A coward dies a thousand deaths; a hero dies but once."

Because the word *coward* comes with such terrible condemnation, we are hesitant to use it. Instead, we might say someone is meek or timid. How many times have you heard a homosexual man referred to as timid?

In Scripture we have some notorious acts of cowardice, but some of them were committed by men who otherwise showed great courage. Many of us wince at the story of when Abraham found out that Pharaoh was attracted to his wife, Sarah. He told her to tell the Egyptians that she was his sister rather than his wife so that if Pharaoh wanted her for a wife, he would not first kill Abraham. On these terms Sarah moved into Pharaoh's house (Genesis 12). And yet this was the same Abraham who courageously left his land and people for an unknown future on the basis of God's promise.

Peter's three denials of Jesus are perhaps the best known act of cowardice in the Bible. But Peter's overall life and death give clear evidence that he was a man of courage. God in His mercy did not rebuke Abraham, and Jesus had Peter three times profess his love for the Lord, thereby healing the wounds that Peter felt for what he had done.

I have gone on about cowardice for a reason. There is an enormous power in words, and the right word is most powerful when we confess. In confessing, using the correct word—a word that carries no sugarcoating or excuse, a word that stares us in the face with all its naked ugliness—can bring the greatest freedom we can ever experience. Pray about this. If cowardice has been one of the things that has kept you from becoming the man God has called you to be, take it before the Lord. If this is your sin, He will lift it from you.

Courage is the willingness to risk being hurt for a purpose. What are those things for which a man would take such a risk? Three are fundamental to Christian manhood: the protection of others, truth, and God's honor.

Courage allows a man, first of all, to be a protector, one of his noblest callings. A Christian man is called to be a protector of his wife and children, of his parents, and of others to whom he is related by blood. A man is called to be a protector of younger, less experienced men and of single women in the fellowship of believers. He is called to be a protector of his community and of his nation. Author Leon Podles, in his book *The Church Impotent: The Feminization of Christianity,* says that the real purpose of manhood is the protection and provision of the community.[44] Courage and the role of protector are inseparable.

The second thing for which we need courage is to stand for the truth. Previously, we described how a focus on truth is a hallmark of the masculine.

Standing for truth is much more than mere idealism. Truth is a far more glorious thing; it is what brings light into a dark world. Jesus said that He *is* the Truth. Truth is a powerful force that has the capacity to set people free. In our culture we are surrounded by human suffering, the result of trying to apply human solutions to the problems of society.

"For many years I led a homosexual life, but Jesus set me free." Think of the risks that come with such a statement. The culture doesn't want to hear it and will label the speaker as naive, deceived, or a not-so-bright fundamentalist. The liberal church, wedded to the culture, will do the same. Some conservative churches will lock up the young boys when such a speaker is around. The Christian man coming out of homosexuality faces unique risks when he speaks the truth. What a privilege that he has been given special opportunities to glorify God.

The prophets spoke the truth without any knowledge of whether their words would change circumstances. In the case of Ezekiel, God told him to speak to the people of Israel, and at the same time told him that they would not listen to him (Ezekiel 3:7). We speak the truth courageously, not only to bring about a result, but because we are people of the Truth. We serve God, who is Truth.

Third, we need courage to defend God's honor. God does not "need" honor any more than He "needs" our love, but it is due Him. He is worthy of all honor. The first four of the Ten Commandments have to do with honoring God. Although we have opportunities almost hourly to honor or not honor God, the circumstances in which this entails risk and requires courage are not frequent, but they should not be overlooked. Walking out of the room when you are with a friend watching a video that mocks the Lord or asking a friend not to use the Lord's name in vain in your presence can bring you all kinds of negative responses, but that should not matter. We can choose to be pleasers of God or pleasers of men (Galatians 1:10).

Men overcoming homosexuality have every reason to believe that they can become men of courage. Many of the manly characteristics and qualities, such as leading or being decisive, require training; they are developed over a period of time. But we exercise courage by making individual decisions. Once we have decided, both intellectually and before the Lord, to be risk takers, once we have specifically acknowledged the risks that we are willing to take, showing courage is a matter of individual decisions. And if one time you fail to make the courageous choice, other opportunities will surely occur. Succeed and you will have strengthened yourself just a little bit for the next decision. It is probable that you will not get many opportunities to train yourself in courage through risking life or limb. Most of your chances will come in the areas of risking embarrassment or humiliation. As you learn to walk through these fears, you will also become strong for the physical dangers should they arise.

Of the manly virtues discussed here, the one that I believe the homosexual overcomer can acquire in the fullest measure is courage.

A MAN IS DISCIPLINED

I started to write that a man is *self*-disciplined, but it struck me that something must precede a man's being self-disciplined; he must first place himself under another's authority. To be disciplined implies that we live our lives in accordance with certain principles, and unless we choose to live with total autonomy, those principles will come from some source other than ourselves. Interestingly, the nature of sin (and the spirit of this age) grounds itself on the principle of total personal autonomy. As Christians, though, we give up this right, and we place ourselves under God's authority, seeking to live according to the principles He has laid out in His Word and in the teachings of His church. His Word also makes it clear that He has established other authorities, such as parents, the civil government, employers, and the church.

Even before a man starts to exercise self-discipline, he willingly places himself under the authority of God and the agents of His authority. This is essential for God's order to be maintained. Like the centurion who asked Jesus to heal his servant, we acknowledge that we are under authority. I find it interesting that there are six different centurions mentioned in the New Testament, and all of them are portrayed positively. Four of them showed admirable traits: The one just mentioned had faith in Jesus' power (Matthew 8:5-13); the one at the cross declared that Jesus was surely the Son of God (Matthew 27:54); Cornelius, an early convert, was hospitable to Peter (Acts 10); and another one took Paul's nephew to the tribune to warn him of Paul's pending ambush (Acts 23:16-18). Centurions, commanders of a hundred men, were the second lieutenants of the Roman armies. Such men, who knew what it meant to exercise authority and be under authority, must have been pleasing to God for Him to have placed so many of them in positive roles in the biblical narrative.

In most situations and with some degree of success, we can refuse to acknowledge legitimate authority. We can rebel. To a certain extent, our homosexuality was a rebellion against God's order. Now we willingly live under His authority. This willingness is expressed in the discipline with which we live out our lives. The self-discipline part enters in when we believe that there is no one around to enforce the discipline, and this includes our knowledge that God probably will not punish us immediately for our transgressions. Parents are present to enforce discipline on their children with the hope that when they are not around, the children will still live according to what they were taught.

Because men tend toward hierarchical systems,[45] men have a greater appreciation for discipline. Because men are more truth focused than relationship focused, they tend to place a high value on obedience to authority and discipline.

To teach you how to become more self-disciplined would be far beyond either the scope of this book or my abilities to teach, but let me suggest just one thing for any man who is seeking to grow in manhood. Start viewing discipline as a good thing. Stop fighting it; stop resenting it.

All discipline flows from God's authority. Sometimes I wonder how much homosexuality comes from our having rejected the authority of our imperfect fathers instead of from our fathers rejecting us. Whether it is self-discipline or submitting to legitimate authority, remind yourself of God's role in it. Be like the centurion who knew both his responsibility for those under his authority and his own place when he approached the Lord.

A Man Demonstrates Humility

All people are called to humility, but for men this is a crucial issue. It is crucial because men are vulnerable to the sin of pride. Those things which man is called to do—to lead, to build, to protect—all of these accomplishments can easily become a source of pride. What should be our privilege and joy can become a stumbling block.

Men from a homosexual background, however, have a special propensity to pride, not a pride that genuinely sees oneself as superior, but a pride that covers up deeper feelings. As we will discuss later, the healthy, solid man is the same person at every level. The stereotypical homosexual man, however, is "layered." Buried deep within him is the person God created him to be. Resting above that is the frightened boy, the man who feels he has little worth. This is the area where the wounds and pains reside, the quivering jellied layer. To cover it up and avoid feeling the pain, he creates the next layer, a hard but brittle layer of fantasy, defense, and denial. Then there is the outermost layer, the one that interacts with the world, the one he wants people to see. It is often gifted and attractive, sometimes flamboyant or highly accomplished.

All men are susceptible to creating an image that covers up deep insecurities, but in many homosexual men the center quivers so much and the shell is so brittle that they spend an extraordinary amount of energy maintaining the outermost man. Occasionally the shell does crack and the fearful man leaks through, but the most "successful" homosexual man is the one who manages to live almost totally out of the outermost man. He has the best clothes, the classiest apartment, the most perfect body and teeth and skin, the most outstanding accomplishments, and he is the most fun to be with. When watching someone on TV, I've heard my wife or a friend say, "He's gay." I'll ask how they know, and they'll say, "Because he's so perfect."

This attitude toward looks and possessions and accomplishments is called pride. It is a sin not because a man recognizes that he has these things, but because he takes his value from them and believes that they make him a superior person.

Unless God so instructs, the answer to pride is not to get rid of the beautiful furniture, to stop bathing and shaving every day, or to give up one's leading role in the opera company. The answer is to seek to live out of the inner man. For some it may take inner-healing prayer to discover who the true inner man is, but many of us simply need to remind ourselves regularly of who we are. We are stumbling, bumbling sinners who have nothing except what God has given us, and at the same time we are His beloved creatures and are precious beyond measure in His sight. We are His sons. We are far from having "arrived" yet, but His plans for us will take us far beyond our greatest hopes. We have a long way to go, but daily we are becoming more Christlike.

Letting go of the outermost man and starting to live out of the real, inner man is much of what sanctification is all about, and it can be a long process. Pursuing true male humility can help greatly. Identify it in some of the Christian men you most admire, and emulate it. Such men may or may not be blessed with many accomplishments or with great looks, but if they are, these things won't be important to them, and what you will see in them is not pride but a grateful heart.

Here again, it helps to have a sense of humor about ourselves. In effect, as we grow into manhood, we are going through delayed adolescence, and adolescents are notorious for alternating between feeling foolish and being prideful. Develop the capacity to stand off and look at yourself as a good father looks lovingly at a son who is struggling to grow into manhood. Show yourself a little grace.

A MAN EXUDES JOY

Did you ever know a Christian man whose presence seemed to make a room light up when he walked in? My friend Roger is such a man. A physician, he was formerly a member of our church and is now a medical missionary in Ecuador. Roger's joy and love for the Lord is so present, it is almost contagious. Any man can have a joy of life. It is a special characteristic of men because of the way they face the world. The world is something to be challenged, savored, and conquered. But when the man is a Christian, this joy that comes from challenge glows far brighter. It becomes the joy of the Lord.

Where does Roger get his joy from? Many people know the Lord but don't shine with such joy. In trying to figure out where his joy comes from, I have made a few observations about Roger. He does not focus on himself but looks out for the interests of others. He cultivates a grateful heart. He longs to serve the Lord, and he believes deeply that God can use him. His joy is a fruit of the Spirit, not something he works up in himself. Trying to act this way when it doesn't come from within rings hollow. This joy, like all fruit of the Spirit, flows from Roger's seeking Jesus in every part of life.

Another characteristic of his joy, though, is not related directly to his walk with Jesus. Roger believes that God can use him, and this flows out of his strong sense of manhood. As we grow in our manhood, as we develop courage and determination, a passion for truth and self-discipline, and as we come to know Jesus, we gain a sense of our becoming more than conquerors. We know that Jesus has already won the victory, and this victory spills over into our lives. This is cause to be joyful.

Though Roger has a naturally outgoing personality, which makes his joy more noticeable, we don't have to be extroverted to be men who are full of the joy of the Lord. My friend and model in ministry, Frank Worthen, is quite reserved, but when you talk with him, this same joy is evident. Joy is knowing that, in the end, all is well, and joy expresses itself not as happiness but as confidence: a confidence in the present that comes from our assurance of future glory.

A MAN LOVES JESUS

Again, if we look at the men we most admire in our Christian fellowship, one quality that often shines through is that they obviously love Jesus. This is a huge subject—some would say that it is the purpose of one's life. But there is one facet of loving Jesus that is especially applicable to the message of this book. That is the inseparable relationship between loving Jesus and obedience.

> "If you love me, you will keep my commandments. And I will pray the Father, and he will give you another Counselor, to be with you for ever, even the Spirit of truth, whom the world cannot receive, because it neither sees him nor knows him; you know him, for he dwells with you, and will be in you.
>
> "I will not leave you desolate; I will come to you. Yet a little while, and the world will see me no more, but you will see me; because I live, you will live also. In that day you will know that I am in my Father, and you in me, and I in you. He who has my commandments and keeps them, he it is who loves me; and he who loves me will be loved by my Father, and I will love him and manifest myself to him." Judas (not Iscariot) said to him, "Lord, how is it that you will manifest yourself to us, and not to the world?" Jesus answered him, "If a man loves me, he will keep my word, and my Father will love him, and we will come to him and make our home with him. He who does not love me does not keep my words; and

the word which you hear is not mine but the Father's who sent me."
(John 14:15-24)

Many of us, in reading this passage as the great promise of the Holy
Spirit, may have overlooked how many times obedience and God's love are
tied together for those who have received the Spirit of God. As we are obedient, we will grow in the love of the Lord. As we grow in the love of the
Lord, we will grow in our capacity to be obedient.

Every man who battles homosexual temptations out of obedience to
God is allowing himself to be drawn more and more into the sphere of
God's love. You will find victory in this love, and then you will love Him
even more. What a great journey we are on.

overcoming the obstacles

One day when I was a relatively new Christian, as was my usual practice when driving, I was listening to my favorite Christian radio station in Baltimore. A preacher was talking about what we need to do to raise our children properly. Mostly, he said we needed to hold high standards for our kids, to set clear boundaries for them, and to be firm in our discipline. He scrolled off a long series of Bible quotes, most of them from Proverbs, supporting these views. I agreed with everything he said—how could I disagree with Scripture? But the more he talked, the angrier I became. Finally, in frustration, I yelled at the radio, "I know all this stuff; its so obvious. My problem is I've tried and tried to do these things, but I've failed over and over. Not one thing you have said has helped me in any way."

It turned out that this little irrational exchange with the radio would guide my teaching and writing from that time forward. I had discovered that we can describe a problem perfectly, with all of the subtle nuances that others may not see, and then show clearly with perfect logic how if A is the problem, then B must be the answer. And with that, almost always, we have offered our listener or reader absolutely nothing. Most people understand what the problem is, and they can readily recognize the logical solution to that problem. The problem is in being able to do what the solution requires.

At this point you may see that the reason why you don't feel like a man is that you never did the things that men do as you were growing up; you skipped major steps that boys go through on their way into manhood.

That's the problem, so obviously the answer now is to go out and start doing the things that men do. With this advice all of your problems are solved, right? Hardly.

The real problem is not that we don't know what the solution is; the real problem is that we face huge obstacles in applying the solution, and we don't know how to overcome these obstacles.

This chapter and the next will be among the most important in the book because we will discuss the obstacles and suggest how they can be overcome. If you have felt some frustration as you have read thus far, I hope this will assuage some of it. The obstacles you face may be formidable, and they may be faced on several fronts. In this chapter, we will examine certain spiritual barriers that can stand between us and growth into manhood, and in chapter 12, we will look at the roadblocks thrown up by our emotions and our wills.

BENEATH MANY OBSTACLES LIES A SIN

Anyone who reads my newsletter articles or who has gone through Regeneration's New Directions program knows that I am big on sin. Not that I am in favor of it, heaven forbid. But I see the discovery of specific sins and the repentance that follows as the keys that unlock the door to vital and lasting change. I further stress that repentance is easy; it is the discovery and acknowledgment of the sin that makes the road to sanctification so long and difficult. (This was part of the preparation for tests we talked about in chapter 9.) Recognizing that seeking out our sins is a lifelong process, I am going to discuss it further here in the context of overcoming obstacles to growth.

My twenty-five years as a Christian have been marked by a series of life-changing encounters in which the Holy Spirit convicted me of sins that in one way or another held me in some type of bondage and blocked my growth as a Christian man. These were not the easily recognized sins like lust or greed but the much deeper ones that tended to corrupt my character. As

I have grown in Christian maturity, such discoveries have not become less frequent. Rather, they have shed light further into the darkness of my soul. This is a journey that every Christian must take.

I said that the recognition of the sin was the difficult part, that repentance was easy. Let me qualify this somewhat. Repentance is easy if we are not in rebellion. Rebellion recognizes a sin but refuses to do anything about it. But rebellion is its own sin, one that has the perverse ability to allow other sins to live under its cover. Rebellion, which we'll discuss later, may be one of the hidden sins that will have to be owned up to and confessed if growth into manhood is to be achieved.

I am a strong advocate of looking for the sins that undergird life's problems because I know that in Jesus and His blood we have a clear and ready remedy for those sins. This is immediately available to us as believers, whereas overcoming the destructive effects of our habits, hurts, and hangups can be a much more complicated matter. In this therapy-oriented world (and therapy-oriented church, I might add), our preference for dealing with wounds rather than sins can become a major factor in the persistence of our problems.

As you read what follows, ask the Holy Spirit to shed light on any dark areas of sin that you need to bring to the cross. For the time being at least, try to let go of thinking about the circumstances that influenced you to take a certain direction, and focus more on your responses to life's difficulties. Our early lives may have provided many setups to steer us toward homosexuality, but our responses to these setups are what ultimately made the difference, and our responses were often sinful.

OVERCOMING THE OBSTACLE OF FEAR

This is the big one. Over and over again in counseling men dealing with homosexuality, we meet up with the fears that controlled their lives in adolescence and still leave them paralyzed in certain areas today. I am certain that most homosexual overcomers can look back at their adolescence and see a clear picture of themselves figuratively or literally walking off the field where interactions with other boys were too threatening.

To meet and overcome any fears, we must first identify what they are. With respect to the fears that we carried over from adolescence, this may not be as clear-cut as we suspect. What specific fear caused you to get off track, to run away from the process of growing into manhood? What fears today keep you feeling as if you can never measure up in the world of men? Because our fears are often quite nebulous, we may never have tried to adequately define them. You may be able to identify *activities* that cause fear— you may be fearful of playing softball or fearful of speaking before a large group—but this doesn't tell us much about the fear itself. Fear is based on anticipated harmful or unpleasant consequences. What consequences do you fear? For most men there are three basic fears: the fear of rejection, the fear of being hurt, and the fear of humiliation. Each of these fears is actually a family of fears.

The *fear of rejection* is the fear of not being loved. Traditionally, this has been seen as central to the homosexual condition, particularly among men. This fear is based on actual (justified or not) feelings of pain coming from not having felt loved in the past. The pain was so intense that we dare not risk ever having to endure it again. This fear is most often resolved by dealing with the past, facing the situations that gave rise to the original pain. You will not "grow out of" this kind of fear, but it is best resolved through counseling and healing prayer.

The *fear of being hurt physically* can be a fear of pain, a fear of deprivation, a fear of being out of control, and ultimately a fear of death. With lesbian women, past sexual abuse may lie at the root of such fears, but this is seldom a factor with men. Although many homosexual men have backgrounds of sexual abuse and this abuse may have left scars, seldom do we encounter a homosexual man who fears he is going to be sexually molested.

We often associate the wimpy homosexual man with a fear of getting hurt physically, and this may keep him from doing some of the physical things that men do. He may be terrified of picking up a chain saw or of going hunting. This type of fear can be a real hindrance to growth, but it is far less debilitating than the third type of fear: the fear of humiliation. Furthermore, if we successfully attack the fear of humiliation, it is quite likely we will find ourselves overcoming the fear of being hurt physically.

The *fear of humiliation* is the core issue that kept us, and may still be keeping us, from doing the things that men do. Here, too, we encounter a family of fears that disable men seeking to overcome homosexuality. In addition to humiliation itself, the family of fear includes the fear of failure, the fear of not measuring up, the fear of looking incompetent, and the fear of feeling worthless.

Growing up, our fear was not of baseball; it was of appearing incompetent when we tried to play it. Our fear was not that we might be teased, but that we might be considered worthless. Our fear was not that we might not be as physically strong as other boys, but that we might not measure up on the whole scale of values that measured manhood. These fears may be rooted in pains suffered in the family, but most likely the real humiliation came with peers, the broader world of men and boys.

If we are to do the things that men do, we are going to have to deal with—no, more than that—we are going to have to *conquer* these fears. Although the years of peer rejection may lie decades behind us, the fears may still be controlling us. Conquering them doesn't mean that we won't feel them but that they will no longer control our lives. Fear can be an enormous obstacle, but overcoming it may be the key to our renewed growth.

At the company where I worked for many years, every spring there was a men's outing at which the middle-management men were expected to participate in a softball game. As June and the outing came closer, I would literally get sick at the thought of this. A few times I found ways to avoid the whole outing. When I did go, I was so anxious and miserable that today I can remember little about those outings except that we played softball.

Interestingly, I don't recall how I did in the actual games; what I remember is the awful fear beforehand. This is significant.

How does one come through such fears? You certainly won't do it by reading a book, even this one. No author, not even your own logical thinking, will bring you out of it. I knew rationally that my fear was exaggerated, that I would live through the experience without identifiable scars. I knew that playing softball wasn't really the measure of a man, but none of this did any good.

If you have a small child who is afraid of the water, how do you get him to overcome his fear? Do you read him books on swimming? Do you explain why it doesn't make logical sense for him to be so fearful? No, you take him into the water. Maybe it's only three inches deep and you are holding his hand at first, but the only way he is going to overcome his fear is to get into the water. So it is with us. If we are going to overcome our fears, we have to do the things that could bring us humiliation, the things that would prove that we don't measure up.

A little boy grows into manhood by doing the things that men do, and you missed the boat. You tried to do those things and failed, or, more likely, you made a few small efforts, and finding failures to be too painful, you dropped out of the race. So who says anything is going to be different this time?

Try again, resume the journey now, and won't you be setting yourself up for more failure, perhaps even driving home more intensely than ever the reality that you don't measure up to other men? Besides, won't you make a bigger fool of yourself now, when others' expectations for your performance are much higher than they were when you were a young boy? This time you are not expected to perform like an eleven-year-old, but like a thirty-year-old. What is going to enable you to succeed now when the hurdle is so much higher? What is going to be different this time?

There will be differences this time, and they are tremendously significant, so let's take a deeper look at them.

1. Now You Know the Purpose for It All

When I was an athletically and socially inept teenager, my parents would urge me to get involved with some teenage group or in some physical activity. If the suggested activity was a threat, and it almost always was, I would simply tell them, "I can't stand doing that," and that usually ended it. They didn't really see the full importance of the activity, and besides, it was not their way to push me in any area of my life.

More importantly, *I* didn't see the importance of these activities. I had no idea that if I didn't do these things, I would grow up shy, fearful, withdrawn, prone to live in my own little fantasy world, envious of other boys and craving their manhood. There was no way that I could see that avoiding such unpleasant activities was advancing me more and more into homosexuality.

But you know differently! You know that there is a purpose—a great benefit—in doing some of the things that men do, things that you really don't want to do. If you truly and earnestly desire to experience the fullness of your manhood and if you know of no other way of doing this except by doing the things that men do, you will do those things. When asked to come over and watch the Super Bowl with a group of men, you will smile and say, "Sure, I'll be there." No one will hear the voice inside you saying, "Man, I don't want to do that, but I know I need to." Just as an athlete works out—something he may not like doing at all—for the purpose of gaining a skill or making a team, you are ready to exercise your manhood for the purpose of experiencing full manhood. No one exercises without a purpose. You now have a purpose.

God seemed to provide the setups that forced me into activities with other men and that thrust me into leadership roles. There was no one around telling me that I needed to do these things so that one day I could be a proper husband and father or an acceptable ministry leader. I did not know the greater importance of these things. Had I known, especially after I had become a Christian, I might have embraced them more fully and achieved a far faster growth. I might even have sought out such situations for my own good. God may or may not provide setups for you in a similar way, but opportunities will be there.

Now you know that you have powerful reasons to embrace the opportunities that arise. Do so, and if necessary, seek others out.

2. Now You Are in a Better Position to Select the Arenas in Which You Will Be Tested

Now there is no Mom telling you that you must go out and play with the other boys, no physical education teacher telling you that you must climb the rope. You can decide what you are up to trying, where and with what group of men. You can wade through the three inches of water before you are ready to jump into the deep end of the pool. You can choose safe places. This was the principle behind our Regeneration softball games.

These games were started after I had spent years hearing one man after another describe how painful sports were for them in their teens. And it was always softball or baseball that was the worst. Our guys got chosen last. They were put out in right field where they prayed that the ball would never come to them, because if it did, they couldn't catch it, and when they did get it, they either couldn't throw it far enough or would throw it to the wrong base. And that was just the defensive half of the game. The times at bat would prove without a doubt their incompetence as boys or men. The pain from these experiences was enormous in these men. I knew the pain firsthand, so I could empathize with them. It was the pain of humiliation.

Our Regeneration games have given our men an opportunity to walk through an arena that for many evoked their greatest fears of humiliation. They selected a safe place to do it, and they were with other Christian men who understood what they felt. But believe me, even in this setting the first time out all of the old fears came up. But they conquered them. Few of our men went on to make softball a major pastime in their lives, but quite a number were willing at the next church picnic to go out on the field with the other men, ready to take the next step. They had found a relatively safe environment, so they were willing to take their first steps into an area of great fear, and in the process, the power of fear loosened its grip just a bit.

Perhaps you are not with a group that is interested in playing softball. Bruce McCutcheon, the leader of Quest Ministry in Atlanta, suggests a simple way that his overcomers can approach the men's world of sports. He urges them to spend five minutes a day reading the sports section of the local paper. Who knows when a little knowledge picked up there might enable one of them to take one small step into the world of men?

3. Now You Can Decide That You Are Willing to Fail

As negative as this might sound, it is a corollary to seeing the purpose. It might be paraphrased by the old cliché, No Pain, No Gain. You cannot take one step down the road to manhood unless you are willing to face the possibility of failure. When you were a little boy, you didn't want to play baseball likely because when a ball was hit to you, you could not catch it, and you felt humiliated. So you decided not to play ball. But it never occurred to you that every other little boy, at some point in his development, dropped most of the balls hit to him. What was different with those other boys that made them willing to take the embarrassment and try again?

There may be any number of reasons why we weren't willing to risk the embarrassment and others were. Maybe we were more sensitive by nature. Maybe we had a heightened sensitivity to rejection rooted in real or perceived rejection by our fathers. Maybe for some reason we got a late start in sports and were embarrassed primarily because we lagged behind the other boys. Whatever the cause, the fear was intense, and it was enough to make us want to avoid failure in the eyes of our peers at almost any cost.

You may now see how high the cost was and is. But more important, you can now take a more objective look at the cost of failure. It is almost always less than you felt it would be. You will not die; almost certainly you will not be devastated. If you do encounter pain, it will only last for a short while, and you now know that the pain has a purpose: No Pain, No Gain. Try to think of the last time you failed in a manly role: in engaging in small talk with other men, in being decisive, in a leadership role: in catching a ball. If you can remember any specific times when you appeared incompetent to your peers, were the consequences so dire? Do you think anyone else remembers those incidents? Probably not; it probably wasn't all that important to them. Remember how I have no memory of looking incompetent at the company softball games, only memories of the fear?

There is no doubt that you will sometimes fail when you try to do things that men do. Make the decision now that you are willing to fail on some occasions, that you will endure the consequences of failing. First, however, think of what those consequences might be. Look at the worst-case scenario. Will you die? Will you be devastated? Or will you simply have to go through a rather unpleasant experience that will soon be forgotten? There is a deceitful voice in many of us that says, "If I try and then fail…" and then never completes the statement. We feel that the consequences will be horrendous, but somehow we never put them into words. We are threatened by a great amorphous cloud of disaster, but we really don't know what it is. Make yourself finish that sentence, project what the consequences might be, and then determine whether or not you can handle them.

You can afford to fail. In almost every situation the consequences of failure will not be that terrible. And unless you make the decision to risk failure, you will never do the things that you must do to grow. Nor will you ever experience the successes that will provide the building blocks of your manhood. Your failures will be forgotten in a short while. Your successes will bear fruit for as long as you live.

4. This Time You Are Not Alone

The first time through, I was alone. The second time I sought to grow up, I had a friend to help me. He encouraged me every step of the way. When I slipped and fell, he picked me up, dusted me off, and applied balm to my wounds. When I cried, "It is too much, too difficult," he held me, and through the strength of his arms, new strength flowed into mine. He was with me every step of the way. I could not have made it through without him. With him, the ultimate completion of the project was a certainty.

I'm sure you know my friend was Jesus. He did call us friends (John 15:15). He did say that we could endure in Him (John 15:1-11). Scripture tells us that we can do all things through Him who strengthens us (Philippians 4:13).

Quite likely, the first time through you did not know Jesus, or if you did, you were unaware of His desire and willingness to help you in every struggle of life. He is the perfect father, the perfect older brother, the perfect friend. He will make possible every step you need to take. He will comfort you in the midst of failures and give you what it takes to want to try again.

At the beginning of this book I offered to walk with you down the difficult road to manhood. I should say that I will start the journey with you, but after a while I will let go of your hand and place it in the hand of Jesus. He is the one who will be with you all the way. He is the one who will bring to completion the work that was begun before you were born.

I know that many men overcoming homosexuality, men who are born-again believers, have not known the living Jesus in a way that makes Him seem truly present as a friend, encourager, helper, and comforter. If you are such a man, seek such a relationship with all your heart. You will find it, and it will be the key, not only to your growth into manhood, but to your total healing from homosexuality. The most important truth that I can express in this book, the truth that has served as the foundation of our whole ministry is this: *Healing comes through our relationship with Jesus Christ.*

A life-changing personal relationship with Jesus is possible for every Christian. I believe this for the simple reason that He has shown us that He wants it. Read John 14–16 and listen to how deeply and personally He loves you. Remember how much the Father loves you. He sent Jesus to the cross because we were estranged from Him and God wanted us to be reconciled to Him.

The most important thing you can do to establish a living relationship with the Lord is to spend time with Him, a daily quiet time. This is so important, so central to the theme of this book, that I have put my teaching on the subject in appendix B.

I mentioned earlier that we need to look for the sins that underlie the problems that beset our lives. What is the sin that is behind our fear? Fear itself is not sinful. God gave us fear as an emotion that would cause us to avoid danger. The emotion of fear activates our physical fight-or-flight mechanism. God made us this way. But He did not give us fear to help us avoid those things that were good for us or shirk our duties as men. In such circumstances, fear is a sin because ultimately it reflects a lack of trust in God.

When Steve was a little fellow, one of the things he loved to do was climb the stairs and jump through the air into my arms. As he got older and braver, he would climb a step higher so that he kept alive the feeling of daring, perhaps even a feeling of flying. He loved it, and I did too. For him it was a chance to impress us all with his bravery. For me, it was the pleasure of witnessing his joy, and even better, the blessing of seeing the absolute trust he had in me. He was confident I would always catch him, and I always did.

We—you and I—have a Father who loves to be trusted also. In fact, there is probably nothing that brings Him greater joy than our trusting Him, for when we trust Him, we show more clearly than in any other way that we know His character. We show that we know He is faithful, trustworthy, able to do all that we need Him to do. In a way, trust is the highest form of praise.

Fears, however, can be a statement that we believe He is not trustworthy. Repent of such fear, and let every challenge, even those that could bring humiliation, be the cause for an exercise of trust in the One who loves you and is above all trustworthy.

OVERCOMING THE OBSTACLE OF WILLFULNESS

Brian, a member of our ministry, was approached by one of the men at work.

"Hey, Brian, three of us are going fishing for rockfish on Saturday. You want to go?"

"No, thanks. I don't do that; no fishing."

"Why not? We'll have a great time."

"Sorry, I don't like boats, it may rain, and there's no way I'm going to bait a hook. What do you use? Bloodworms, squid? Ugh!"

"Brian, you are such a priss. Every time we ask you to do something, you turn us down."

"Well, I'm sorry. That's just the way I am."

Brian's approach to life could be summed up in those two statements: "I don't do that" and "That's just the way I am." Many of our men have developed self-protective lifestyles in which these statements are the cornerstones. Possibly this grew out of early hurts, but it could be just human self-centeredness carried another step. Whatever the cause, these men place a huge premium on avoiding anything that makes them uncomfortable. They create a safe world and refuse to venture outside of it.

The determination to have life on our terms and no other way is willfulness. I use this term in a negative sense. The stubborn determination to do things our own way and sometimes to intentionally remain ambivalent—wanting things both ways—is sinful. It is using God's incredible gift of a free will for selfish purposes. It is a declaration of "My will be done."

Contrast Brian's willfulness with the approach to life that many healthy teenage boys have. When my son, Steve, was asked to do something he had never done before, the mere fact that he could do something new was often all the motivation he needed to do it. His was a world of challenges.

Kevin, who for years ran our Regeneration softball season, decided he would take a group of our men to a turkey shoot. (They don't shoot turkeys; frozen turkeys are the prizes for hitting targets with a shotgun.) A number of the men had all sorts of reasons for not going: "It's too far." "I can't stand the noise." "The gun has a kick, doesn't it?" Kevin asked Steve, who was about fourteen at the time and often participated in Regeneration events. Steve couldn't wait to go, and he and several of the Regeneration men had a wonderful time. When Steve got home around midnight, he woke us up to show us the turkey—and the ham—he had won. Steve and these men had expanded their manhood just a little more.

Situations of childhood trauma may leave a man with an almost irresistible need to be self-protective in certain situations. For example, a boy falls off a roof and is forever afraid of high places, or he is bitten by a neighbor's dog and remains fearful of dogs. But these fears are based on specific risks. What I am addressing here is the habit of always choosing safety and comfort over challenge and growth. The man who has developed such a lifestyle is his own worst enemy. Like Pogo, he should be saying, "We have met the enemy, and he is us."

To resume growth, you will have to make the decision that you are not always going to choose safety and comfort over challenge and growth. A conscious decision must be made to view the world, not as something from which you need protection, but rather as an adventure to be experienced. It is a matter of exercising the will.

It is important not to call something psychological paralysis when it is essentially a matter of choice. Many men could do things that would help them, but they simply won't because it would be inconvenient or uncomfortable.

This willful attitude can express a spirit of rebellion. From early childhood, a man may have reacted against the things that men do. With a childish attitude and a degree of anger, some of our men have reacted against the whole world of men as expressed in the culture around them. They want no part of it. Homosexuality itself is, after all is said and done, a form of rebellion—against our parents, against the standards of our culture and church, against God's fundamental order for life on this earth.

Another sin that willfulness might express is a spirit of extreme individualism: not being willing to see oneself as a part of a community, a family, a body; being unwilling to recognize that God made us social creatures and that this requires a give-and-take in which life is not always lived on our terms. Such men see manhood as an option that they can accept or reject, not as a positive influence they can have on the people around them, not as a part of God's fundamental plan for their lives.

When I encounter such an individual and see that his inflexibility is keeping him from growing as God would have him grow, I will look closely at his individual situation, I will try to consider all of the psychological ramifications present, and then after much prayer, I will give him this advice: Stop it! You want to get healed? Then get a life. (I don't say it quite like that, but in a more loving manner.)

The human will is a mighty thing. We are *not* totally programmed to behave in a certain way by our genes and our past experiences. The will is a force that has the power to overcome our natural instincts. God gave each of us a truly free will that allows us to choose in most situations. Use your will to make choices that will take you out of your comfort zone and will place your feet on the path that leads to manhood.

As I have grown as a Christian, I have come to recognize more and more that God doesn't always give us control over how things will end up; He often saves that for Himself. But He does give us control over the means that will work toward His end. Through His grace and through His power, we have the means to overcome our fears and to change our most stubborn ways. If we earnestly seek to do these things in pursuit of the manhood He desires for us, He will be with us, and His goal will be accomplished.

overcoming the past

"Therefore, if any one is in Christ, he is a new creation; the old has passed away, behold, the new has come" (2 Corinthians 5:17). The changes that come upon us at conversion are indeed extraordinary. The spiritual consequences of our old life are washed away, we enter into a new and marvelous relationship with Jesus, and all of a sudden we have a future that we need not fear. Our past, our present, and our future have been radically transformed.

If our conversion was sudden and dramatic, we may feel for a time that absolutely everything about us is new and that all the consequences of our past life have been nullified. At some point, however, most people come to see that parts of our "new creation" are not experienced instantly; they must be lived out. Not all of the old things have totally lost their grip on us; they must be released as we grow in our relationship with the Lord.

What is extraordinary about our future, however, is that whereas the debris of our sin and brokenness so littered the pathway of our old life that progress often seemed all but impossible, now we find that God has placed our feet on a new path, and we can and do start changing. Furthermore, we find that He has equipped us with all the means that we need to overcome the obstacles that stymied us before. We have the means—the strength—to overcome the fears, the willfulness, the ambivalence that marked our earlier lives.

The past's power to control us is not broken on every front at conversion. We may have to live out our release from the "old things," and this may be a slow process, much slower than we would like. We find that this is a two-stage process: We must discover what it is that still has its grip on us, and we must decide to forsake it. Neither step is easy.

For men overcoming homosexuality, I see three "ghosts" from the past that commonly still control them and keep them from growing into their God-ordained manhood. They are childhood vows, unforgiveness, and a false identity.

CHILDHOOD VOWS

Most of the things that we did that contributed to our homosexuality were, by their nature, self-protective. We removed ourselves from situations that were threatening. We broke off relationships where we felt rejection. We made decisions in specific situations to keep ourselves from getting hurt. When similar decisions were made over and over again, patterns for our lives became established.

Some decisions we made, however, were especially far reaching. In our ministry we call them childhood vows. That they were intended to be far reaching is seen in that they always included the words *never* or *always* or their equivalents.

I made two vows early in my childhood that are perfect examples of what I am talking about here. From my earliest years I can remember hearing my mother and father engaged in frequent heated arguments. These arguments probably came out of the family dysfunction that grew out of my father's depression. One evening, when I was quite a young child lying in bed listening to them in an especially loud and angry battle, I told myself, "They can't hurt me. Nobody can ever hurt me." I remember the smug satisfaction that I felt as I made that determination. It worked. From that point on their battles never again hurt me. But my decision to shut my heart off to them was to have far-reaching consequences that a little boy could never anticipate. I had made a vow never to let anyone hurt me, and this meant that I would never be free to love anyone. Loving always makes us vulnerable, and I had determined never to be vulnerable.

My second childhood vow was that I would meet my own needs at all costs. My years of pursuing homosexual contacts were an outgrowth of this vow. I needed physical contact with a man. I needed a dose of some man's manhood. At the same time, I knew that what I was doing wasn't right. I knew that I was being unfaithful to my wife. I knew that, long range, the consequences of my actions could prove disastrous. But they were my needs, and come what may, I was going to meet them.

Although the power of such childhood vows may be broken at conversion, as mine were to some extent, or they may go by the wayside as the Holy Spirit leads us to make new decisions that nullify the old ones, too many Christians in our ministries continue to live under the power of their own childhood vows. Prayerfully examine your life and heart, and determine if a "never" or "always" decision from your early life still has a grip on you. If so, ask the Lord to show you the vow you made, and then go before Him and renounce it. Ask Him to take away its power and to place in your heart new commitments and new decisions that will bring forth life rather than stifle it. Better yet, find someone to pray this prayer with you. Let him or her be a witness to your declaration of independence from your old ways of self-protection, and have that person affirm your place as a son who now lives in the shelter of his Father's protection.

Unforgiveness

The second ghost, unforgiveness, holds countless Christians captive to events of the past. Over and over again, Jesus stressed how we are to forgive as we have been forgiven. Many Christian writers have taken the Lord's command to forgive and have shown how freedom cannot come until we forgive those who in some way hurt us. For our purposes I will not deal broadly with forgiveness here but will discuss the one area in which unforgiveness seems to be the greatest obstruction to growth into manhood: the failure to forgive one's father.

Leanne Payne has written that the greatest hindrance to healing is the failure to forgive. I agree. But I want to take the issue back one step. Our greatest hindrance to forgiving is not owning up to the wrongs that we did in our relationships with others. Until we recognize *our* sin in a given situation, our forgiveness will be muddled. It will be mixed up with casting blame. Our forgiveness cannot make a situation or a relationship right if there are still other matters to be dealt with. What I am about to bring up is not universal among homosexual overcomers, even among those whose homosexuality clearly stems from an inadequate father relationship, but it is so common, and we have such a strong tendency to overlook or deny it, that I offer it here hoping that each reader will prayerfully consider its applicability to his own life. I will describe it by sharing a personal story.

One year on a day early in June during my quiet time, it occurred to me that it was around the time of my late father's birthday. I didn't know the exact date. I always had to ask my mother, and somehow I always got it mixed up with Father's Day.

I don't know my father's birthday! In an instant the awful significance of that swept over me. I felt like a hot poker was being driven through my heart as truth after truth overwhelmed me faster than words could express them.

I didn't know my father's birthday because my father was of no significance to me. He never had been. He had been a reality in my life, but he was of no importance. I knew my mother's birthday, my brother's, my children's, even some of my close friends', but in all those years I had never remembered the exact date of my father's birthday.

All of a sudden I had a picture of my father. He was a good-looking man. He was kind to everyone. He had a sense of humor. He worked as a counselor for handicapped people, whom he really tried help. He loved fishing, and when I was young, he offered to take me with him. I usually refused.

How different these thoughts were from my usual memories of my father. My memories almost always centered on the depression from which he suffered during most of my life: his drawing into himself, his crying, his trips to the psychiatrist, my picking him up after his electric shock treatments when I was a teenager. How different these new thoughts were from the memory of one time when he was going into the mental hospital and he showed me how to light the pilot light on the gas furnace in case it went out. I remember thinking to myself, *Thanks Dad. This is all you have to show me. I'm already doing everything else that you should be doing in the family.* Utter contempt.

"Honor your father and your mother, as the LORD your God commanded you; that your days may be prolonged, and that it may go well with you, in the land which the LORD your God gives you" (Deuteronomy 5:16). It seems strange that only this and the prohibition on adultery are included in the Ten Commandments as directives for family relationships. How about "Parents love and pay attention to your children"? Or, "Husbands, love and cherish your wives"? And why is this the only commandment with a promise?

The commandment doesn't say we are to honor our father and mother if they are good parents or if they do their best. In this, the commandment is consistent with how we are told to relate to others in the New Testament. Paul didn't say obey and respect the government if it is fair, just, and democratic. Wives aren't told to obey their husbands only when the husband shows wisdom and consideration for them. Husbands aren't told to love their wives if they are lovable. God's commandments are not conditional. If they were, we would be setting ourselves up over the law because we would have to be the ones to determine if the conditions were being met. God says to love, obey, honor. That's it.

I had failed to keep one of the simplest and most basic commandments. I had not honored my father. As the painful reality of the sin swept over me, I started to think, *Yes, I didn't, but it was understandable. I was a little kid and I was needy. He was not being a father to me.* The Holy Spirit seemed to say, "There may be some truth in that, but it is totally irrelevant to what I am calling you to deal with now. You did not honor your father."

Strangely, memories started coming back to me of ways in which he did try to be a father to me. He did want me to go fishing with him. Sometimes, on Saturday mornings he would take me into the office with him. True, in his depressed state, he couldn't be much of a father, but what was being laid before me was that *I never let him be my father*. I had not honored my father, and I had never repented of the sin.

And so, in the quiet of that early June morning, I repented. I wept and asked God to forgive me for not letting my father be my father, and for not honoring him. A few days later I went to his grave—for the first time in the ten years since he had died—and asked him to forgive me. I am forgiven, but some sorrow lingers on. I still mourn the lost opportunities to be a son and to let him be my father.[46]

It was necessary that I release my father before I could come into the fullness of my manhood. To release someone always means forgiving him, but for me the forgiveness had to be preceded by repentance. I had to repent for having rejected him. I had to repent for having sat in judgment over him for so many years. That is never a son's role.

The commandment to honor our parents does come with the promise that things will go well with us. This has a powerful application to the homosexual struggle. Our failure to let our fathers be our fathers is a primary cause of homosexuality. You cannot become a man until you have been a son. You cannot be a son until you have acknowledged, or honored, your father.

Some reading this book had fathers who were truly abusive, physically, sexually, or verbally. By verbally abusive I mean they demeaned your manhood openly and cruelly. I never went through any of this, so I don't feel competent in this context to deal with the special problems of those who were abused. I suspect that many victims of real abuse need healing prayer before they will be able to forgive their fathers, but ultimately, even they must release their fathers.

My experience in ministry tells me that most homosexual men were not abused by their fathers. Most of us had fathers who wanted to be good fathers, but because of something in them, in us, or in the circumstances of our lives when we were growing up, they weren't the fathers that we needed. But we are not in a position to judge them. Who is to say, given how they were dealt with by their own fathers, or given the circumstances of their lives when we were growing up, that they could have done any better? We cannot sit in judgment; we can only forgive.

Each of us, biologically or otherwise, is destined to be a father. For me it was to be the father of Laura, Beth, and Steve. You, like Paul, may be called to be a spiritual father of other men or to assume some other fatherly role in the church or community. The true essence of manhood is found in the capability of being a father.

If we do not release our fathers, we will continue to live under the power of whatever wrong they did to us. If we do not release our fathers but continue to demand (albeit retroactively) that they be perfect fathers, then we will never dare to become fathers ourselves, because we know that we won't be perfect fathers either. As you forgive others, so shall you be forgiven.

How do we forgive our fathers? We start with the decision that we are willing to forgive. Then we go before the Lord. You might want to pray something like this:

Heavenly Father, I want to forgive my earthly father. Help me to do it. I am willing to take responsibility for my own life and for the decisions that I have made, and I release him from responsibility for who I am today. Lord, show me where I have sinned against my father. Show me if I rejected him or if I have sat in judgment of him. If so, I repent of these sins. Lord, I forgive my father for any harm he might have done me—intentional or unintentional—and I release him into Your hands. I pray that in practice or in memory I will be able to honor him as father so that I may be set free to become that man and father You want me to be. In Jesus' name, amen.

If your father is still living and circumstances will allow it, you need to seek reconciliation with him. This means facing him with the acknowledgment that you sinned against him and, if you have truly forgiven him, with no demand that he repent of his sins against you. You will be blessed is he accepts your forgiveness. If he doesn't acknowledge that he has done anything to be forgiven for, God will minister to you anyway. The burden of unforgiveness will still be lifted from you, and you will be free from this part of your past.

If your father is deceased or if reconciliation is out of the question, you still need to repent. But then seek to be the son of another—your heavenly Father. After becoming a Christian, I had always related easily with Jesus, but since going through the experience I just shared, I was more and more able to approach the Father. It became a joy to experience real sonship and to experience the healing that came with it.

A FALSE IDENTITY

At conversion, as we are told in Ephesians 4:22-24, we put off our old, corrupt nature with its deceitful lusts, and we put on the new nature that reflects the righteousness and holiness of God. By identification with Jesus Christ, this is a spiritual reality for each of us. One day we will be like Jesus; we will have put Him on totally. But meanwhile, in many parts of our life, the reality of the new nature is not yet manifested. Rather, we have been empowered to enter into a series of putting offs and putting ons. Where once we were locked into our sins of selfishness and self-protection, now, empowered by the Holy Spirit, change has become possible. Although it may not occur without intense struggle, we can put off—let go of—our old ways of coping with life and put on—accept—new ways that are pleasing to God and conform to our new nature.

This putting off and putting on applies to every aspect of coming out of homosexuality. It is a central factor in the growth part of overcoming homosexuality.

What we are putting on is clear. We are putting on our manhood: mature, godly, confident, outpouring manhood. We are becoming what our true nature calls us to be and what our Lord wants us to be.

But what are we putting off? This is not quite so obvious. If a male is not a man (or a man in process), what is he? He is a boy. If your homosexuality is rooted in an identity problem, you can be almost certain that you are "living out of your little boy." This means that by every physical criteria you appear to be a man, but a little boy inside of you calls the shots, controls your feelings, and throws up roadblocks when you want to move ahead in some direction. Often you feel as if he is the real you.

In the early years of my healing I felt like a boy most of all in the presence of men, especially Christian men who appeared confident and comfortable with their manhood. I have heard many male overcomers say the same thing. Contact with men, particularly in an informal group setting, brought back the old feeling that was so powerful and so painful in childhood: "I am different." *Different* always translated as "less than" or "inferior to." It hurt and it was painful, and even after the decision had been made to come out of homosexuality, it was debilitating. It came as an unwelcome reminder that I was not yet healed. This is the negative side of "living out of the boy." I hated it and wanted to get rid of it.

But there is another side, a positive side that we might not be so eager to give up. A boy is dependent. A boy is self-protective. A boy has excuses for why he can't do certain things. He can avoid some of the responsibilities that come with manhood. Viewing oneself as a boy can be comfortable. It has its compensations.

Before going on with the idea of the boy within, let me mention that I am not referring to the positive *boyishness* that breaks forth from time to time in all healthy men: the playfulness, the lightheartedness, the capacity to be carefree and to have fun. This is a positive trait, something that most of us find appealing in men.

I am discussing a boy-ness that reflects an emotional immaturity. This is an integral part of male homosexuality. We see it expressed by the gay community itself in "The Boys in the Band" and in the reference to the "boys" in the chorus of a Broadway musical. In a man who dresses in a way more appropriate for a teenager than a thirty-five-year-old man or in a man who is trying to effect a look of boyish innocence, the boy identity keeps breaking through. Looking at a man in the gay community, we often see someone who at the level of his deepest feelings has no sense that he is a man. He knows that he is not a woman, although occasional cross-dressing or campy talk might make him feel like "one of the girls." He is, at the bottom line, a boy.

Look at a gay pride parade and what you see are great numbers of men behaving like adolescents. You see immature exhibitionism, adolescent narcissism, childish rebelliousness. The tendency of gay men to dramatize the tragedy of their lives, to enjoy the role of victim, is a manifestation of immaturity. No healthy man wants to be a victim. Homosexuality is, indeed, arrested development.

I mention these things because it is important for every overcomer to recognize the inherent immaturity in homosexuality. Most of you probably did not flaunt your immaturity as I described it here. You probably did what I did: You tried to act and live like a man, all the time feeling like a little boy inside.

Of course, not feeling and not acting like a mature man is not the exclusive province of the homosexually oriented. Our father-deprived culture is producing vast numbers of immature, irresponsible, narcissistic, silly heterosexual men. Unable to control themselves or to take responsibility for what they do—most tragically for the children they have fathered—they display a manner and lifestyle hardly any more desirable than what the gays have to present.

There is a difference, however. These heterosexual boys seem to be locked into late adolescence. Most of us became stuck in preadolescence. As far as their identity is concerned, they went through puberty. We never did.

We will never know whether Peter Pan was homosexually oriented or not. J. M. Barrie is no longer around to tell us. But Peter Pan was a boy who chose never to grow up. A few years ago he was the rage in pop psychology as the model for the man who refused to act like an adult. The Peter Pan syndrome has faded from popular view as these things do, but he is still a model for what we are discussing here.

A little boy is comfortable. A little boy avoids responsibility, because responsibility can be uncomfortable. But God gives us responsibility. He gave us, as men, the primary responsibility of caring for His garden, all of creation. He made us in His image to have dominion over all that He created. We were given this responsibility by God Himself. And when sin entered into the world, we were not relieved of this responsibility; we were simply told that taking care of the garden would now be hard work. Originally, tending the garden must have been a total joy. Man would have enjoyed the comfort that comes when we can fulfill our purpose for being here. But then the Fall came, and the natural world, along with our fallen nature, started working against us. Responsibility became a burden—but we were not relieved of it. We who chose to remain boys decided to choose comfort (or the avoidance of pain) over our call to grow as men and take over our God-given responsibility. In this sense, homosexuality is rebellion against God.

Responsibility flows out of love. We take responsibility for God's creation out of love for Him. We take responsibility for women, for children, for other men who need us, and for our neighbors out of love for them. It is interesting that 1 Corinthians 13, Paul's great treatise on love, culminates with "When I was a child, I spoke like a child, I thought like a child, I reasoned like a child; when I became a man, I gave up childish ways" (1 Corinthians 13:11). Obedience to God demands that we forsake childishness, that we give up living out of the little boy inside us.

Until now, we have been speaking of the little boy within, but now we want to remove that little boy from inside you and put him alongside you. (Don't worry; there won't be any radical surgery.) Of course, both images, the little boy within and the little boy alongside of you, are metaphors or pictures created to express truths that are difficult to express in any other way. Men, especially with their ability to perceive visually, can be helped by this.

Leanne Payne in *Crisis in Masculinity* described the story of Richard using the image of a man walking alongside himself.[47] The image of walking alongside ourselves is appropriate because there is a way in which the boy is almost another person. I have worked with men who grieve over the pain their little boy went through just as they would if they were to witness a little nephew or neighbor child whom they loved going through great suffering.

In my teaching at Regeneration support groups, I have said that a man may bear some responsibility for the wrong decisions that he made as a young child, even when there were extenuating circumstances, situations of rejection or abuse that made those decisions understandable. The men will invariably pounce on me in defense of the child. Although they may have valid reasons and my position is radical, more than they would like to admit, they are jumping to the defense of their own little boy.

To become a man, you must let go of the little boy. You may be one of the men for whom this will be terribly difficult. You have genuine sympathy for the little fellow, or perhaps he provides the shelter behind which you can avoid the harsh demands of manhood. Letting go is painful and frightening, but this putting off must be done before you can put on. There is no room in you for both the little boy and the grown man.

Like most significant steps we take in life as Christians, this will first and foremost be a transaction between you and God. You must give the little boy to your heavenly Father, just as ultimately you will receive your manhood from your heavenly Father. Much prayer should precede the yielding. Prayerfully count the cost of what you are doing. You are giving up a certain sympathy for yourself. You are giving up the right to say no when manly things are expected of you. You are giving up a means whereby you were able to justify some of your selfish behavior.

Counting the cost means experiencing some of the grief and pain right now, before you have entered into the transaction. This is important in order to make it less likely that you will change your mind and nullify the transaction later. Counting the cost means saying to God, "I am willing to never, never, never take back that little boy again." Yes, you may fail and find yourself living out of the little boy from time to time, but such failures need not nullify the decision. If it was firm in the first place, you can repent and get back on course.

In prayer God will show you when and how to let go of your little boy. Quite likely, if you think in pictures at all, the transaction will have a sacramental or physical quality to it. Let me share with you a spiritual device that can help you see this letting go as a holy transaction. Imagine this: You and your little boy are walking down a long road that goes across a broad, level plain. He is beside you, holding your hand. You feel a certain security with him right there beside you. You are conscious of how happy you are that he is there. In the distance a figure appears to be walking toward you. As he gets closer, you recognize that it is Jesus. After a few moments He is standing before you and your little boy. Not a word is spoken. He extends His hand forward, not to shake hands, but his arm is lower and his hand turned upward as if to take hold of something. You know exactly what the gesture means. With a heart that is pounding and seeming to cry out, "No, no, don't do it," and with eyes filled with tears, you take the little boy's hand and put it in the hand of Jesus. Still, not a word is spoken as they turn and start walking down the road away from you, hand in hand.

You stand there feeling sorrow in every inch of your body. You have never felt so alone, so weak, so naked. Your tear-filled eyes never leave them, the man and the little boy. Then, just as they fade from view completely, you feel a hand on your right shoulder, a strong, firm hand. The warmth from it starts to flow through your whole body. You dare not turn around lest you discover that it is *not* Who you believe it is. Then the hand moves across your back and rests on your left shoulder. You feel His arm around your back, and then you realize that He is standing right beside you. Now you dare to look. Yes! It is Him. It is Jesus! With a slight smile, a nod of His head, and a little nudge from His arm around your back, He says simply, "Let's go." You and He start walking down the road together.

What happens to your little boy? I don't know. You may know immediately, or God may reveal it to you later in prayer. If there was some sort of trauma in your early life, such as sexual abuse, severe rejection, or an experience of devastating humiliation, I am certain that Jesus is healing your little boy from the effects of this experience.

I had no early trauma that I am aware of, but for whatever reason, I carried with me for much of my life a deep sense of worthlessness. Some years ago, in my most vivid experience of inner-healing prayer, the Holy Spirit took me back to when I was four or five years old, and He gave me a picture of Jesus carrying me around the block on which I had lived as a child, the block that pretty much encompassed my whole world at the time. We went into the drugstore down at the corner and into the barbershop. We went into the houses of a couple of friends. He held me up high as though He was proud of me and wanted everyone to see me. I felt extremely proud. This man was Jesus, and He was carrying *me* around the neighborhood. After rounding the block, He carried me into my own home. That was all. It was simple, but I believe that it was in this prayer that Jesus was healing the little boy in me, giving me an inkling of self-worth that was to grow and grow in coming years.

When I first tried to imagine in pictures what could happen when we give up the little boy, not surprisingly the first thought that came to me was of Abraham's placing his boy Isaac on the altar as a sacrifice and as a test of Abraham's faith (see Genesis 22). There is no better imagery of how we are called to offer our most precious things—our idols and our sins—to the Lord. But somehow, this did not fit. When we lay our idols and sins on the altar as Abraham did Isaac, we have to know that we may never have them offered back. This is not so with our little boy.

God wants you to know that He will give you back the little boy. Unknown to you a different kind of surgery will take place, and the little boy will be placed back inside of you, but not for him to be the child out of whom you will live your life. This time, within the existing shell of your manhood, you will feel the little boy start to grow. The healed little boy, the boy who now belongs to God, will start to grow, and he will fill your arms and legs and your chest. The little boy within and the outer man will start to come together until they are one solid being, one solid man created in the image of God. Every part of your manhood that had been growing all of your life and the matured, redeemed little boy will have come together. You will have put on your full manhood.

Letting Go of the Homosexual Identity

One of the things I learned at my first Exodus—North America conference more than twenty years ago was that overcomers should not define themselves as homosexuals.[48] In other words, *homosexual* was not to be used as a noun. It could be an adjective, as in "homosexual man" or "He is homosexual." But not a noun. I could understand the reasons for this. Who wants to define themselves by their particular form of brokenness? What overcomers are trying to do is get away from being homosexual, so why perpetuate the identity by calling themselves by that name?

Later, however, I came to see that not calling ourselves homosexuals— and not thinking about ourselves as homosexuals—is more than a matter of choice or strategy; it is also a matter of truth and logic. Homosexuality speaks to a person's feelings or behavior, not to who he or she is. Let me illustrate this by a little dialogue:

> John: Dad, I think I'm a homosexual.
> Dad: John, why do you think that?
> John: Because I'm emotionally and sexually attracted to men
> and not to women.
> Dad: Why do you think you are attracted to men?
> John: Because I'm a homosexual.

I challenge anyone to give John a better answer to the question of why he thinks he is a homosexual. As hard as the gay community and their supporters have tried, no one has been able to define a homosexual person by anything other than their sexual attractions and behavior. If there was a widely recognized physiological difference between homosexual men and heterosexual men, John could have used this as his reason. But there isn't,[49] and so we must stay with the concept that homosexuality defines what someone feels and does; not who they are.

You may agree with this but still find that letting go of the homosexual identity is an extremely slow and difficult process. For so many men, being gay or homosexual has been the filter through which they have viewed their entire lives. If they had a "coming out" experience in which they moved from self-hatred and shame to accepting themselves as gay, the identity may have brought with it tremendous feelings of freedom and relief. And if you don't feel like a man, who are you? Most men will have to work hard at removing the homosexual identity from their deepest sense of who they are. But it can be done.

One thing that supports the idea that a person can let go of the homosexual identity is the fact that for thousands of years homosexuality was *not* an identity. Even before biblical times, people knew about homosexual behavior, and surely many knew that some people had sexual attractions exclusively for people of the same sex.[50] But until the nineteenth century, even the word *homosexual* did not exist. There were words for the behavior, but none for the condition, and certainly no one was known as a homosexual. So as hard as it may seem, we can live in a world of reality without believing that anyone is a homosexual. In fact, reality is distorted by turning attractions into an identity.

The gay or homosexual identity was promoted first by the psychiatric community to give legitimacy to certain feelings and behaviors. More recently, the gay political movement of the past twenty years has been essentially an effort to give an identity to people who feel same-sex attractions and to gain widespread social recognition of this identity. Their success with this goal in the broader culture makes it all the more difficult, even for us, not to think of homosexuality as an identity. But we can change our thinking. Here are some suggestions that might help:

1. As a first step in clear thinking, start distinguishing between being gay and being homosexual. Dr. Joseph Nicolosi writes of homosexual but not gay people who have homosexual feelings but choose not to identify themselves with the gay movement. This distinction narrows the meaning of homosexual, removing from it much of the cultural trappings that tend to make homosexual people a breed set apart.

2. In your own thinking, consciously try to abandon the division of mankind as heterosexual and homosexual. In your thinking and speech resist making this distinction and resist using homosexual

as an identity. This will seem awkward at first, but over time it will become fairly natural. (I don't believe I used *homosexual* as a noun anywhere in this book. This wasn't hard to do.)

3. Carefully and precisely list the problems that hinder you from functioning as a man in accordance with God's plan for your life. These might include same-sex attractions, a lack of opposite-sex attractions, feelings of inadequacy around other men, compulsive masturbation, a longing to be held by another man, whatever is true to your specific condition. These, or others like them, are your problems, not that you are a homosexual.

Taking this approach is not denial. I am not suggesting that you deny the real problems you are facing. Being attracted to men and not to women is a major problem and should not be dismissed lightly by anyone. But the problems don't determine who you are. Ironically, real denial enters in when a person says that these attractions, longings, and compulsive behaviors are not problems—because he is a homosexual.

What we have here is not just a debate on semantics. The difference matters. Holding on to a homosexual identity will hinder your growth. It makes it easier to accept other false beliefs. The intrinsic sinfulness of homosexual behavior can get thrown into question. "Maybe it's not God's best, but how can He condemn me for acting according to who I am?" Accepting the homosexual identity narrows life and its options. There will be a stronger identification with the homosexual community, possibly cutting off the other 95 percent of mankind. What I am saying here can also apply to holding on to an "ex-gay" identity. Holding on to either identity makes change less likely. How much more difficult it appears to change who you are as opposed to changing what you do or what some of your feelings are.

You are a man. You are not a homosexual. Hold on to this truth. Fight for it. Knowing this truth will be an important part of your growth into manhood.

you are acceptable

When I set out to write this book, I wondered how I could I write a whole book so focused on change without sounding like a hypercritical father. "Do this, do that, straighten out!" Many readers have known such fathers. But we who have seen good fathers operate know that beneath their criticism and correction, behind the advice and encouragement to do better, there dwells a loving acceptance of the son who is being called to grow and change. In fact, we can see that it is a father's love for his son that makes him yearn to see his son be all that he can be. We—you and I—have a perfect Father, and He wants us to grow and change. But more so than the best father here on earth, He loves us just as we are. Our realization of this love and acceptance is essential in order to gain the hope and the strength that we need to carry us down the difficult road to manhood.

A WORK IN PROGRESS

From the perspective of almost anyone not familiar with Exodus ministries, my profession— helping men and women overcome homosexuality—is an odd one. When someone asks me what I do for a living and I tell them, often there is a pause. I assume they are wondering if I had been homosexual but are a little afraid to ask. Often they try to move beyond the awkward pause without getting too personal by asking, "How did you get into this field?" Genuinely curious about my background, but assuming that they will get an answer relating to my training, perhaps in psychology or in ministry, they really don't know what to say when I respond, "I am a certified public accountant, a CPA." After enjoying their consternation for a minute, I break the ice by adding facetiously, "Of course, that qualifies me to deal with people's deepest emotional and sexual problems." My little game over, if they are willing, we then can start a serious discussion.

Except for helping me set up and maintain a fine set of books for Regeneration, my accounting training hasn't borne much fruit in this second part of my life. So it is with some excitement that I use an accounting principle to bring out a main thought for this chapter.

One of the things you learn in first-year accounting is that a manufacturing company has three types of inventory, each of which must be accounted for separately: raw material, work in progress, and finished goods. If a firm is manufacturing wooden chairs, its raw material might consist of lumber, screws, glue, stain, and varnish. Its work in progress would include pieces of wood cut to shape but not yet assembled, chairs that have been assembled but not yet stained and varnished, and so forth. Finished goods, of course, would be completed chairs that are ready to be shipped to retailers. A number of factors are involved in the transformation of the raw materials into finished, useful chairs. There must be a plan or design, labor or effort will have to be expended, and the process will take time.

The analogy to our growth into manhood is probably clear. We come into the world with the raw material to become a man. God has designed a final product, and He has a plan for completing the final product. Making the man will certainly involve some effort, and it will take time.

I did not think of this analogy until after I had come out of homosexuality and was resuming my journey into manhood, but reading *Crisis in Masculinity* helped me see how I was following a path similar to a chair at the chair manufacturer. I could not do all of the things that I felt I should do, particularly as a husband and a father, because the masculine side of my personality just hadn't been fully developed. I was not in the finished-goods column. Coming to understand this through reading Leanne Payne's book was like a lifesaver to a drowning man. The forming of a man is a long and complicated process, and I had gotten off track somewhere, and the process had stopped. But it could resume, and meanwhile I could give myself a little grace.

All of the raw materials are on hand. Even if you are small, smooth, slight, and a sensitive person, you still have all of the raw materials needed for manhood. Every cell in your body carries the chromosome markers for a man, you have genitals, to some extent you have the muscle-to-fat ratio, and you have the brain differentiation. Certain of your parts are already completed and ready to be put into the final product. You have all of what it takes to be a man.

In fact, today you are much more than raw material. Time and training and experiences have already matured you in many ways. But you are not a finished product, the complete man that you want to be or that you believe God has called you to be. You are a man in progress.

It's okay to be a man in progress. Given all that has gone before, God is delighted that you are a man in progress. That's all He wants for you today. This phrase, *given all that has gone before,* is important here because the past is a given. There is nothing you can do about it. That's why God calls us to live in the present. There may have been some factors that caused your growth to go slowly, even to stop for a time, but they are in the past. Nothing can be done about those things. Regrets will accomplish nothing and, in fact, will be harmful if they distract you from the job at hand. You are who you are today, and God accepts you as you are—a man in progress, a man being formed according to His plan.

When Stephen was five years old, I delighted in him as a five-year-old. I don't think any father could have been more pleased, but of course I did not want him to stay five; I wanted him to grow. The same was true when he was eight and when he was fifteen. I loved him and accepted him as he was, but I didn't want him to stay where he was.

If I, an imperfect father, could be that way with Steve, how much more will our perfect heavenly Father be with us? What was most important to me with Stephen was not so much where he was at any given point, but rather whether or not he was growing. A God who accepts each of us as we are must surely be the same way. He accepts us here, and He loves us here, but the desire of His heart is that we move onward and upward.

Let the knowledge that you are loved and accepted by the Father just as you are be the starting point for you as you resume your journey into manhood. But remember that it is the Father's deepest desire that you be a man in progress, not that you stay where you are. Such love and acceptance are totally compatible with a desire for change. His love for us makes Him desire that we grow into the fullness of our manhood. Without a deep knowledge of God's acceptance, the road out of homosexuality may be too hard for us, the hurdles too great, the journey too long, the struggle too painful. So keep coming back to the truth of his love.

Some words of Martin Luther—spoken to men of all sorts and conditions—can be helpful here:

> This life, therefore, is not righteousness, but growth in righteousness, not being but becoming, not rest but exercise. We are not yet what we shall be, but we are growing toward it. The process is not finished, but it is going on. This is not the end, but it is the road. All does not yet gleam in glory, but all is being purified.[51]

YOU ARE UNIQUE

You might now be asking, "Okay, accepting that I am a work in progress, what will the finished goods look like? What am I becoming?" You are becoming a man unlike any other man who ever lived.

How is that going to help you fit into the world of men? Is that good? Yes, it is good because our uniqueness is a part of God's plan; it is not an accident. God loves diversity. After creating each part of creation, He said that it was good, and He created literally thousands of species of plants and animals and insects and birds and fish—and no two of them were alike. God loves diversity, and the fact that you are like no other man who ever lived on this earth reflects His desire for His creation.

You are free to be who you are. But freedom flourishes when it dwells within boundaries. Anarchy does not bring freedom; it causes chaos. God has established a framework within which we are to dwell as men. Other men respect this framework, and so to gain admittance into their world you will have to comply with certain behaviors. But once in that world of men, you will find that your uniqueness is what makes you interesting and fascinating to them. No one is looking for male clones. Men who are outstanding in men's eyes are men who have the courage to be somewhat different.

A wonderful thing will happen to you as you go down the road to manhood. As you develop your masculine qualities—as you become more of an initiator and less of a responder, as you gain the freedom to focus outward rather than inward, as you become a man of truth—all of the pressures that forced you into compliance in the past will weaken. The stronger you become, the more freedom you will feel to be the man you truly are.

What we have here is not unlike what C. S. Lewis described as happening to a man as he becomes more Christlike. "The more we get what we now call 'ourselves' out of the way and let Him take over, the more truly ourselves we become."[52] The more you become the man God designed you to be, the more unique you will become.

FOR THOSE ON THE LEFT-HAND SIDE OF THE CURVE

I often marvel at how far God has brought me in the growth of my manhood in the years since I first set out on this journey. But you know, I am still not an Arnold Schwarzenegger, and I never will be. And if I tried to be, besides looking foolish, I don't think I would be pleasing God.

I fit over on the left side of some of those bell curves, and in some respects this will never change. It's the way God made me. Part of His plan for me is that I would manifest more of certain feminine qualities than most men and a few less of the masculine. That's part of what makes me unique, but it doesn't make me less of a man.

Sy Rogers is one of the best known leaders in the Exodus International network. He has spoken all over the world on overcoming homosexuality. For a number of years Sy lived as a woman, and he had the characteristics that enabled him to pull it off quite well. Now, years after his conversion and healing, Sy still bears some feminine characteristics. They are noticeable when you first hear him speak, but after listening to him for a few minutes, you find that these characteristics fade from view. Sy's genuine manhood—something that now dwells at the core of him—starts to emanate with power and authority.

After I had had a mustache for about ten years, one day, without telling my wife, I shaved it off. When I walked into the room where Willa was, she looked at me and said, "What have you done? Why do you have that silly grin on your face?" She did not recognize that I had shaved off my mustache. When we get to know someone, we look beyond their outer appearances and mannerisms; we see the true person who dwells within. You may never be an Arnold Schwarzenegger, far from it, but those who know you will see the man within. And you will know he's there. The man within is being formed, and he will shine for all to see.

relating to women

A woman is a glorious creature. She is created in the image of God, and she uniquely reflects the eternal feminine side of God. She is totally equal in value to man. Although her nature is to be in response to men, her essential worth comes from God, not from man. As much as woman needs man, so does man need woman. She, unlike men, is the bearer of life.

In a book so completely focused on manhood and addressed to readers who as a group may have had an inordinate focus on the male, I mention these truths just to bring some perspective to our subject. Although I address women as potential objects of our attractions and affections, in no way should we have a frame of reference that always sees man as the subject and woman as object. A woman has her glory and value apart from and even totally without man.

The purpose of this chapter is to offer the overcomer help in growing into a healthy, heterosexual view of women, that he might see women as "other"—his wonderful complement—first women in general, and then the specific woman God may bring to be his wife. But first, as with so many things, you may need to clean up some debris from your past. Your past decisions and experiences with respect to women, especially your mother, may have left you with feelings and attitudes that will keep you from entering into healthy relationships with women or that will sabotage relationships that get under way.

I will address three topics: "woman" problems that are common among men overcoming homosexuality, releasing our mothers, and the broader subject of relating to women.

"WOMAN" PROBLEMS FROM THE PAST

We cannot deal in great depth with the resolution of deeply rooted woman problems, but such issues need to be addressed here because where they are present, they will inevitably block a man's full growth into heterosexual manhood. If after prayerful consideration, you believe that any problems like those mentioned here are a part of your life, pursue Christian counseling or healing prayer. They can be resolved, and when they are, major roadblocks to growth will come down. Here are the three most common:

1. The man is still bonded to his mother. Such men either never fully passed through the stage of separation from their mothers or, more likely, they sought out their father and, finding him unresponsive, retreated to the safety of their mother, in effect rebonding with her. For such men Mother's values are his, her feelings are his, her tastes are his. This man may be solicitous toward women. He may delight many of them because he is so understanding of where they are, so sensitive to their needs. In fact, this type of man may especially appeal to certain types of women, those who have trouble with the truly masculine men or with male sexuality. He may be effeminate, or even if he is not, certain male things—mud, sweat, and chain saws—may be unattractive to him. Such a man may have difficulty seeing a woman in any capacity except as his mother.

Most men, if this unhealthy bond exists, can recognize it if it is pointed out to them. Breaking the bond is, for the adult man, more than anything, a spiritual transaction. It is done prayerfully and under the guidance of the Holy Spirit. I recommend seeking spiritual guidance in this either through a Christian counselor or through the books of Leanne Payne and others.[53]

2. In the man's eyes, women have no value. This is at the other end of the scale from the man who too closely identifies with the woman. This man combines idolatry toward men and the masculine with an almost total devaluation of women and the feminine. There is a good, simple word for this attitude: *sin*. To not value half of the humanity made in the image of God is sinful. The solution is repentance. This might be best facilitated by reading through and meditating on all of the Gospel accounts of the encounters that Jesus had with women, heeding how He respected and honored, loved, and protected them. Then the man needs to pray that God will change his heart.

3. A man has great anger toward women. Such a man often represses this anger, the roots of which are usually in having too often complied with the wishes of a dominating mother. The typical man who manifests this was a "good boy," always doing what his mother wanted, but inside he started to rage. His manly urge to be free and independent battled for control of his character against the good-little-boy whom mother always affirmed. The people pleaser usually won out. Living out of his good-little-boy image, he could not even acknowledge to himself the anger that he felt toward his mother.

Where there is anger toward the mother, denial of the problem seems to be the norm among homosexual overcomers. Look for symptoms in yourself. One symptom is that you experience unreasonable anger when any woman tells you what to do or even suggests what you might do. Another symptom is a pattern of breaking off female relationships regularly, usually because "she changed" or "I didn't know this about her." If you suspect at all that you might be carrying such repressed anger and you have a friend who is the kind of person who will speak truthfully to you, ask him or her if they see it in you. Many times it is obvious to other people.

You don't just grow out of woman problems like these. They require healing or repentance or both. If you recognize such problems in yourself, the common channels of healing to pursue are books on healing and professional or prayer counseling. The best help usually comes from a professional who incorporates prayer as a central part of his or her counseling.

Releasing Our Mothers

Earlier we addressed the issue of releasing our fathers, stressing the need to own up to and repent for any role we played in not relating to our fathers. We talked about how essential forgiving them is for our healing. Now let's do the same with respect to mothers. As with fathers, what is offered here may not apply to the extreme cases—the highly manipulative, overly controlling mother or the mother who made her son her surrogate husband—but rather to the mother who had very human faults, especially those that are common in the family situation in which a homosexual son is raised. As with fathers, I will use my story, and describe how my view of my mother was changed, hopefully helping you cast your mother in a new light.

There was a popular country song some years back that went something like this: "Daddy, you've been a mother to me." The singer was praising his dad for filling in for his mother after she died. Many of us could sing, "Mom, you've been a father to me." We could sing it as either praise or condemnation. Many of us didn't lose our fathers to death, but they were not there for us in many important ways, and many times Mom did fill in. My mother fit this pattern.

My mother had a difficult life. She grew up in England, the daughter of parents who thought that children existed totally for their benefit. She was compelled to quit school early to work so she could bring more money into the home, money that was not really needed. She served in the Woman's Royal Air Force in World War I, and after the war, out of loyalty to her parents, she broke off her engagement to a handsome British Army officer to emigrate to America with them. In the U.S., it took her a long time to find a husband. Then, not many years into the marriage, his mental illness surfaced.

My mother was definitely the strong one in our home. She made most of the big decisions, and she was the one who guided and disciplined my brother and me. Was she "domineering," or was she simply filling in where a vacuum existed? In counseling wives in our ministry, we have struggled with this issue: If a husband doesn't fulfill his God-given role in the family, should the wife step in and try to fill it, or should she step back and let things fall apart, hoping that out of necessity the husband will come forth and play his proper role? There may be no universal answer to this question, but I am grateful that my mother stepped in.

A lot of my mother's guidance came to me from her favorite quotations from the Bible and from Shakespeare. (Only years later, after becoming a Christian and not finding many of the quotes in the Bible, did I assume that most of them were from Shakespeare.) One of her favorites came from neither; it was from Lord Nelson: "England expects that every man will do his duty." I would remind her that she is the Englishwoman, and I am an American, but somehow this still rubbed off. I grew up with a strong sense of duty. In fact, most of the good attributes that I brought into adulthood came from my mother's guidance, much of it coming from her blessed quotations.

I did not mind her playing this role at the time. I know this because one of my favorite songs when I was about ten or twelve was "My Son" by English singer Vera Lynn. I liked it so much I bought the record. One of verses that Vera Lynn sang in her full-bodied, motherly voice went "My son, my son, just do the best you can, and you will find you'll face life like a man." I was hearing my mother's voice in that song, and I valued it. Like most boys, I craved guidance and direction, and I thank God that when my father did not or could not give it, my mother did the best she could.

Looking back, I can see that when things were really bad in the home, my mother would occasionally pour her heart out to me. She could not have done otherwise. I know the temptations of wanting to gain sympathy from our children when I am upset with my wife.

Most parents wish they had done some things differently with their children. Willa and I certainly feel that way with respect to all three of ours. We all make mistakes. Let's give our parents the same grace that we would want given to us.

In our world of pop psychology it is easy to take memories from our childhood and filter them through current psychological theories and come up with all sorts of trauma—trauma that sometimes never really happened. Pray earnestly about this. Your mother may indeed have exerted more influence than she should have, and like my mother in her distress she may have made you her confidant, a role you should not have had to play. If this happened, consider praying a prayer something like this:

> Heavenly Father, I thank You for my mother, the woman You chose to give me life. I thank You for the love, care, and concern with which she helped raise me. If I failed or used her in any way, show me this. If so, I repent of these sins. Father, I do forgive her for any ways in which she failed or used me, and I release her into Your hands. I pray that I will always be able to love and honor her. Bless her, Lord. In Jesus' name, amen.

How much healthier it is to have a grateful heart than to be forever the victim. To move toward this, you must forgive your mother and release her. If your mother is still living, you may find great opportunities to exercise your manhood in her life. You are no longer her little boy, even if she thinks you are, but now you are an important *man* in her life. What a blessing it can be to both of you if you can find ways in your relationship with her to be the initiator, the protector, and the one who speaks truth in her life.

RELATING TO WOMEN IN GENERAL

Strangely, homosexual men are often among the worst users of women. I say this despite the fact that, for a majority of single homosexual men who have come to Regeneration, their best friend has been a woman. They are users of women because in so many of these relationships, at the emotional level, the woman gives so much to the man, but the man has nothing to give in return. I do not discount the value of friendship or buddy relation-ships, but I have found over and over again that homosexual men not only cannot meet the emotional needs of women but too often are totally indif-ferent to them.

Women are a mystery to men, and to a lesser extent men are a mystery to women. But in a relationship of two heterosexually oriented people, there is a natural complementarity between his masculine and her feminine that covers over a lot of problems while the man and woman are truly dis-covering one another. A man with a homosexual past, however, who lacks a well-developed masculine side, cannot rely on this natural complemen-tarity. His relationship with a woman will have to be, at least in the early years of healing, a more conscious and deliberate thing.

For the man coming out of homosexuality and growing into man-hood, there are two primary issues to be dealt with here: the way he relates to women in general and his capacity to love a specific woman in a way that encompasses both romantic feelings and sexual desire. Change in both ways of relating will come about as his manhood develops and woman becomes more and more "other." But this will not happen automatically; so he should expect to put some real effort into the process.

To a certain extent, relating to women as a man can be considered one of the things that men do, and it may thereby increase a man's sense of manhood. However, this is an area in which he should exercise great caution. It borders on using the woman and could do great harm to her. Many homosexual men have started dating women as a part of their healing process or just to see what would happen, and what for them was a form of therapy became a huge emotional investment for the woman with tragic consequences for her. On the other hand, the male overcomer may need to push himself for the reason that he may never come to fully appreciate or desire a woman until he has started to relate to one in a way that involves some intimacy. The operative word here is *caution*. Be cautious and always seek to put her interests above yours. This means telling her the truth about yourself before too deep a relationship has developed. This is the manly thing to do.

Regarding the first issue, how you relate to women in general, once you have dealt with any of the debris just discussed, there are a number of things you can do that are helpful. These are done cognitively, but if they are also done prayerfully, you may not only experience a change in habits and perspectives, but the Lord may start changing you in deeper ways. Furthermore, as your manhood grows in other ways, these changes will start to become natural to you. Here are some things to help you grow in your appreciation of women as women.

Seek to Grow Out of Buddy Relationships with Women

This is not to say to break off friendships that are of this character, but seek to change them. She is not one of the boys, and you are not one of the girls. Subtly start to treat her as "the weaker vessel" who is deserving of special honor and consideration. Start to establish a degree of modesty in the relationship, maintaining the boundaries that would normally exist between a man and a woman. Where certain activities that you and she have done together would usually be considered men things, start doing them with men. Encourage her to do women things with women. Stepping back a little in the relationship can bless you both as you begin to see her not as a friend, but as a friend and a woman.

Start to Contemplate and Meditate on the Feminine
As It Is Embodied in the Woman

Go back to chapter 7 and reread the part about the contrast between the masculine and the feminine, only this time focus on the feminine. Think of the beauty of responsiveness, the exciting mystery of a woman's inner directedness, the noble strength of the woman who holds families and relationships together, the loveliness of the mercy that flows out of the feminine. Picture these attributes in the women you know, and thank God for them. In your mind picture each woman whom you know well, and try to identify the aspects of the feminine that she manifests. Picture each attribute interacting with the masculine in perfect harmony. Thank God for His wonderful plan.

Start to Meditate on the Physical Attributes of Women

Don't start at the purely sexual, but focus on all of those things that make her "other." Picture her softness, the smoothness of her skin, the rounded-ness of her figure, her hair, her lips. Contemplate what beauty God has created in woman. Recall the delight that Adam expressed when God presented him with Eve. Ask God to start working such delight in you.

There is also an inner beauty—a specifically feminine beauty—in every woman God has created. God revealed this to me some years ago, when I was attending the funeral of a friend's mother. The officiating clergyperson was a woman Episcopal priest. In the way she carried herself and the way she spoke, she was almost a caricature of a butch lesbian woman. Further fueling my suspicions, she had brought with her a very "femme" partner. My objections to this woman being a priest spilled over into powerful feelings of animosity toward her personally. She symbolized so much of what I believed was wrong in the church.

But then, in the midst of my resentment toward her, God gave me a picture of her as a little girl, a girl who was very heavy and quite plain, a girl whom boys taunted mercilessly. No wonder she had grown up this way. While starting to feel shame for the way I was sitting in judgment of her, my heart melted, and I started to see things about her that were quite beautiful. I started to see the feminine in her, which had been so crushed that I was sure she could not see it herself. And I realized that if God would allow me to see beauty in this woman, then I could see beauty in every woman. I've tested this ever since and have found God faithful to show me womanly beauty in all sorts and conditions of women. We can see with the eyes of the Holy Spirit.

Start to Practice Some of the Traditional Male Courtesies Shown to Women

As appropriate, start to open car doors for women, stand when a woman enters a room, help her with her chair when she sits down. When walking down the street with a woman, place yourself on the street side. These are simple things, perhaps silly and antiquated things in the eyes of many today, but each is a way in which a man honors and shows value to a woman. We are changed by what we do! Our actions can change our thinking and our perspectives. Act as though a woman is something special, and she will become that to you.

Seek Insights About Women from Women

To gain insights about women, ask one of them. You don't want to seek such insights from a woman who might have a romantic interest in you. The wife of a male friend might be appropriate. Such a woman could help you dispel any wrong ideas you might have, particularly with respect to how women might view you. She could give you positive suggestions as to how to approach women.

Coming to appreciate women as women is not only a part of your growth into true manhood but is an important prerequisite to your being able to appreciate *the* woman when God brings her into your life. Furthermore, God may use the exercises suggested here to show you specific areas in which you need healing if you are to relate to women in a positive manner. In addition to mother issues, you may discover that you have an attitude that denigrates women, or you may encounter feelings of repulsion toward women's bodies, feelings that could be rooted in childhood sexual abuse or in episodes of inappropriate intimacy by women toward you when you were very young. An effort to focus on women—on the feminine and on those things that make women different—can open the door for you to pursue the healing that you need before you get seriously involved with one woman.

So far, in addressing the way we relate to women generally, we have not addressed the way in which we find women sexually attractive. As important as this subject is, other Christian books on overcoming homosexuality have not addressed it as fully as it needs to be. Perhaps the fact that other writers have not dealt with the sexual-attraction issue reflects our view that homosexuality, at its core, is not a sexual problem. Others might say that if we deal adequately with behavior and identity, the sexual issue will take care of itself.

Neither of these reasons provides adequate justification for not directly addressing the sexual attractions issue. Homosexuality *is* a sexual issue. It is the lack of opposite-sex attractions that causes the most grief for many of the men in our ministries. Do sexual attractions change automatically as behavior and identity change? No. The steps of growth into manhood offered in this book are not likely to automatically produce heterosexual feelings. These steps will certainly help open up the possibility of feeling sexual attractions to women, but the fact is that boys go through certain experiences that develop their heterosexual attractions, and most of us did not go through them. So the question arises whether a man should seek to go through them in adulthood.

We will address this important issue first by describing the stages that most men overcoming homosexuality go through quite naturally as they enter into good marriages. Then we will discuss a major area in which homosexual overcomers seldom become "just like other men." In the next chapter I will discuss the sensitive issue of what can be done with respect to encouraging sexual attractions toward women, and whether or not it is even right to encourage the increase in such attractions.

ATTRACTIONS TO *THE* WOMAN

One of the great distresses that the Christian overcomer feels has to do with his lack of sexual attraction to women. He wants this to change, and before he has thought about it much, his assumption may be that being sexually attracted to women is really the beginning and the end of what ex-gay ministry is all about. In fact, the majority of Christian men who come to Regeneration do seem to want to exchange their homosexual lust for heterosexual lust. They know that most men struggle with heterosexual lust, and they want to be like most men. It sounds perfectly logical until we realize that God is not in the business of giving out lust. He is not interested in our exchanging one form of sin for another. So what does happen? What can the man who is growing into manhood reasonably expect to experience?

Most men overcoming homosexuality find that a strong sexual attraction to women does not arise until that one special person comes into his life, and then the sexual attraction flows naturally out of loving her. It might go something like this. You know a woman and like her, and you are healed enough so that you can truly appreciate those womanly things that make her different. You start to get to know her better, and the desire to be with her increases and increases, finally blossoming into romantic love. As this happens you want to be close to her, to hold her, and finally you want to be totally one with her—in mind, spirit, and body. Your desire for union with her has flowed naturally and beautifully out of loving her.

It seems that one of the things that happened to man in the Fall was that his wholeness—the unity of mind, body, and spirit—was shattered. One effect of this for the man was that his sexuality became broken off from the rest of him. (This did not happen so much with women; they had other problems.) This is why most men, not just the addicted or perverted, can thoroughly enjoy sex without a relationship. This is why men will pay a lot of money for a few minutes with a prostitute, why a homosexual man will hang around a rest room and risk arrest for a momentary sexual encounter with another man. Man's sexuality became a free-floating force unconnected to its original purposes: the bonding of a man and woman in a permanent loving relationship and the creation of new life. A high percentage of heterosexual men in good, loving Christian marriages struggle with attractions to disconnected, impersonal sex: to pornography or maybe to the body of a neighbor woman whom he doesn't even know. This almost never happens to male overcomers with respect to women. This is the reason why I believe that we are actually in a better place than most men. We are closer to God's original intent for our sexuality.

VISUAL ATTRACTIONS OR THE LACK THEREOF

The pattern we follow—love first, then sexual desire—often works just the opposite in men who are heterosexual in their attractions. Sexual attraction may come first, then love, or the two may be so intertwined that it is difficult to separate them. This is one way in which we may be different. And there is another way, one that if not recognized early could lead to discouragement and to unawareness of the actual work that God is doing in us.

Most male overcomers I have encountered continue to differ from other men in that they do not become sexually stimulated by the sight of a woman's body. For many—perhaps most—heterosexual men, the most immediate sexual stimuli are visual. We all recognize that the swimsuit issue of *Sports Illustrated* really has nothing to do with swimming. Ads directed at men often feature scantily clad women, whereas ads in *Good Housekeeping* and *Woman's Day* seldom feature partially naked men. Gay publications, on the other hand, abound with them.

Let me inject one encouraging side issue here. Being readily turned on sexually by visual images is a male thing, coming out of the male brain. The fact that most homosexual men are turned on visually—albeit by men—shows that their brains are essentially male in their formation.

Men overcoming homosexuality have an expectancy that they will become "just like other men." The thought that they might not can be a cause of real distress. But this is a situation, like many, in which the real problem is not the deprivation (the lack of heterosexual visual stimulation) but the belief that things should be one way and finding out that they are not. The cry "I ought to…and I'm not" reveals the distress.

I don't know the reason why, when so many other changes take place in the man overcoming homosexuality, this one generally doesn't. There may be a certain time in a boy's psycho-physical development when attractions are learned and programmed into the brain, and if this is missed the programming will not take place later. This could be compared to the belief that a child learning a language at a certain age has a heightened ability to learn that language, and a language learned at that age will never be forgotten.

Regardless of the cause, fortunately we do find that the other side of the equation is not nearly so rigid. Homosexual men who have formed a strong stimulus-response pattern with respect to the sight of a male body do find that, as healing progresses, these responses diminish greatly and, in fact, sometimes totally disappear. The homosexual visual stimulus–response pattern, although it certainly has some programming in it, seems to be closely tied to envy and feelings of weakness, and as these elements are done away with, the male body becomes decidedly less an object of sexual attraction.

This lack of heterosexual visual stimulation is not just confined to single men. From what we have experienced in our ministries thus far, this condition generally stays with overcomers after they marry. At a conference Regeneration held for married men, of the fourteen male overcomers present, only one said he was aroused by the sight of his wife's body. I was among the thirteen, and my years of ministry experience validate the results of this little sampling. Larger surveys may reveal somewhat different results, and our continued growth in understanding how to minister could lead to new areas of change, but for now, I believe it is practical to assume that the sight of a woman's body will not be a source of sexual stimulation for us. *This is the only clearly noticeable difference that I have observed between homosexual overcomers and men whose attractions have always been heterosexual.*

How can we say that we are healed when we are not visually "turned on" like other men? It's very simple. Sexual attraction need not arise from visual stimulation alone. There are two other major prompters of sexual interest: touch and emotional feelings. My strongest sexual desire for my wife comes when I feel most loving toward her. Many times I feel those desires when we kiss or when we are simply sitting on the sofa watching TV and my arm is around her. There is no question that these are spontaneous sexual feelings.

Our experience in ministry has indicated that sexual response to a woman through emotional feeling and through touch is the normal state for men overcoming homosexuality. This is why we declare so strongly that a man overcoming homosexuality can experience every joy of a heterosexual life.

relating to women sexually

What was addressed in the previous chapter may be fine for the married man. Now, what about the single man? This would include the man who believes he probably never will get married, the man who would love to get married and is looking, and the man who thinks he may have found God's woman for him but is worried about his ability to relate to the woman sexually. Is there anything an overcomer should be doing between the day he starts to appreciate woman's otherness and the day he finds himself in the honeymoon suite with his bride? Is there anything he can do to develop a sexual attraction to women, or should he just wait and hope that the attraction will develop? Is it right for him to even try? There is little doubt that many men seeking to overcome homosexuality try to nurture in themselves a desire for sex with a woman. They think about it, not just wondering what it would be like, but trying to light a little fire, perhaps even fantasizing that they are having sex with a woman while masturbating. Is this helpful? Should this be encouraged? Is it right at all for a Christian man?

These questions can be tremendously important to the male overcomer, and yet they are questions not addressed in any of the Christian books dealing with the healing of male homosexuality. As succinctly as I can put it, the question is this: Should the single man overcoming homosexuality seek to develop in himself erotic or sexual attractions toward women?

Many people would respond with a strong no for reasons such as these:

- It would simply create another problem. If successful, wouldn't he be setting himself up with a whole new field of temptations?
- There is no way to get from here to there—from no attractions to having attractions—without passing through sin. The process would involve fantasy, lust, probably masturbation, and possibly even pornography.
- If an ex-gay man's desire for a woman will eventually flow out of love for her, why would this be necessary?

But there are also strong reasons on the other side:

- Being sexually attracted to women is an integral part of manhood, and an overcomer who has these feelings will grow in his identity as a man.
- Heterosexual thoughts can be a replacement for homosexual thoughts. The alternative is a form of asexuality, which just may not work. Nature—and man's libido—abhors a vacuum.
- The process of seeking to develop sexual desires for a woman could reveal certain blockages (mother problems, for example) that might not otherwise turn up until a man is married, and this could be disastrous.
- Having even a limited sexual attraction toward women could greatly speed up the day when a man will spot that one special woman whom God has chosen for him. He would be much more apt to be looking for her.

The arguments on both sides are powerful. Orthodox, biblical Christians are going to come down on both sides of the issue. After prayer and thinking at length about it, I come down on the side of actively trying to develop the attractions.

Before I explain why, I want to introduce one important caveat. I do this not to stop the letters and e-mail from coming in from those who disagree with me, but because I believe in what I am saying.

First of all, I believe that Christians must recognize that there are essential matters in the faith and there are secondary ones. There is a body of belief—largely expressed in the historic creeds—that we must believe or we have no right to call ourselves Christians. Then there are Christian moral teachings that are made so clear in Scripture and that have been so overwhelmingly affirmed by the church for two thousand years that they cannot reasonably be questioned. The sinfulness of lust and any sexual intercourse outside of marriage would fall into this category. Further down there are matters that may seem of vital importance and unquestionable clarity to one group of believing Christians but which other committed believers see quite differently. The matters discussed here fall into this category.

I also believe strongly that every Christian is bound to honor the teaching and the authority of the part of the body, or the community of believers, to which he belongs. As Christians, we are not fully autonomous individuals. We are joined to one another, and everything I do in some way can affect my brothers and sisters and the entire community to which I am joined, even in such private matters as my sexuality.

Nothing could be more personal than masturbation. If a man masturbates, how could it affect anyone else? If he is in a church that teaches that masturbation is always a sin and he masturbates, he is weakening the body of which he is a part by defying and demeaning its authority. He himself will grow in disrespect for its leaders. He has either set himself up as a higher authority than his leaders, or he is in rebellion against them. This weakens the body and harms the man.

Based on these two beliefs, my caveat is simply this: To the extent that it is possible, follow the teachings of your church. No matter how incredibly logical my arguments may be and no matter how much you want to follow my proposals, you are better off in the long run obeying your own church, for this body of believers is your source of strength. If they are weakened by your actions, your support structure will slowly erode.

Now, as to the matter of the single person seeking to develop or increase his heterosexual desires, here's why I believe that seeking the development of such desires is a good thing and that we can go about doing it in ways that are not sinful. First, the desired end is good. The goal of attaining heterosexual desire is a good one. Five times we are told in Scripture that a man is to leave his mother and father and to be joined to his wife and the two are to become one flesh. God commanded Adam to populate the earth. God created marriage, and it is a good thing. There may be a higher state than marriage, such as singleness for the purposes of ministry, but God's general principle is that it is not good for man to be alone. And I don't believe that God intended that some should not marry because they *could not*, which is the state of many homosexual men. If anything in God's creation is out of order and we can correct it, I believe that God would have us make the correction. To seek to develop heterosexual attractions is to seek to be the men God created us to be.

Regarding the possibility that God will give us the sexual desires after we meet the woman, this does happen for many men, but I see many more overcomers who, because of their total absence of heterosexual attractions, are not even surveying the field. Their eyes are not open to seeing the woman whom God may have chosen to be their wife. God did not create sexual desire in man so that it can be turned on the minute the preacher makes the pronouncement that he is married. God created in man a sexual energy that is meant to draw him to a woman. As we are recognizing in our culture today, the reasons for men not to get married are many (personal autonomy, freedom to wander, general selfishness), and if they don't have to get married to find sexual satisfaction, many will not get married. God placed this strong urge in man and He created the family, and the two are complementary. God intended sexual energy to draw men into marriage, and although his attractions may be somewhat different from those of men who have always been heterosexual, I believe that this would apply to the homosexual overcomer also.

Use of the Imagination

It is hard to picture how any boy growing through adolescence could come to desire a woman sexually without having at some point pictured in his mind what it must be like to have sexual intercourse with a woman. In fact, I would think that the only boy who might not have such thoughts would be one who received a message growing up that all sexual intercourse is evil. As puberty increases his capacity for sexual feelings, whether he consciously directs it or not, his mind will be drawn toward those things that increase sexual pleasure. God's intent for the energy growing in him is that it will lead him to marry one day, and so, hopefully, he will direct his sexual thoughts that way. Is this wrong? Is this lust for an adolescent? I think not. Lust has two elements: a desire that has gotten inordinately strong and a demand for the immediate satisfaction of that desire. Neither of these is *necessarily* present in a boy starting to think about sexual intercourse. Of course, the chance that his natural sin nature will lead him in the direction of lust is quite high. The job of his parents—and of the church—is to seek to channel his sexual desire toward its proper use, not to try and stamp it out altogether.

Not all desire for good things is lust. When I am hungry, I might really want a hamburger, but this does not mean that I lust for food. I desire financial security for me and my family; this does not mean that I lust for money. What marks a Christian man is the ability to keep balance in his life, the capacity to delay the satisfactions of his appetites, and a focus on the truly good, not that he has no desires.

Many of us did not as adolescents go through that stage of imagining that we were having sexual intercourse with a woman. Just as it is unlikely that a boy would ever grow into healthy manhood in which he could be a godly husband without ever having pictured himself with a woman sexually, so we overcomers cannot develop a sexual desire for a woman unless we first imagine it. Further, I believe that we can direct our thoughts in a way that would minimize the likelihood of such imaginings becoming lustful.

Because sexual fantasy was so much a part of our sinful pasts—or of our current struggles—we may have some trouble thinking of the imagination as a gift that God can use. Oswald Chambers said that the imagination is the greatest gift that God has given us—if we will use it for His purposes.[54] I think that goes a little far, but we surely need to consider all the ways in which God can use this gift. The imagination reflects what is in the heart; it is the eyes of the heart. If our heart is set on that which is not of God, the imagination will draw us to that which is evil, to sexual fantasy, visions of revenge, flights of self-glorification. If our heart is set on that which is of God, the imagination will draw us to that which is of God. Mature holy manhood and Christian marriage are clearly of God.

Let me describe how you might imagine yourself being with a woman who is to be your wife. Prayerfully imagine the following:

God has brought you the woman who is to be your wife. She is a Christian, strong in her beliefs, gentle in her demeanor. By every standard that you have she is both outwardly and inwardly lovely. You start going places with her, doing things you enjoy together. You start to feel in yourself a growing desire to be protective of her and to show her that you cherish her. You start doing things that show her this. She responds with warmth and joy. You start to notice things that make her so wonderfully feminine—her responsiveness, her depth, the mystery that there is about her. And you start to notice physical things about her: the smoothness of her skin, her softness and roundness. You feel delight when you touch. More and more you want to be with her. Finally, there is no doubt that you love this woman. You express this to her, and she responds that she loves you also. Romance has come into your relationship.

Skip now to your wedding day. She is coming down the aisle,

all in white, radiant beyond anything you expected. This is the most exciting day of your life. The miracle of two separate people becoming one is being manifested today, first in your vows before God, second in the celebration of the community of believers who have come to affirm this union, and finally in the marriage bed. You picture that scene too. Both of you are modest and nervous, but at the same time eager and excited, almost unable to put off the special moment. But you do. Gently you caress her and she responds. Slowly and naturally, as your hearts are so entwined, your two bodies become one. Finally you know the incredible joy of sexual love.

If you are able to let God use your imagination to stir up in you a degree of sexual desire for a woman, this is not something you want to work on regularly. If it is of the Lord, it will do its purpose, and then it would be best if it is tucked away in your heart, a knowledge of the way you hope one day to use your sexuality.

USE OF MASTURBATION TO DEVELOP HETEROSEXUAL DESIRE

Masturbation needs to be discussed in any book addressing male homosexuality, and I cannot think of any better context in which to discuss it than this: marriage and the encouragement of heterosexual feelings.

A part of me simply did not want to bring this subject up, but it is too important and too relevant not to be discussed in this context. Rarely have I talked with a man about his lack of sexual attraction toward women without having the subjects of masturbating and thinking about women come up.

If you are in a church that believes that masturbation is always sinful, or if you hold that belief strongly yourself, you might do best to skip this section. If you are not sure what you believe about masturbation in this context, my prayer is that God will lead you to His truth, even if it is not what I am suggesting here. Also, I write this for men who do masturbate. If a man does not masturbate, I would not suggest that he take it up for the purpose of developing heterosexual attractions. The risk of addiction is too great to allow me to suggest that a man take up masturbation if he doesn't do so already.

I make my suggestions believing that they are sound ones and are in accord with God's Word, but I do so with a sincere recognition that I could be wrong. I call this one of my 60 percent beliefs. Along with subjects like pacifism, capital punishment, and using artificial means of birth control, I have views because I believe I must, but if I get to heaven and am told that I was wrong on any of these issues, I do not expect to be shocked. I praise God for His grace that is available to us when, as we seek the truth, in our fallibility we don't always find it.

Roman Catholic teaching says that masturbation is always a sin. For many of us who disagree with this teaching, the overweighing factor in forming our view is that the Bible nowhere mentions it as a sin, and God's Word is quite complete and thorough in pointing out sexual behaviors that are sinful. Virtually all Christians, however, believe that lust is always a sin, and we know how masturbation and lust feed each other: lust leading to masturbation and the masturbatory state most often being one of constant lust. So even for those of us who believe that masturbation is not always a sin, the circumstances in which it *would* be allowed are quite limited. However, for most men whose primary sexual attractions are homosexual, the creation of heterosexual fantasies could for a time be hard work rather than the escape that we normally associate with lust.

In discussing masturbation with members of our support groups, the most helpful Scripture passages for me are two similar verses found in 1 Corinthians.

"All things are lawful for me," but not all things are helpful. "All things are lawful for me," but I will not be enslaved by anything. (1 Corinthians 6:12)

"All things are lawful," but not all things are helpful. "All things are lawful," but not all things build up. (1 Corinthians 10:23)

Regarding masturbation, I read these scriptures as saying that it may at times be permissible, but it has the capacity to enslave us (1 Corinthians 6:12), and it is not the behavior of a mature man (1 Corinthians 10:23). If one uses masturbation as a means of trying to develop a sexual desire for women, he must do so with the full awareness of its dangers: He could fall into bondage to it, and he could become locked into an essentially immature act.

When we consider using masturbation as a means of developing opposite-sex attractions, we need to take these cautions seriously. As for the capacity for the act of masturbation to enslave us, the escape that it provides, the release of soothing endorphins in the brain, the way it provides self-comforting, the way it can make a man feel alive for a few minutes, the extraordinary pleasure that it provides—all combine to make it the almost perfect vehicle for addiction. If it is entered into at all, it must be entered into cautiously and held to a minimum.

Regarding the second caution, it does not build up or lead us toward maturity, I believe that Paul's comments imply that it is not something for a mature man. Masturbation is an adolescent act, an almost universal act among teenage boys when they are discovering their sexuality. The pleasure of ejaculation bonds, so to speak, with the image of intercourse with a woman, and the connection becomes forever linked.

Most of us did not go through this. To the contrary, we linked the pleasure of ejaculation with homosexual sex, and if we bonded it with anything, it was with men. It could be helpful for some men who never formed the right connection to now replace the homosexual images with heterosexual ones. However, one caution to mention here is that you might find that you switch from heterosexual to homosexual thoughts during masturbation. If this happens regularly, then this is not an approach for you. Possibly even deceiving yourself, you may be using the heterosexual thoughts as an excuse to get into homosexual fantasy.

I maintain that using masturbation to stir up sexual desire is a good purpose in that one day it may enable a man to procreate, to enter into God's wonderful one-flesh union, and to be able to bring pleasure to his wife. These are good ends. Most Christian teaching would say that it is acceptable to use neutral means to achieve good ends, but for Christians to use sinful means for good ends is never justifiable. Therefore, the question here is whether or not masturbation is sinful. And if a man believes that it is not sinful per se, and he is not doing it compulsively, then I believe he should consider, for a time and for a specific purpose, using heterosexual images with masturbation.

Let me say this again: For most men whose primary sexual attractions are homosexual, the creation of heterosexual fantasies is often such hard work that it does not produce the escape that we associate with lust.

TOUCHING

What has been discussed thus far, the use of the imagination and masturbation to encourage heterosexual orientation, is addressed to all men coming out of homosexuality. This part is for the man who believes that he may have discovered the woman he is meant to marry. How much should he test his capacity to respond sexually to this woman, or should he not try at all?

I have dealt with men at every place on the spectrum in this regard, from men who never kissed their wives until they were married to men who had fallen into sexual intercourse before marriage. Again, this topic needs to be examined within the context of the teaching of one's own church and within the broader context of the church's universal teaching that sexual intercourse outside marriage is a sin.

Most would agree that deliberately putting oneself in the position where it becomes extremely difficult to resist the temptation to engage in sexual intercourse is itself sinful. Within this parameter, is it wrong to engage in physical touching for the purpose of determining whether or not you have the capacity to become sexually aroused by the woman you hope to marry? In other words, is it permissible to test in real life that which to this point has existed only in your imagination?

I believe that it may be permissible to a point. My reasoning is totally different from that offered in discussing the two previous topics. It should be considered for the sake of the woman. No man who has been chaste with his wife-to-be knows how he will "perform" (a terrible word, but nothing else fits as well) on his wedding night. Many men who are exclusively heterosexual and have remained chaste all of their lives have a great fear of how they will do.

But most of these heterosexual men have looked forward to this for much of their lives, whereas the homosexual overcomer has entered into these desires by an entirely different route. He has sought to develop them, and they may be fairly recent. He may—quite likely does—still feel some sexual attractions to men. His reasons for apprehension are, therefore, much greater. He might find that the romantic sexual scenarios of his imagination are not yet transferable to the real world of loving a wife. The one whom we should be most concerned about in such a situation is the wife. It is rare, but she could find herself in a sexless marriage. If the man truly loves her, he would want to protect her from this.

In regard to protecting the woman he hopes to marry, a man needs to consider her sexual vulnerabilities also. Even with the best intentions, he could be stirring up sexual feelings in her that will give her great problems—if not causing her to want to pursue the physical relationship further. Therefore, physical contact must be pursued carefully.

Now, when talking about physical contact, I mean holding hands, kissing, hugging. I would suggest even going so far as embracing, standing up with the couple's bodies pressed together. If this causes the man to feel a surge of sexual arousal, then the purpose has been accomplished, and the couple's focus can now be on restraint. If the man experiences no arousal, then for the sake of both of them he may need to seek further healing before pursuing marriage.

I do not make this suggestion of "testing" of physical contact because the men in our ministry who marry have found themselves unable to function sexually in the marriage. To the contrary, the overwhelming majority of our marriages—where the man has received some healing, where both parties are Christians, and where he was totally honest with her before the marriage—have worked out sexually. However, the deciding consideration came for me when I realized that if one of my daughters had married a man from our ministry, for her sake, I would have wanted him to be as certain as possible that he could be a husband for her in every way.

But will knowing that arousal can take place remove the overcomer's anxiety on the wedding night? Probably not. For overcomers who are getting married, Frank Worthen has good advice. He tells the couples to agree beforehand that they not have sex on their wedding night. Inevitably, they come back and tell Frank that they did. The lack of pressure did its job.

Marriage and fathering children is not the completion of our growth into manhood; it is the product of completed manhood. Completed manhood is in part measured by our being ready to marry and become fathers.

full manhood

At the beginning of the book, I promised to lay out a road map for your journey into manhood. The map is almost complete now. After warning you about one more possible pitfall on the journey, I want to describe the destination for you. Regarding this destination, let me just say for now that the journey does have a destination, and you—every man reading this book—can reach that destination, the point at which your manhood is a given and you no longer need to make growth into manhood a focal point and purpose for your life.

Now, one last possible pitfall remains.

MAN'S ACHILLES HEEL: NARCISSISM

There is an irony in this book, one that could become a major pitfall if not addressed. The very process suggested here could be self-defeating if we cannot see manhood with the clarity available to the Spirit-filled believer. Ironically, the process of seeking to develop our manhood requires that we look inward, but allowing ourselves to be primarily inward focused is the antithesis of manhood.

Homosexually oriented men, by and large, are excessively inwardly focused. The homosexual man, often overly conscious of his appearance, his physique, how he comes across to others, how he compares with other men, develops traits that are fundamentally narcissistic. So closely are narcissism and male homosexuality intertwined, we could almost say that male homo-sexuality is a variation of male narcissism. By focusing on our deficits as men, by establishing measurements of manhood, by suggesting that we seek role models, and by concentrating on what we do, as suggested in this book, there is the possibility that we will compound our problems with narcissism rather than rectify them.

The issue lies partly in the fact that the program laid out here in many ways constitutes going through delayed adolescence, and adolescent boys are notoriously narcissistic. In adolescence, a degree of male bravado—seeking to prove oneself as a man, always looking to see how others are responding to you—reflects the narcissism that is a normal part of teenage development. It is expected. It can even be endearing to the adults who know and love the adolescent. But it is expected to pass. In an adult man it is not attractive and can be counterproductive. We need to resist feeding our narcissism.

The narcissism discussed here is not the clinically described regressive state of development found in psychology books, but the generally recog-nized form of excessive interest in one's appearance, comfort, importance, and so on. It is a most unattractive characteristic that exalts the narcissist as he becomes blind to others or sees others primarily as a means of feeding his own need for attention or pleasure.

We should recognize that narcissism is an overriding flaw to which men in general, not just homosexual men, are prone. We could come into the fullness of our manhood and then find that one of the features of our manhood that made us "just like other men" was our narcissism. Many heterosexually oriented men never seem to emerge from their adolescent narcissism. Constantly needing to prove their manhood to themselves as well as others, they pursue any outward manifestation that will show that they are men: bodybuilding, womanizing, excessively aggressive behavior. Unlike the homosexually oriented man, who at some level has given up on attaining his own manhood, the narcissistic heterosexual never gives up try-ing to prove his. But like the homosexual man, he is doomed to failure. The fact that he is focused on himself, that he gives such great importance to outward appearance, dooms him to perpetual adolescence.

How are we who have decided to come out of homosexuality and are determined to become men in the truest sense of the word to avoid this narcissistic trap? How can we examine ourselves—necessary steps if we really want to change—without perpetuating, even intensifying, our self-absorption? It is difficult but possible.

I discovered a key answer to this problem in the statement of a young man who was a newcomer to one of the groups in our ministry. As a passing comment, one evening he said, "Manhood is something we give away." We grow as men when we see our manhood as something we desire for the sake of others. When we desire manhood so that we can protect and defend, help and serve, provide safety and security for others, we will grow into men. And it is the practice of helping, protecting, and serving that does so much to develop our manhood.

An active member of one of our sister ministries was a woman with severe cerebral palsy. When I visited the ministry, I observed the men regularly lifting her in and out of cars, from a wheelchair to a sofa and back. Their manhood was wonderfully visible in this act of helping and serving.

In the book *And the Band Played On,* gay author Randy Shilts describes, perhaps unknowingly, a beautiful example of this.[55] A homosexual man, mild and passive in nature, comes down with AIDS. The person who takes care of him in his final months is a bold, aggressive lesbian woman. The two are close friends; in fact you can soon see that they genuinely love each other. As the man becomes increasingly sick, his tough lesbian friend becomes more and more tender and fragile. Her strength seems to fade away as her love for the dying man cuts deeper into her heart. For his part, the more vulnerable she becomes, the more the man desires to protect her. Wanting to shelter her fragile heart, he grows stronger and stronger. What Randy Shilts was describing was the forming of a man and a woman.

For a good many years at the national Exodus conferences, on Fridays before the closing banquet, we had makeovers in which hairdressers (mostly men) did the hair and makeup for women, for many of whom such expressions of femininity were very threatening. Watching these men gently and sensitively serving these women, I always knew that I was observing a beautiful display of manly strength.

Jesus was the ultimate man. He never had to prove it, but how clearly He demonstrated it. Gently talking with the woman at the well, protecting the life of the woman caught in adultery, kindly humoring His mother when she insisted that He do something about the wine at the wedding in Cana, taking the little children into His arms, Jesus shone forth with full manhood. Washing the feet of His disciples, He provided the men He had chosen with an example of manly strength put under control for the purpose of serving others.

If I were a creator of advertising, there is one picture I would use every chance I could because it is an image that will draw the attention of almost every man, woman, or child. It is a picture of a young man walking down a path holding the hand of a little two- or three-year-old child. It symbolizes manly strength under submission for the purpose of guiding and protecting someone who is much smaller and weaker. It is almost irresistible. It is an expression of God's purpose for manhood: that it be in service to others.

A man is most completely a man, a man is his most wholesome and appealing, when he is outer directed, when he has little consciousness of himself. His face is toward the world, toward others, toward God. For him the world is a joyous challenge, something to both overcome and be delighted in. His lack of self-consciousness draws people to him.

The irony of all this is that you cannot become this kind of man by concentrating on it. This is self-defeating. You cannot become outer directed by constantly looking inward at what you are doing. It is like the person who so energetically pursues his own happiness; he never finds it until it comes upon him as a by-product of other things. We must focus outward to become outward focused. The simplest way to do this is to take into our hearts—and remind ourselves over and over again—that our manhood is given to us to give away, something that God created in us that we might use it to bless others.

The End of the Journey: Bringing It All Together

At the beginning I said that the road that leads to manhood would be a long and difficult one. By now, you probably believe I understated the challenges that the journey would present. And this book has only provided a road map, a course to follow; the real work comes in running the course by doing the things that men do.

Two goals for the journey have been implied in this book. The first was laid out in chapter 1: to become sons who are pleasing to the Father. I have just described the second one: to possess a manhood that can be used to serve others. "Love the Lord your God with all your heart, and with all your soul, and with all your mind.... Love your neighbor as yourself" (Matthew 22:37, 39). Our goal is to fulfill these two great commandments through our manhood.

But there is even more. Manhood is more than just a matter of relating; it is also a matter of *being*. Being is everything that is wrapped up in our personhood. God, the Great I AM, is the ultimate being. He IS without respect to any other thing or person. God can say I AM, and no words need follow this statement. Other words would only serve to qualify who He is. We cannot do that.

We are made in God's image and so we have being also, but our being differs from His in one important way: We exist only in relationship to Him. We have no being apart from Him. We may be disobedient sons or prodigal sons who try to ignore Him, or we may be sons after His own heart, but regardless, our being is always in relationship to Him.

A reward awaits you at the end of the road toward manhood, and it has to do with your being. The reward is called *integrity*. Integrity is what you have when it has all come together, when there is an inner sense that all of the pieces have been put in place.

Most people think of integrity as being a characteristic of someone who doesn't lie to his friends or run around on his wife or cheat on his income tax or someone who is not a hypocrite. True, these are marks of a man of integrity, but integrity is something much more than mere honesty.

The word *integrity* has the same root as the word *integer*. It means "one." It also means "whole." A man of integrity is a man who is *one* in terms of his body, his mind, his spirit, his beliefs, his feelings, his actions. What he says, he believes. What he believes, he is not afraid to say. His actions reflect the values that he holds. His beliefs as to what is right and what is wrong are not constantly at war with his feelings. His whole being has come into line with the body that God gave him. He is whole. He is of one piece, or as my grandfather, who was a tailor, would say, "He was cut out of one piece of cloth." His being is not scattered. The pieces fit together to make a whole.

Regardless of his physical appearance, handsome or homely by our standards of beauty, a man of integrity is startlingly attractive to almost anyone. In common parlance, he's got it "together." In him we do not see an assortment of pieces tenuously clinging together, so we feel we know who he truly is, and he is comfortable to be around. He is reliable, faithful, a good partner, father, brother, friend. The man of integrity is a man at peace with himself. He has a solid core of being, out of which he lives, out of which he functions with a high degree of confidence as a husband, father, worker, citizen, church member, leader.

The man of integrity knows who he is so well that much of the self-consciousness and narcissism that men bring over from adolescence has faded away. He knows who he is meant to be, and he finds fulfillment in being that person. He has a destiny. We all were created to be fully developed in our manhood. The man of integrity is approaching his destiny.

Like all spiritual journeys, this one won't be totally completed in this life—there has been only one complete man—but the fulfillment that the man of integrity feels is not realized only at the end of the journey; it is experienced with greater and greater frequency along the way. As you go down this road, even when you are far from your goal, over and over again in the midst of the struggles and the defeats will come glorious moments when you start to feel your manhood emerging, when you know that you have moved to a higher level. Victory will lead to victory, and not only will failures become less frequent, but their power to hurt you will fade.

Manhood is good, and you will feel good as a man.

"I am sure that he who began a good work in you will bring it to completion at the day of Jesus Christ" (Philippians 1:6).

moving on to further completion

Your journey through life certainly isn't over when you have attained a solid, sure manhood. Rather, your manhood will serve as a platform on which you can place your feet, firmly and solidly, as you turn your eyes to even greater rewards. Remember how Peter could walk on water until he looked down, and then he started to sink? That's the way it can be with you. Standing on the firmness of your manhood, you will no longer be looking down at yourself, constantly introspective. You will be able to look upward and outward toward the world and beyond. From this platform, you are in a place to find your further completion in two other glorious ways: in woman, who was created to be your "other," and in Jesus Himself, who is your ultimate goal.

God said it was not good for man to be alone. He has built into man a permanent incompleteness, an empty place that every man longs to have filled. It is the place that can be filled only by one who is different, the one who is his complement. Man, even before the Fall, was given a longing to find his completion in a woman. Further, as befits one with a natural desire to create and build, a man has a longing to, with this woman, create and tend to the growth of new lives.

Most men are intended to marry, and I believe that most men coming out of homosexuality will marry. A few are called to a ministry in which the single state is better, and peculiar circumstances make marriage impossible for some others, but God's whole man will want to marry. Some men may not find their freedom from homosexuality until they are past the years when fatherhood is a practical consideration, but the joys of being one with another can still be there. And many of us have found that in the joys and challenges of sharing our whole lives with another, we have continued to grow in our manhood.

But even in this, in a good marriage in which two have become one in mind, body, and spirit, in a marriage that has joined with God in the creation of new life, the longing for completion does not end. Even the man who has found great fulfillment in this life knows that he is not yet complete. He still longs for one more thing: oneness with God. He longs to live in total obedience to God, to love God with all his heart, to have the mind of Christ, and to dwell immersed in the love of God. We know that we will not find such total completion in this life, but we have the promise that it will one day be ours, and we know that even this longing for more and more of Him is a joyful thing.

When the journey to full manhood is complete, you have only just begun to reap the rich rewards that your Father has for you.

The final challenge: Manhood is something that is meant to be passed from generation to generation, from father to son. Sadly, we have come through a series of generations that have, through complacency, self-indulgence, and simply not knowing any better, failed in this stewardship and allowed the legacy to be frittered away. It will take radical men to begin to restore it. My prayer is that this book will encourage a group of men who have struggled mightily in becoming men to take on this task. By God's grace these men, who have known the pain that comes with incomplete manhood, who have experienced the longing to see the empty places filled, and who have been witness to their own belated coming into adult manhood, can become the new fathers, the radical warriors who will raise up a new generation of men formed after God's perfect design.

God gave me a son and helped me grow up to be his father. And Steve became a strong Christian man. God will do no less for you. Set out on this journey. Prepare to become a part of God's new generation of fathers: fathers in the family, fathers in the church, fathers in the community. Just step out onto the road to manhood. It will be the journey of your life, and God's plan will be restored in you and in a world that is crying out for men to be fathers.

reflections on twenty-five years of healing: alan medinger's story

"Perverse and foolish oft I strayed, but yet in love He sought me; and on His shoulder gently laid, and home rejoicing brought me." These words from an old hymn based on Psalm 23 express perfectly what happened to me twenty-five years ago when I encountered the Lord and He brought me out of homosexuality.

My journey into homosexuality fit the pattern that we see over and over again in ministry. I was an unplanned child, born to parents who would have preferred a girl. My older brother was more athletic and generally fit the "all boy" model far better than I did, and somehow he became Dad's and I became Mom's.

Our family lived in a row house in northwest Baltimore. My parents were good, kind, conscientious people who did all they could to raise their sons to become successful, well-adjusted men, but one problem tended to shape all of our destinies: My father was subject to severe depression, so severe that he was under psychiatric care for many years and on a few occasions had to be hospitalized. He could barely cope with life, much less be the husband and father we needed him to be. In his bad times, he drank heavily, and he and my mother fought verbally quite often.

My mother's life was difficult, and to a limited extent I became her comfort and confidant. I certainly identified with her more than with my father.

If you are familiar with the most common early childhood roots of male homosexuality, you can see that, except for sexual abuse, they were all there for me. But no parent makes a child homosexual. We have learned that a child's early home environment may provide the setup, but other significant factors always come into play in steering someone toward homosexuality.

For me, a couple of those factors were decisions that I made quite early in life. I have a vivid memory of lying in bed one night as a young boy, listening to my parents fight, and saying to myself quite smugly, "They can never hurt me. No one will ever hurt me." I believe that I made a decision that night to never be emotionally vulnerable. As a consequence of that decision, until my conversion years later, I would never be free to truly love anyone.

Another decision I made quite early in life was that I could meet all of my own needs and would meet them at any cost. This further insulated me from the kind of life-giving relationships that we all need.

I retreated into a world of fantasy, sexual and otherwise. It became my secure retreat from the pain of life. In a typical fantasy I would be a boy hero leading men into battle, and then when the fighting was over, the men would use me sexually. I both longed for my own manhood and for the manhood of other men.

At first my longings weren't sexual, they were simply a craving for a man's attention and interest in me. I remember a family Christmas gathering when I was only four or five years old, and the boyfriend of an adult cousin held me on his lap and played with me for what seemed like hours. For years after that, I would go to bed and in my mind relive that wonderful experience.

A few blocks from our house there was a neighborhood fire station, and I would regularly walk there just to stand around, hoping that one of the men would come out and talk to me. They had a set of weights in the firehouse, and I loved to look in and see the firemen's muscles as they exercised.

Eventually these longings for male contact did turn sexual. A strong, aggressive neighbor boy, who was about a year older than I, found out I was more than willing to take care of him sexually and was delighted to let me do so. Although my fears of being found out limited my activity, I was homosexually active with other boys from about age thirteen through high school.

My sexual activities stopped when I went to college. My brother had gone to Johns Hopkins University before me, and he had not joined a fraternity—to his later regret. He urged me to get into one. Although my recollection of myself is one of having been a classic nerd, somehow I managed to get into a fraternity. At that point I had about forty other young men who almost had to be my friends. My craving for male contact was at least partially satisfied through sharing typical college-boy activities with my fraternity brothers.

Still, the direction of my sexual desires never changed, and my fantasies abated very little. Although I dated some girls, there was never any doubt that my overwhelming desire was for a man.

I was blessed to grow up in a time and culture in which there was no gay alternative lifestyle out there calling me into it. I knew that there were a couple of homosexual bars in Baltimore, and I would visit pornographic bookstores to glance at the magazines in the "male" section, but it never really occurred to me to bail out of the only world I knew and let homosexuality determine the course of my life. Like so many homosexually oriented men of that time, I would get a job, marry, have children, and cope the best I could.

That's exactly what happened. Willa Benson had been my friend from elementary school days. We dated through high school, then off and on during college, and two years after college we were married. I told Willa nothing of my homosexual desires. Although I might rationalize this by the fact that when we married I hadn't had sex with another man for six years and wasn't really in fear of acting out in the future, in retrospect, I can see that this was really another manifestation of my determined self-protection. It was also a reflection of the fact that my inability to really love anyone made me incapable of putting her interests ahead of mine.

The first years of marriage went well. We had two daughters, and I started to move up in the business world. We were active in our little neighborhood Episcopal church, and we led an active social life. But gradually the pressures of career and family started to build up on me, and at the same time a faulty thyroid gave Willa some emotional problems. My response was to retreat into my old means of finding comfort: homosexual fantasy, pornography, and, five years into the marriage, sex with other men.

At first I drove forty-five miles to Washington, D.C., to go to a gay bar to find a contact, but as time passed I became more and more reckless until I was openly going to gay bars and gay-cruising places in Baltimore. A major part of my homosexuality was masochistic, and I started answering ads for sadomasochistic sex.

For ten years I led the classic double life. Successful in business, vice president and treasurer of a prestigious Baltimore company, a pillar of my local church—church treasurer, vestry member, and Sunday school teacher. The front was masterfully constructed and maintained. In reality, my life was out of control, and my marriage had become a sham. I was drinking heavily and turned much of my guilt on Willa. We fought frequently. For the last two years of my homosexual activity, I was unable to function sexually in the marriage.

Although I believed in God and had an intellectual acceptance of most of the basics of the Christian faith, my faith seemed to have no impact on my life. I prayed routinely, and I did pray that I would be able to stop my homosexual behavior, but I was never aware of any of my prayers being answered. I suppose I prayed the way I did most things, out of duty.

I never justified what I was doing, but I felt powerless to stop it. Gradually sinking into a fatalistic attitude, I saw my life as being on a downward spiral that eventually would cost me my family, my job, maybe even my life, and there was nothing I could do about it.

But God could. Two things happened. Willa, searching for help, got into a prayer group. Unbeknownst to her, she had stumbled upon a group of older women who were mighty prayer warriors. The leader of the group was Helen Shoemaker, author of a half-dozen books on prayer and cofounder of the Anglican Fellowship of Prayer. She was the widow of the great evangelical Episcopal priest, the Reverend Sam Shoemaker.

Willa did not tell them the exact nature of our problems, but they started praying for me and for our marriage.

Not long after this, a friend at work, Jim, had a profound religious experience. One night, at his children's Catholic parish school, he came upon a large prayer meeting being run by the Lamb of God Community, an interdenominational, but mostly Catholic, charismatic group. Jim was captivated by what he saw and went in and joined them. He went back the following week, and at that meeting he surrendered his life to Christ.

As Jim tried to explain to me what had happened (neither of us understood it exactly; being born again was not then in our theology), I became certain that he had had a true encounter with the Lord. Somehow I knew that I could too, but this was the most frightening thing I could think of. I knew that such an encounter would involve my homosexuality. Perhaps I would have to confess who I really was. Maybe God would give me just a little more strength, and I would be able to hold on with white knuckles for the rest of my life. Perhaps He would somehow enable me to give it up, but even this seemed terrible. As much as I hated it, I didn't think I could live without it. It had been my way of coping with life for as long as I could remember.

But things were desperate enough that after six or seven weeks of agonizing, on Tuesday, November 26, 1974, I went to the meeting with Jim. He didn't know my problem, nor did anyone there. At some point during the evening, as the two hundred or so people were praising God out loud, I said quietly, "God, I give up. My life is a total mess. I can't handle it anymore. I don't care what You do; You take over." And He did.

Within a few days, I knew that some profound changes had taken place in me. First of all, I fell head over heels in love with Willa, and I desired her physically. My homosexual fantasies, which had almost never left me, were gone. And most important, I knew that Jesus was real, that He loved me, and I was starting to love Him.

A few weeks later, I told Willa the whole truth about my life. Her years of denial came crashing down, and in the months ahead she encountered the wounds that my years of rejection, deception, anger, and blame casting had caused. Her healing was just beginning and would take a number of years. Being able to trust me and receive my love came very slowly. A part of the new start in life that we were both given was the birth of our son, Stephen, eighteen months after my conversion.

It was about four years before I heard of anyone else who had been set free from homosexuality, and then I read of Love in Action, a ministry for healing homosexuality, then in San Rafael, California. I started to correspond with Frank Worthen and Bob Davies of Love in Action. It would be another year before I actually met another "ex-gay" at my first Exodus conference in Seattle, Washington.

Exodus leaders were wary of my testimony at first. They had encountered others who claimed to have received sudden, miraculous healings from homosexuality, only to find out in a year or two that these healings had been far from complete. Their caution was justifiable, but not because I had not been set free from compulsive behavior and sexual attractions to men. I had. Today, twenty-five years later, if God were to bring me the best-looking man in the world, and say, "Here, you can do whatever you want with him," my response would be, "No, thank you, I'm not interested."

But homosexuality is more than just sexual attractions and behavior, and I had barely begun to experience healing in other areas. One area that had not been touched was my emotional neediness. Although it was no longer sexual, I still had a powerful longing for some big, strong man to take care of me. That little-boy need faded in the early years after my conversion, however, as I entered into a deep personal relationship with Jesus. He poured into me the man's love that I had never felt. Today, I believe that my need for male friendships are as normal and healthy as anyone's.

Homosexuality is also a matter of identity, and here again I had miles to go. I was thirty-eight years old at the time of my conversion and healing, but in the development of my masculinity and sense of manhood, I believe I was about eight years old. I had to start growing up. This process took years, but again it was a mighty work of God. Today I am confident in and at total peace with my manhood.

Within the past couple of years I have gained another insight into how God changed me, one that goes back to the original sexual healing. I always saw that healing as a miracle. I don't anymore. I now see it as *three* miracles.

Homosexuality is not an affliction like mental retardation or cancer; it is a group of problems that together produce homosexual attractions and behavior. Each of these problems must be dealt with individually. Here are the three problems that God dealt with at the time of my initial healing, my three miracles.

First, He broke down my wall of self-protection, and I was suddenly able to love. And who would have been a more logical object of my love than Willa, the person who had loved me and stayed by me all of those terrible years? I fell in love with her, and as happens with many men who come out of homosexuality, out of that love came sexual desire for her.

The second miracle is that God "desexualized" my unmet needs. For a time, I still longed for a man's love and attention, but that longing was no longer sexual. I still longed to be a man, but this longing was no longer expressed in a desire to possess another man's manhood.

Third, the sexual addiction was broken. This is perhaps the hardest miracle to understand, but it is the one we encounter most often. Every successful twelve stepper will tell you how his surrender to God is what broke the power of his sexual addiction.

Although not too many people experience change the way I did, everything that happened to me can happen to any man or woman overcoming homosexuality—being set free to love, desexualizing my unmet emotional needs, breaking the power of my addiction, having the deep needs of my heart met by Jesus, and growing into manhood (or womanhood). I know this because I have seen it happen hundreds of times.

In 1979, five years after the initial healing, I started Regeneration, a Christian ministry for men and women overcoming homosexuality. Willa progressed in her healing and ministers with me. Our two daughters have grown up, married, and provided us with six wonderful grandchildren. Steve, our child of the promise, grew to be a strong Christian man, was recently married, and is teaching school.

When I look back and consider what might have been, compared to what my life is today, I can barely contain my gratitude. What a gracious God we serve. I am reaching the age where it will soon be time to let go of some of my ministry-leadership responsibilities, but I cannot imagine ever wanting to stop helping people find the freedom and abundant life that our glorious God has given me.

the most important thing you can do to grow into manhood

Spend time with God. It is a radical thing to say, but I absolutely believe that the most important thing you can do to further your growth into manhood is to spend time with God. I wish there were some way I could say this without it sounding like a tired old Christian platitude. It is so important, more important than anything else I have to say in this book. I firmly believe that if I had not over the years faithfully spent regular times alone with the Lord, my manhood would not have advanced far beyond where it was at my conversion twenty-five years ago. It has been in my quiet times that I have experienced everything that a father should pour into his son.

As I write about spending time with God or as I teach on it in our Regeneration groups, I always feel as if I am saying something so obvious that it will seem trite. Doesn't every Christian already know this? I felt this way when I included a teaching on "Quiet Times" in New Directions (our ministry's basic program for men and women overcoming homosexuality), and yet it is the one teaching that more people have told me has changed their lives than any other.

Perhaps my teaching on this has had a powerful effect on people in our groups because it is the only teaching I do in which I could in good conscience say as Paul did in 1 Corinthians 4:16, "be imitators of me." For the past twenty-five years, on an average of five or six days a week, I have spent close to an hour and a half alone with the Lord in prayer, meditation, and reading Scripture. Without these times, I would never have become the man who could found Regeneration and see it through all of the challenges it has brought over the years.

It is in my quiet times that I have been sustained through all circumstances. It is in those daily times alone with the Lord that I hear His call to repent for the deeper sins that I could easily overlook, that I sense His inexplicable love for me, that I hear His words of encouragement, the Father's call for me to fight the good fight in both my life and ministry. It is with Him that I am put into a state of mind in which I can write and be creative. It is my quiet time that sets my direction for each day. It is the most important time of my life.

A central theme of our teaching in Regeneration is that healing comes through our relationship with Jesus Christ. I believe that most of our people accept this. They would also recognize that to be in a real relationship with someone, we must spend time with him. And yet, when I ask group members how many have a regular, significant quiet time with the Lord, only about half of the hands go up. They know that they should do it, but they don't. Why is this?

Looking beneath the surface, here are some of the reasons I have found why many Christians don't spend significant regular time alone with the Lord:

1. *Priorities.* Although the individual may never have acknowledged it, other priorities are higher. It might be something as simple or mundane as the comfort of a warm bed in the morning or the "need" to watch the eleven o'clock news at night. It could be the busyness of life, even the demands of important ministry work.

2. *Troubles with discipline.* A person doesn't have the ability to defer an immediate good for a greater long-term good.

3. *Spiritual problems.* Perhaps God always seems distant. Perhaps the enemy is at work. There is nothing Satan would rather do than keep someone away from the Lord.

4. *Rationalization.* You pray in your car or you listen to Christian radio. You are doing the Lord's work all day, so you don't need special times.

5. *Past failures.* You have tried it so many times and failed. What's the use of trying again?

Struggling to do something we know that we should do is not much different from struggling to stop doing what we shouldn't do, so there may be no easy answers. However, in regard to having a daily quiet time, we can be certain that God wants it as much as we do—He created us to be objects of His love—so there must be answers. Let me suggest some:

1. If the problem is priorities, try this exercise. List everything that you do in a typical day from getting out of bed to retiring at night. Then scratch out those things that are necessary for survival, like eating, going to work, etc. Then ask yourself: Should anything left on this list have a higher priority than spending time with the Lord? This would include shopping, resting, taking care of your aged mother, even attending support-group meetings. The answer should be obvious. Start to prioritize accordingly.

2. If the problem is a lack of self-discipline, I have a couple of suggestions. The first is to find someone to whom you can be accountable for this purpose, someone who for a time will faithfully ask you if you are fulfilling your intention. Second, at the end of any day in which you didn't have a quiet time, say this prayer: "Father, forgive me. I didn't think enough of You today to spend some time with You." Keep this up until the reality of it gets through to your heart.

3. If the problem is the enemy, you may need to engage in spiritual warfare. Out loud, in the name of Jesus Christ, rebuke Satan and

his tactics. Remember, he is a defeated enemy and is no match for the power of Jesus.

4. If the problem is that something is making God seem unapproachable or very distant, you will need to find the reason for this. This may be a spiritual journey in itself and may require help from a pastor or counselor.

5. If the problem is rationalization, stop it! Be honest with yourself and acknowledge that nothing in your life is as important as the time you spend with the Lord and that for at least a part of the day, He deserves your full attention.

6. If you have tried before and failed, try again. This time utilize some of the suggestions that follow. You may find that making this new "habit" is like breaking old ones; you simply have to bite the bullet and do it—regardless of how you feel—until the new way sets in.

There are many resources available to help Christians experience fruitful quiet times. Let me suggest some things that have worked for me and others.

What Is the Best Time to Have a Quiet Time?

Generally, this has to fit your bodily rhythms. There are morning people and evening people. Early morning is best if you can do it then. It makes the Lord your first priority, and it can set the tone for your day. Besides, early morning is least subject to interruptions or competing obligations.

How Long Should It Be?

Here, I may disagree with some others who would say start with ten minutes or so to just develop the habit. I suggest starting with at least half an hour. It takes most of us some time to settle down, clear our minds and start to make some sort of contact with God. In ten minutes this probably won't happen, and so your quiet times will seem meaningless and you are likely to give up quickly.

Where?

If at all possible, let it be a private place, one where you can feel free to kneel, sing, pray out loud, or whatever else you feel led to do. Make it a comfortable place, and it is good if it is the same place every day, your private meeting place with the Lord.

What Do You Do in a Quiet Time?

There are as many answers as there are people, but again, let me suggest what works for me.

1. *Start with praise.* This is totally focused toward the Lord so it puts us in the right relationship with Him. When I was a new Christian, praise seemed awkward and difficult. About all I could do is say, "Praise You, Lord. Praise You, Jesus," over and over again. I am sure that the Lord was as pleased with these clumsy words from my heart as He is with the most eloquent words I could compose today. After time, praise comes more easily and diversity starts to come naturally. Reciting psalms of praise can help.

2. *Then go to thanksgiving and confession.* These also focus on the Lord, but they bring us into the picture. They put us into a proper relationship with Him—sinners who have much to be thankful for. They acknowledge that He is the source of everything we have, that on a daily basis we need forgiveness and cleansing.

3. *Intercessions*—prayers for the needs around us—are part of almost everyone's quiet time, but if we are not careful, they can become very routine. Also, there being so many needs around us, they can take over our prayer time. I find it helps to keep a written schedule for intercessions. Of course, I pray every day for my family, for my pastors, and for our staff at Regeneration, but then I have special prayers for different days of the week. On Mondays I pray for the church around the world, on Tuesdays for our country and the world, on Wednesdays for other Exodus ministries, and so forth. For each staff member, I have a special day of prayer.

4. *Scripture reading* is essential, but without taking time to pray and

reflect on it, it can become a legalistic exercise. I like to use a Scripture guide, something that suggests readings from the Old Testament, Psalms, the Gospels, and the Epistles each day. Without a guide, I would tend to read only the familiar passages that are my favorites. I would miss out on much of the richness of God's Word that I have not yet discovered. Reading straight through the Bible can be helpful on occasion, but in doing it we are giving the same weight to the dimensions of the Tabernacle as to John 17. A good guide or lectionary will have you going through more important parts more frequently. Use other helps, such as Oswald Chambers's *My Utmost for His Highest,* but never let them be a substitute for the pure Word of God. You will discover a power in the Scriptures that you can find nowhere else.

5. *Petitions*—prayers for our own personal needs—seem very appropriate after reading Scripture. God's Word can guide us into praying for those things we really need. Don't overspiritualize and not ask for what is on your heart. A good father wants his sons and daughters to express their desires to him.

6. *Keep a journal.* Of those who tell me that they have regular significant quiet times, more than half say that they also journal. I have a mind that is always racing and going from thing to thing, but writing slows me down so I am better able to hear God. It clears my thinking. It helps me come to grips with my innermost life by capturing thoughts and emotions that are whirling around in my head.

My journal is where I record the lessons I have learned, and I am less apt to have to learn them over and over again. My journal is a history of where God has taken me. Our growth into manhood is mostly a slow, gradual process. As such, we sometimes don't see the changes that are taking place in our lives. With a journal, you can look back and see that certain "manhood" areas that you struggled with for years have suddenly stopped appearing. What a great faith builder this can be.

People use journaling in many ways. I don't write in my journal every day, only when there is something I believe I need to record. I give each entry a brief title so that if in the future I find myself going down a familiar road, I can look back and find how God dealt with me on this issue earlier. My journal is a simple loose-leaf book.

You may have difficulty getting started with regular quiet times, but don't despair. God wants it and you need it. If you struggle on and on with certain problems, and you only throw up occasional prayers for help, you are not developing the relationship that is going to bring lasting victory and healing. We have seen many people struggle with their problems for year and years, essentially by themselves, but when they have allowed the Lord to come in by spending significant time with Him, glorious things have happened.

Having a meaningful quiet time will be the most important thing you do in growing into manhood. In your quiet time you will be with the wisest Counselor there ever was. You will be with the perfect Father and the perfect Brother, the perfect Friend who will love you and hold you accountable. You will be with the only One who can meet your every need, and you will become the man He wants you to be.

other resources

BOOKS

Growth into Manhood: Resuming the Journey is not intended to be a complete book on overcoming homosexuality. The reader is urged to take advantage of other books that cover different aspects of homosexuality and the change process. The following are recommended:

On Healing and a Spiritual Understanding of Homosexuality

The Broken Image, by Leanne Payne (Baker, 1996). This is the book that opened Exodus ministries to the healing power of Jesus Christ for homosexual people.

Crisis in Masculinity, by Leanne Payne (Baker, 1995). This book opened the door to the process of growth that is described in *Growth into Manhood.*

Pursuing Sexual Wholeness, by Andrew Comiskey (Creation House, 1989). The author, who developed the Living Waters Program, provides a deeply spiritual approach to healing from sexual brokenness.

Setting Love in Order, by Mario Bergner (Baker, 1995). In sharing his ten-year journey out of homosexuality, the author provides living proof of the reality of what Leanne Payne, Andy Comiskey, and others have written about.

For a Broader Understanding of Homosexuality
and Ministry to the Overcomer

Homosexuality: A New Christian Ethic, by Elizabeth Moberly (James Clarke, 1983). This was a groundbreaking book in describing how detachment from the same-sex parent is a primary root of homosexuality.

Coming Out of Homosexuality, by Bob Davies and Lori Rentzel (InterVarsity, 1993). This may be the best book available for a general understanding of homosexuality and ministry to those who seek freedom from homosexuality.

Homosexual No More, by William Consiglio (Regeneration Books, 2000). This is one of the most practical helps for men overcoming homosexuality.

You Don't Have to Be Gay, by Jeff Konrad (Pacific Publishing, 1998). This is an excellent resource for the male overcomer. The book is written as a series of letters in which the author shares his own journey out of homosexuality with a friend who is struggling with the issue of change.

Reparative Therapy of Male Homosexuality, by Joseph Nicolosi (Jason Aronson, 1991). The author, a professional therapist, provides excellent insights into the unmet needs that underlie the homosexual condition, offering help for meeting those needs in legitimate ways.

Helping People Step Out of Homosexuality, by Frank Worthen (New Hope, 1995). The author, the father of ex-gay ministry, draws on his twenty-five years in ministry to offer an outstanding workbook on overcoming homosexuality. For individual or group use.

Homosexuality and the Politics of Truth by Jeffrey Satinover (Baker, 1996). The author, a psychiatrist, provides a brilliant explanation of how society should respond to homosexuality based on its causes and its consequences.

Straight and Narrow? by Thomas E. Schmidt (InterVarsity, 1995). This book offers what may be the best description that we have of the multi-causal roots of homosexuality.

For Family Members and Churches

Someone I Love Is Gay, by Anita Worthen and Bob Davies (InterVarsity, 1996). This is the most helpful book available for parents, spouses, and other loved ones of homosexual people.

Unwanted Harvest, by Mona Riley and Brad Sargent (Broadman & Holman, 1995). This book addresses the role of the church and Christian individuals in the lives of homosexual strugglers who seek to change.

All of these books and many other Christian books dealing with homosexuality from a healing perspective are available through Regeneration Books. Contact Regeneration for a catalog: P.O. Box 9830, Baltimore, MD 21284. Phone: (410) 661-4337; fax: (410) 882-6312; e-mail: regenbooks@juno.com, or to review books or order them on-line: exodusnorthamerica.org/resources.

CHRISTIAN MINISTRIES FOR MEN AND WOMEN OVERCOMING HOMOSEXUALITY

Exodus International—North America: This is the U.S. and Canadian part of the worldwide Exodus network of ministries. Exodus does not do direct ministry itself but can direct you to more than one hundred ministries in the United States and Canada that help people overcoming homosexuality, serve their loved ones, and assist churches in dealing with homosexual issues. Exodus also sponsors a major annual conference—over one thousand attend—on ministry to homosexual people. Contact them for a list of member ministries and for information on their next conference:

P.O. Box 77652, Seattle, WA 98177. Phone: (206) 784-7799; fax: (206) 784-7872; Web site: exodusnorthamerica.org.

Exodus International: Contact them for a list of member ministries outside the U.S. and Canada. There are Exodus-affiliated ministries in Europe, Latin America, Africa, Asia, and the Pacific. P.O. Box 21039, Ajax, Ontario, Canada L1H 7H2. Phone: (416) 283-9797; fax: (416) 283-3383; Web site: exodusintl.org

Regeneration: A ministry offering support groups and one-on-one help for people dealing with homosexuality and sexual addiction, as well as help to family members and churches. Regeneration conducts conferences and retreats and publishes a monthly newsletter (at no charge) offering helpful articles for men and women overcoming homosexuality. Regeneration makes available to other ministries the New Directions Program, a basic support-group program for homosexual overcomers. Contact the main office and Baltimore ministry: P.O. Box 9830, Baltimore, MD 21284. Phone: (410) 661-0284; fax: (410) 882-6312; e-mail: regenbalto@ juno.com; or the Northern Virginia ministry: P.O. Box 1034, Fairfax, VA 22030. Phone: (703) 591-4673; fax: (703) 591-6540.

Courage: A Roman Catholic ministry providing spiritual support for persons with same-sex attractions striving to develop a life of interior chastity in union with Christ. Courage has 86 chapters/contacts worldwide. Contact them c/o Church of St. John the Baptist, 210 W. 31st Street, New York, NY 10001. Phone: (212) 268-1010; fax: (212) 268-7150; Web site: http://world.std.com/~Courage; e-mail: NYCourage@aol.com.

Homosexuals Anonymous: A network of "Fourteen Step" groups for men and women dealing with homosexuality: P.O. Box 7881, Reading, PA 19603. Phone: (610) 376-1146.

OTHER RESOURCES

Living Waters is the most widely used program for men and women dealing with sexual and relational brokenness. For information on the program, conferences, or equipping seminars for leaders, contact Desert Stream Ministries at (714) 779-6899; fax: (714) 701-1880; e-mail: info@desertstream.org.

Healing Conferences with a Special Focus
on Healing from Sexual Brokenness

Pastoral Care Ministries (Leanne Payne): P.O. Box 1313, Wheaton, IL 60189-1313. Phone: (630) 510-0487; fax: (630) 510-7659.

Clay McClean Ministries: P.O. Box 98DTS, Boone, NC 28607. Phone: (828) 297-1877.

notes

1. Leanne Payne, *Crisis in Masculinity* (Grand Rapids, Mich.: Baker, 1995).

2. William Consiglio, *Homosexual No More* (Baltimore, Md.: Regeneration Books, 2000), 61.

3. Joseph Nicolosi, *Reparative Therapy of Male Homosexuality* (Northvale, N.J.: Jason Aronson, 1991), 58.

4. Leanne Payne, *The Broken Image* (Grand Rapids, Mich.: Baker, 1996), 41-2.

5. Some years ago it became a popular notion to believe that 10 percent of the world is gay. This has been thoroughly discredited by a 1989 University of Chicago National Opinion Research Center (NORC) poll showing that overall less than 1 percent of the population is exclusively homosexual. Most recent studies have reported a 2 to 4 percent incidence of homosexuality—higher among men and lower among women.

6. Uriel Meshoulam, "Homosexuality As a Construct: Implications for Therapy," paper presented at the NARTH Annual Spring Conference, 22 May 1994; reprinted in *Collected Papers of the NARTH Conference 1994*, 55.

7. The strong homosexual influence among the early Nazis, especially the brownshirts, is documented by Scott Lively and Kevin Abrams in *The Pink Swastika* (Salem, Oreg.: Lively Communications, 1997).

8. Elizabeth R. Moberly, *Homosexuality: A New Christian Ethic* (Cambridge, Eng.: James Clarke, 1983).

9. Ruth Tiffany Barnhouse, *Homosexuality: A Symbolic Confusion* (New York: Seabury, 1979), 157.

10. Nicolosi, *Reparative Therapy*, 34.

11. Anne Moir and David Jessel, *Brain Sex: The Real Difference Between Men and Women* (New York: Delta, 1992), 21.

12. As quoted in Nicolosi, *Reparative Therapy,* 45.

13. Thomas Schmidt, *Straight and Narrow?* (Downers Grove, Ill.: InterVarsity, 1995), 151.

14. John Piper, *What's the Difference? Manhood and Womanhood Defined According to the Bible* (Wheaton, Ill.: Crossway, 1990).

15. Phillip Johnson, *Darwin on Trial* (Downers Grove, Ill.: InterVarsity, 1993). Dr. Johnson, a professor of law at Berkeley, has written a number of books on evolution, but this one has had the greatest impact.

16. Carol Ann Rinzler, *Why Eve Doesn't Have an Adam's Apple: A Dictionary of Sex Differences* (New York: Facts on File, 1996).

17. Moir and Jessel, *Brain Sex,* 15.

18. Rinzler, *Why Eve,* 85.

19. Rinzler, *Why Eve,* 21.

20. Rinzler, *Why Eve,* 152.

21. Rinzler, *Why Eve,* 81.

22. Rinzler, *Why Eve,* 62.

23. Rinzler, *Why Eve,* 19.

24. Rinzler, *Why Eve,* 24.

25. Rinzler, *Why Eve,* 11.

26. Moir and Jessel, *Brain Sex,* 43.

27. Moir and Jessel, *Brain Sex,* 43.

28. Moir and Jessel, *Brain Sex,* 16.

29. From a report on a Johns Hopkins University study, "Gray Matter of the Sexes," cited in *Johns Hopkins Magazine,* June 1996: 21.

30. Donald Joy, *Men Under Construction* (Wheaton, Ill.: Victor, 1993).

31. Moir and Jessel, *Brain Sex,* 89.

32. Moir and Jessel, *Brain Sex,* 155.

33. Moir and Jessel, *Brain Sex,* 42.

34. Rinzler, *Why Eve*, 46, 133.

35. Steven Goldberg, *Why Men Rule: A Theory of Male Dominance* (Chicago: Open Court, 1993), 64.

36. Goldberg, *Why Men Rule*, 64.

37. Lewis, *Perelandra* (New York: Macmillan, 1944), 200.

38. F. Earle Fox, *Biblical Sexuality and the Battle for Science* (Alexandria, Va.: Emmaus Ministries, 1988). Dr. Fox is an Episcopal priest who has spoken prophetically to the church and the culture on sexual issues for many years. He is now also director of Transformation Christian Ministries, the Exodus member ministry in Washington, D.C.

39. C. S. Lewis, *That Hideous Strength* (New York: Macmillan, 1946), 316.

40. Fox, *Biblical Sexuality*, 92.

41. Frederica Mathewes-Green, "Men Behaving Justly," *Christianity Today* (17 November 1997): 45.

42. Karen Linamen and Keith Wall, *Broken Dreams* (Birmingham, Ala.: New Hope, 1995). This was formerly published under the title *Deadly Secrets*.

43. George Rekers, "Gender Identity Disorder," *The Journal of Sexuality* (1996): 11-17.

44. Leon Podles, *The Church Impotent: The Feminization of Christianity* (Dallas: Spence Publishing, 1999), 43.

45. Goldberg, *Why Men Rule*, 63.

46. This story is told in expanded form in *Regeneration News*, October 1994.

47. Payne, *Crisis in Masculinity*, 15-40.

48. This subject is addressed more fully in the article "You Are Not a Homosexual," *Regeneration News* (June 1994).

49. What physiologically distinguishes a homosexual person is usually addressed only indirectly, in arguments as to whether or not homosexuality is inborn. Many books address this issue, one of the best being Jeffrey Satinover, *Homosexuality and the Politics of Truth* (Grand Rapids, Mich.: Baker, 1996).

50. David F. Greenberg, *The Construction of Homosexuality* (Chicago: University of Chicago, 1988). This is a study of the occurrence and recognition of homosexual behavior throughout history.

51. Although every effort was made, the exact source of this quote attributed to Martin Luther could not be determined.

52. C. S. Lewis, *Mere Christianity* (New York: MacMillan, 1979), 189.

53. Payne, *The Broken Image.* The story of Jay (pp. 73-76) offers an excellent illustration of a man bonded to his mother and of prayer to bring release from that bond.

54. Oswald Chambers, *My Utmost for His Highest* (1935; reprint, Westwood, N.J.: Barbour, 1963), 42 (Feb. 11).

55. Randy Shilts, *And the Band Played On* (New York: St. Martin's Press, 1987), 408-9.